MW01493681

SEX OFFENDER

My Father's Secrets, My Secret Shame

DANICA HUBBARD
Ph.D.

Copyright © 2022 Danica Hubbard, Ph.D.
All rights reserved
First Edition

Fulton Books, Inc.
Meadville, PA

Published by Fulton Books 2022

ISBN 978-1-63860-404-4 (paperback)
ISBN 978-1-63860-405-1 (digital)

Printed in the United States of America

DEDICATION

This book is dedicated to my husband. You are my heart holder and life partner. Your encouragement lifted me over the finish line. Yes, this counts as a hike! And to our daughters who always inspire me. May you continue to lead the way in standing up for truth and justice. Finally, this book would not be possible without my parents' commitment and love in raising me. Their life lessons are their legacy.

A portion of the sales from this book will be donated to Prevent Child Abuse America, an organization committed to preventing child sexual abuse through several practical solutions in creating conditions for safe, stable, and nurturing relationships and environments for all children, families, and communities.

Prevent Child Abuse America promotes programs and resources informed by science that enables kids, families, and entire communities to thrive today, tomorrow, and for generations to come.

https://preventchildabuse.org Child Abuse Hotline 855-444-3911
Prevent Child Abuse America is a
registered 501(c)(3) organization
Tax ID/EIN number is 23-7235671

PRAISE FOR SEX OFFENDER: MY FATHER'S SECRET, MY SECRET SHAME

Imagine having someone you've known your whole life, someone you've looked up to, tell you about a heinous crime they committed. Imagine if that person is your father. When Dr. Hubbard's father told her about his indiscretions, she had a choice—to continue the relationship with her father or to turn the other way. She decided to maintain the relationship, support him during his incarceration, and learn as much as possible to make sense of it. This book provides her journey into understanding, forgiveness, and inner strength to tell this very personal story. Many people who have a family member convicted of a sexual crime don't talk about it. Understandably, there's a lot of shame and guilt associated with it. It makes you question everything in your life. There's no question here; put your judgment aside and read this book.

—Julia Lazareck, Author, Speaker, Podcaster,
Prison: The Hidden Sentence®

Dr. Hubbard opens her heart to share with us a beautifully written, touching, informative, and brutally honest book about the intricacies of having a father who was a sexual predator. She opens our eyes to the enormous difficulties of not only living with that legacy in the fabric of a family but also describes the complexities of continuing a relationship with a family member who is incarcerated. This book is a must read for anyone who knows that life is not black or white and is willing to grow by exploring the gray.

—Amy Zabin, PhD, New York University Music Therapy
Program and author of *Conversations with a Pedophile*

When someone you love has been arrested, tried and convicted, there are a myriad of feelings. We feel frightened and helpless. We feel as though the world is looking at us in judgement. And, we feel alone and vulnerable. When the offense is a sex crime, these feelings are exacerbated. This is a sensitive and delicate subject that is seldom explored. It is a testament to Dr. Hubbard that she has the courage and willingness to share her journey with us.

—Barbara Allan, Founder: Prison Families
Anonymous and author of *Doing Our Time On the
Outside: One Prison Family of 2.5 Million*

Dr. Danica Hubbard shares her raw, yet studied, journey as an unsuspecting child of a child sexual predator to an adult dealing with the harsh realities of her father's hidden life. She writes, "My father was a pedophile who appeared to live a 'normal' life while terrorizing young girls in secret." Honest, vulnerable, and courageous, Dr Hubbard shares her emotional path from normalcy through shock and shame to recovery and advocacy. Her knowledge and perspective provide insight into the rarely examined impacts that a child predator has upon his unknowing family and friends.

As a survivor of child sexual abuse turned child advocate, my life has been focused on understanding how to prevent abuse and aide survivors. This book provides a unique glimpse into the pain suffered by another group of previously overlooked victims—the predator's family and friends.

—Suzanne Greenberg, Speaker, Survivor, Executive
Director of Prevent Child Abuse Michigan
and Michigan Children's Trust Fund

Our society too often treats criminal justice issues—and, particularly, issues surrounding how to treat individuals convicted of committing sexual offenses against children—as cut and dry, with right and wrong answers. In her book, Professor Hubbard shows us the fundamental complexity and difficulty of addressing and living with the legacy of serious crime.

In her touching, personal account, we peer at the problem from revealing new angles. We see the virtues and weaknesses in offenders; the perseverance, healing, and forgiveness of victims and families; and the good intentions, failings, and casual cruelty of the criminal justice system. This book will pave the way toward a deeper, nuanced understanding of criminal behavior (especially sexual offending) and its aftermath for readers of all stripes.

—J.J. Prescott, University of Michigan Professor of Law, Co-director, Empirical Legal Studies Center, Henry King Ransom Professor of Life

CONTENTS

Prologue 13

Chapter 1: Sink or Swim 17
    Your Dad Did What?......................................18
    To the Letter 20
    Drop Me a Line...21
    Prison Pen Pals...23
    Hush, Hush..24
    Greetings and Salutations 26

Chapter 2: Caught between the Devil and the Deep
           Blue Sea...28
    Shocking Secrets...29
    Complex Definition 31
    Geriatric Sex Offenders 34
    Repulsed or Rehabilitated? 36
    SOT Meeting...38
    Revered and Feared..43
    Pattern of Pedophilia......................................47
    Sinister Sleepovers...50
    My Friend, His Fault......................................53
    My Story of Sexual Assault by the Man Next Door 54
    Trust Me, Touch Me.......................................55

Chapter 3: Below Deck.....................................61
    Preamble to Prison 62
    Call My Lawyer 69
    Public or Private Attorney..............................70

Probation and Parole 71
Sex Offender Registration...............................77
Love 'Em or Leave 'Em 80
Sentencing Hearing 82
Lock Him Up 86

Chapter 4: Abandon Ship 88
Running from Wisconsin to Georgia 90
Recidivism Risk...93
Where in the World Are You Going? 97
Cutting Off Contact...98
Knock, Knock—Is Your Dad Here? 100
Caught in Costa Rica 104
First Letter from Prison...................................106

Chapter 5: Man Overboard!..........................116
Fleeting Fame...118
Death of a Salesman.......................................120
Bad Publicity..122
Ripped from the Headlines 123
Most Wanted List and More...........................133
Coping with Press Coverage..........................136

Chapter 6: Capsized 139
New Sights, Sounds, and Smells....................141
Nesting Instinct 143
Are You There, God? 160

Chapter 7: Stem the Tide 171
Not Home for the Holidays.............................172
Missing You 181

Chapter 8: Don't Rock the Boat...................187
Friend or Foe?..188
Don't Talk about Your Case 193

Chapter 9: Run a Tight Ship............................210
   Activities for All 211
   Everyday I'm Hustlin'.........................214
   Chow Down 224
   Visiting Hours 225

Chapter 10: High and Dry 232
   Trouble with Toothaches....................233
   I Can See Clearly Now 235
   Relief for Reflux? 237
   Help! My Hernia!..............................238
   Medicine for MRSA...........................241
   Cancer Diagnosis 242
   Splenectomy in Shackles 246
   On Pins and Needles 251
   Last Stages of Leukemia.....................256

Chapter 11: Mayday, Mayday 259
   Monarch Mom 262
   She's Gone, but Not Forgotten.............264
   Last Rites 266
   Obituary 270
   Memorial Mass 273
   Ashes...277

Chapter 12: All Hands on Deck...................279
   Grieving Is a Gift 280
   Telling Our Daughters the Truth 281
   Forgiving My Father 284
   Survive and Thrive 287

Chapter 13: Safe Harbor...........................290
   Homework for Reluctant Writers...........290
   First Installment of My Life.................294
      My Comments and Critique 308
   Second Installment of My Life 309
      My Comments and Critique 319

Third Installment of My Life 320
   My Comments and Critique 323
Fourth Installment of My Life 324
   My Comments and Critique 328
Fifth Installment of My Life 329
   My Comments and Critique 334
Tough Questions Remain Unanswered 335

Chapter 14: Lifelines 336
   Road Map to Resources 337
   Books 339
   Social Media, Blogs, and Podcasts 339
   Is There an App for That? 341
   Communication Is Key 342

Afterword...343
Acknowledgments..347
Glossary 349
Bibliography 353
About the Author..362

PROLOGUE

There are currently 917,771 registered sex offenders in the United States according to the National Center for Missing and Exploited Children. Approximately 150,000 adult sex offenders are serving time in state and federal prisons, with up to 30,000 released into the community each year. Although there have been other case studies of sex crimes in the spotlight like Larry Nassar, Jerry Sandusky, and Jeffrey Epstein, my story is different. My father was a pedophile who appeared to live a "normal" life while terrorizing young girls in secret. In my book I will share his chilling words, extracted from hundreds of letters he wrote to me while incarcerated. This is a different perspective and enables readers to look into the mind of a perpetrator.

Families related to sex offenders often suffer in isolation, engulfed in stress, silence, and shame. I wrote this book to make connections with people like me who may have experienced similar losses and were too reluctant to share. My book can help guide the conversation in sharing this sensitive and taboo subject.

We are not able to control what our parents do, but we can choose how we respond by asking questions like:

- How do you accept a parent who goes to prison?
- How do you cope with the shame and guilt?
- What resources are available to families of incarcerated parents?

These are only a few of the questions family and friends have when someone they love is found guilty of committing a crime, but not just *any* crime. I wrote this book to examine the path my father took from inception to incarceration. This book is a hybrid that combines personal memoir with academic research. Drawing on my memories, interviews, and research, I transcribed five hundred letters my father and I exchanged from his prison cell. I recorded a complex narrative that ultimately led to forgiveness. There is hope and healing embedded in my story. As social justice activist Maggie Kuhn said, "Speak the truth, even if your voice shakes."

Discovering my father's series of offenses was horrifying and demoralizing. At the same time, I felt like I was a helpless child, trying to fit the pieces of a puzzle together that were deliberately hidden most of my life. Every piece held significance in understanding who, what, where, when, and how. I am still struggling with why. It was like I had grown up with dual Dads—doting yet deceitful.

To be clear, my father's actions are not a reflection of our family values. We don't have "monster" in our blood. When he was first convicted, I searched to find a support group to explore how and why external circumstances and impulses may provoke unconventional actions. At the time, I felt alone, confused, and defeated. But today, I believe my story may help form a community to help each other while maintaining dignity and respect.

The purpose of this book can be expanded beyond a support tool for families of incarcerated loved ones. I would like to reach an audience that includes anyone who has ever dealt with loss and trauma. I hope my story sparks a dialogue that educates, informs, and facilitates a pathway to understanding. Finding my voice while navigating the minefield of my father's incarceration was empowering.

As an English professor, I am fascinated by etymology, the study of history and origin of words to communicate clearly and effectively. Each chapter title includes nautical terminology because my father cherished living by the water. The epitaph on his tombstone is inscribed, "The lake is calling, so I must go." This first chapter and all chapters will include some maritime words and phrases to honor my father's passion for living near the water's edge.

My earliest family memory of our Chris-Craft boat named "Happy and Carefree" was cruising on the Chain of Lakes in the Fox River. My parents carefully charted courses starting in the Chicago Harbor into Lake Michigan, exploring the Midwestern Great Lakes region. The lake can be fickle and dangerous with fast-changing currents and massive wave heights during quick weather changes, but my father was a calm captain, a man in charge.

In the first chapter of this book, I imagine sitting on the bow of a boat where I will start to tell his story, my story, our story. Many names have been changed or omitted to protect the privacy and anonymity of individuals who have agreed to share their memories of my father. Although this is my story, it is also their stories, and I am grateful for our phone conversations and e-mail exchanges about how my father impacted their lives. I modified identifying details and changed names to general terms like friend, cousin, or neighbor. I also edited excerpts from my father's original letters for the purpose of brevity in highlighting his prison experience.

I am choosing to share my emotionally charged life as the only child of a successful shape-shifter: a son, brother, husband, father, widow, divorcé, coach, corporate executive, boater, barbecue griller, marathon runner, convicted child molester, and inmate who died alone in prison.

CHAPTER 1

Sink or Swim

*Twenty years from now, you will be more disap-
pointed by the things that you didn't do than the
ones you did do. So throw off the bowlines. Sail
away from the safe harbor.*

—H. Jackson Brown

#389188 hemorrhaged and died from complications in the final
stages of acute myeloid leukemia. It has taken me twenty years to
find perspective and courage to tell this story. I have straddled a
delicate balance between shame and sharing.

As an only child, I am independent, used to fending for
myself, and reluctant to ask for help. But when my mother died of
lung cancer at forty-nine and my father was sent to prison at sixty,
I felt trapped in a cycle of grief. I didn't want anyone to know how
bad things were. So I did what came naturally to me: researched
and journaled. I looked for some sort of instruction manual for
middle-aged daughters whose parents are in prison. No luck.

This is an honest and raw account of the demons my father
faced in spending over a decade in prison, including his frustrations, faith, and confessions. It is a nonfiction memoir, part family
history and part guide for families in the extraordinary process of
maintaining a relationship with a parent in prison. #389188 was
my father's prison serial identification number.

Your Dad Did What?

My father had no prior criminal record until he was charged with three felony counts of first-degree sexual assault of a six-year-old girl in Wisconsin. The first charge stemmed from an incident in July 1999, and the additional two charges were from incidents involving the same young girl in August 1999. He confessed to touching her inappropriately on a reoccurring basis.

He turned himself in to court authorities and pled guilty in August 1999. He was convicted in May 2000 of two felony counts: having sexual contact with a minor under the age of thirteen. My father was sentenced to thirty years of probation with supervised release. In 2003, after eighteen sex-offender therapy sessions, a judge granted my father a state transfer, and he was legally discharged from counseling. Upon moving, he was required to register as a sex offender and schedule regular visits with a parole officer. If he did not follow the rules, he would be sentenced to the maximum thirty years in prison. Within a year, he broke the rules and fled to Costa Rica.

The subject is unsettling and provocative as child predators are often considered pariahs. They are scum in a hierarchal prison system. Lowest of the low. The scourge. I never imagined I would write a book that exposes negativity in my family. Shouldn't I keep those skeletons in the closet that may damage our name? I worried that readers would think of me as guilty by association and draw unseemly connections. Is this story something that would sully my reputation because I am my father's daughter?

I knew my father as a protector, not a predator. I was in my mid-thirties, a young mother and tenured college professor, when he was formally convicted of horrific crimes. He couldn't possibly be the monster described in the newspapers and in the courtroom. No, not him. My father was the man who taught me how to water ski, coached our park district softball team, and bought a round of drinks for the entire bar at my college graduation. Everyone knew him as a charismatic, confident Christian man. He was good, not evil. He left a positive impression on friends, coworkers, and family. He was a different father now standing in front of me. I struggled to feel empathy for him, yet he was still my father, my only living parent. He ended up going to prison for the rest of his life. As the years passed, I found more secrets he was hiding.

Who was this man being accused of exploiting children? Did he suddenly transform? Why did this betrayal happen? There were moments where I questioned still loving my father because he had lost all my trust. Walking a path without a secure foundation brings up a lot of doubt and insecurities. I carried the dead weight of his baggage for years and still reached out to him, comforted him, visited him, and loved him. It was a messy father-daughter relationship, but I eventually learned that his issues had nothing to do with me. I could not change his thinking and was only responsible for my own actions and reactions. I relied upon my family, friends, and faith for their patience, listening, and encouragement to set me free while my father was imprisoned. I worked on rebuilding a shattered life because even when we are broken, we can still become whole.

For many, prisons are only accessible on television or movie screens. I had never seen the inside of a jail or prison. The closest I came to following crime was watching several 1980's popular television shows like *Hill Street Blues*, *Magnum P.I.*, or one of my childhood favorites, *Charlie's Angels*. The predictable plots projected a false sense of comfort that crimes could be solved within the span of thirty minutes, including commercial breaks. I had not even tuned into modern reality television programs like *60 Days In*, *Jailbirds*, or *Lockup*. The main character tackling hard-hitting issues during her prison sentence in the wildly popular Netflix series *Orange Is the New Black* was a delusive snapshot of what really happens when entering a maximum-security prison.

When it's happening in real time with a family member, there is no actual docuseries to reference or ability to watch a recap of a previous episode. The glossy cinematic tricks, makeup, costuming, and rousing musical soundtracks create a convincing atmosphere of authenticity, but being in prison and visiting a parent in prison is nothing like the fantasy portrayed on screen. Instead, it is a full assault to the senses and gets really ugly, really fast. We had no idea how this restrictive and punishing environment would manifest into a new normal for our family.

To the Letter

In the attic closet under a stack of blankets, I kept an over-sized metal bin containing five hundred letters my father and I exchanged, over 1,500 pages of correspondence, from his public prison cell to my private PO Box. I reserved and paid for a PO Box for years in order to protect our two young daughters from possibly retrieving a letter stamped with my father's prison identification number and bold black letters stating, "This letter has been mailed from the Wisconsin prison system" in all capital letters both on the front and back of every outgoing envelope. Week after week, year after year, I would drive to the post office, feeling excitement and shame to secretly retrieve the letters in my PO Box located a few miles from our home.

I would sit in my car in the parking lot and hastily open the white-lined paper folded into thirds tucked into a legal-sized envelope. My heart beat faster as I ripped the gummed flap and faint scents of stale water, moldy laundry, and metallic odors wafted out. I was anxious to read my father's scrawl on the faded blue lines. Sometimes, the letters would also contain colorful pencil drawings, folded prayer cards, or die-cut holiday cards.

Inmates in both state and federal prisons are often issued a handbook during the classification process that contains specific details about writing letters. Some state prisons require a specific color of envelope, and letters must be written in blue or black ink. Restrictions also include, but are not limited to: no paperclips, staples, crayon, stickers, marker, glue, or glitter. No drawings which may be interpreted as signals, gang signs, escape routes, or secret codes. And absolutely no electronics, pop-up or pop-out content. This last rule was personally difficult because my father loved pop-up cards that transformed a flat image to a three-dimensional interactive experience. His amusement with paper engineering of flaps, pull tabs, and wheels to cause movement on a page was a fond memory for my father. Maybe his affinity for inventive folding paper stemmed from his interest in studying architecture. Pop-up cards were the favorite type of greeting cards exchanged during birthdays and holidays in our house.

All routine mail sent to an inmate is opened, examined, and read by designated department staff. I once sent my father a card with a singing Snoopy dog. We used to watch Charles Schulz's *Peanuts* movies and television specials like the animated 1965 *A Charlie Brown Christmas* together. I thought the card may bring him some levity and cheer him up. I didn't imagine the card could be used to commit infractions or even possibly craft a weapon. Construction of a musical card involves a small six-pin processor with a melody played through a speaker and lithium button cell battery, providing the power when the card is opened, turning the music on. I learned this type of card was off limits in prison. My father wrote in his next letter that he was called to the mail room and met by an unhappy correctional officer holding the card up to his face. My father said the officer forcibly split the card into shreds and muttered "Never again" before throwing it in the garbage.

Reading his letters was like riding an emotional rollercoaster. I never knew when the next steep drop would come around the corner as he described his life in prison. I felt like I was peering through a keyhole-sized view of who he was. Some of his letters didn't communicate enough, and others said far too much. The excerpts from his letters that I share in this book weren't filled with finding the perfect words but offered me some sort of record of his daily life as I scurried through my daily routines carpooling, making dinner, and grading assignments. Sometimes, his letters opened a window to his remorse without enduring the same vulnerability and exposure as a face-to-face conversation. His letters had an enormous impact on me.

Drop Me a Line

How can dialogue be increased with a parent in prison? How could I become more involved in communicating? Inmates have very limited lives, so sending letters can offer an escape to the mundane day-to-day life in prison. It took a while for me to start sending my father letters. At first, I was fearful and unaware of how to exchange letters in and out of prison. Eventually, I called the prison, reviewed their website information, and became familiar with the rules. For example, I learned that my letters would be read by security staff before they reached my father. I could not send newspaper clippings and was told to write in blue or black ink. I wasn't allowed to send books, stamps, food, or other personal items in "regular mail," but books can be ordered from an approved publisher and sent directly from the publisher to the inmate. In fact, I sent my father so many books, he started to box them up and send them back to me. Unfortunately, it was prohibited for him to deposit them in the prison library to share with others.

During the holidays, I would send my close friends and family a request to send him a card or letter as well. It was kind of like cold calling in sales—some would agree to write him, some would not. I respected their decision choosing whether or not to communicate with him, but it made a significant difference in elevating his mental health. Eventually, my father asked me to also send him pictures of our active and growing family. At first, I was reluctant and concerned for our safety, not knowing for sure why he wanted our snapshots. But eventually, I sent him pictures, hoping nothing awful would come of it. He told me he took a long look at the pictures I sent and then forced himself to throw them away although he did keep a picture of a sunset tucked into the pages of his *Bible*.

I was consistent in sending a letter every week because if I lost contact, it could fracture the momentum and candid conversations we had in our letters. My father was nervous that another inmate would steal my letters, so he chose to destroy each of my letters after reading in efforts to protect my privacy. Although he could not keep my letters to reread them, he thanked me repeatedly in maintaining our long-term contact with one another.

Prison Pen Pals

Sister Helen Prejean was a leader in establishing prison pen pal programs, making sure inmates knew they were not forgotten. She became pen pals with Patrick Sonnier, a death-row inmate convicted of raping and killing two teenagers. Sonnier's story inspired her to write a book that was later developed into a major motion picture starring Susan Sarandon and Sean Penn.

Sister Prejean came to my workplace, College of DuPage, in 2001 for a speaking engagement. I was awestruck sitting in the audience. I regularly assigned her book, *Dead Man Walking: An Eyewitness Account of the Death Penalty in the United States*, in my English Composition courses. Students responded to her text, organizing arguments in favor or against the death penalty. In her presentation that evening, she said she had no idea that the letters would lead her to visit Louisiana's Angola state prison and meet her pen pal, Sonnier, face-to-face. Years later, she would witness his execution in the electric chair.

I thought of Sister Prejean while rereading all five hundred of my father's letters and extracted the most poignant sections that may resonate with daughters who also have fathers in prison. I categorized his narrative by year as my father tried on different clothes from a wardrobe of despair, hope, religion, nostalgia, denial, loneliness, and shame. In the monotony and stress of living in prison, he processed what a thirty-year sentence means, while including fellow inmates' stories, his work life, and spending time in the Health Service Unit (HSU) suffering a variety of illnesses and disease.

When I was cataloging my father's five hundred letters, I serendipitously discovered a song called "500 Letters" by Finnish singer Tarja from her fourth album *Colours in the Dark*. Listening to the lyrics, particularly the chorus, paralleled my shiver each time I unlocked my PO Box to find another letter sent from prison.

500 letters from a stranger at my door
500 letters words like scars no one can see

It felt so innocent, a childish game
Lines of poetry without a name
Waves of paranoia washed upon the page
And soon obsession turned to rage
Why do you love me?
Why do you want to hurt me?
500 letters from a stranger at my door
500 weapons I can't take it anymore
500 letters words like scars no one can see
500 secrets slowly killing me
At the mercy of a violent hand
Drawing images in my head
I can't escape the way I feel inside
In every shadow just a breath behind
Why do you love me?
Why do you want to hurt me?
500 letters from a stranger at my door
500 weapons I can't take it anymore
500 letters words like scars no one can see
500 secrets slowly killing me
They found the final letter lying by his side
A smile was on his face, cold as ice
One last message written only for me
"Now you won't forget
I see you in your dreams"
500 letters from a stranger at my door
500 weapons I can't take it anymore
500 letters words like scars no one can see
500 secrets slowly killing me

Hush, Hush

The idiom "Don't air your dirty laundry" was first used in English in 1867 and derived from an old French proverb *Il fault laver son linge sale en famille*, meaning, "One should wash one's dirty laundry at home." Shedding light on my father's experience is a risk worth taking to acknowledge the journey that many are forced to take when a parent goes to prison. Am I the daughter of a predator or a member of an extraordinary loving family? It turns out I am both.

I had additional concerns. Did I want to welcome possible embarrassment writing about this taboo subject while I am still moving around in the world as a mother, wife, and educator? How would this published story affect my husband, my children, my friends? These thoughts ran through my mind on a loop until my husband used the shutoff valve, a handle that when tightened, restricted water flow, or in this case, the stream of negative thoughts that resulted from telling my father's story. My husband looked at me and said, "You didn't do this. Your dad did. Know the difference." He was right. I think differently. I respond differently. I carry myself differently.

I was tired of censoring, making excuses, and pushing the mute button. If people asked casually "Is your father coming to your daughter's dance recital?" or "What are you doing for Father's Day?" I felt forced into lying about him being too busy or out of town or sick. Neighborly questions like this put me on edge to keep up the image that my father was absent in socially acceptable ways, not absent because he was a convicted felon behind bars. Although I was reluctant to write a memoir and did not want to further malign my father's legacy, I wanted to be free of the stigma and suspicion. After all, I loved my dad. But I hated what he did.

My father's story cannot be told in a vacuum. There were a lot of people involved, and I felt responsible in seeking approval or consent to tell his story. In checking in with my family and friends while the draft of this book was percolating, one family member warned, "Don't bring the devil back into your life." She didn't want me to get tangled in the trauma again. Throughout the process of writing, I was trying to cause the least amount of heartache, but the idea of keeping it all in the family triggered an image of putting it in a drawer and slamming it shut.

Why not just move forward instead of craning my neck back to stare at the ugliness again? Unsolicited advice urged me to ignore it and maybe it will go away. But dismissing the truth that my father spent the last decade of his life in prison was like carrying around a purse of counterfeit gold coins. I wasn't looking for answers or solutions, but lessons and healing. I wasn't determined to right the wrongs of my father. Instead, I wanted to tell his story from my interpretive lens as a daughter who had lived through unexpected lies, glaring truths, abandonment, extradition, and incarceration.

I swapped isolation for inclusivity. Who was out there like me and my father? Did they also experience the social stigma of having a parent in prison? Not having a father figure in my life resulted in some of the most difficult early adult years, but looking back on the letters we exchanged has increased awareness and validated the decisions I made to continue our relationship instead of terminating it.

Greetings and Salutations

The first thing my father would tell you about himself was that he was born in a blue-collar factory town and was a self-made success story. The youngest of three boys of Polish and German descent, he was a scrapper. He grew up in the shadow of his older brothers, always feeling lesser or smaller than his siblings. He leaned into overcompensating by mowing lawns in elementary school, and later sold pencils door to door after he dropped out of college. He slowly climbed the corporate ladder, reaching prominence in many marketing and sales companies. After my mother died, he left corporate life and became an entrepreneur, opening his own carpet-cleaning business. For as long as I can remember, my father was high energy, a mover and shaker. He couldn't sit still; he was like a human fidget spinner, he whirled around the house, painting, vacuuming, cleaning the cars every Sunday, scrubbing, buffing, waxing. He thrived in creating an orderly environment. He liked planning, list making, and marathon running. And at the center of it all, he demonstrated his deep commitment to the Roman Catholic faith.

When I was growing up, my father gave me a model to emulate. What he did around the house imprinted on me. Every night, an empty breakfast bowl, spoon, and ripe banana was placed on the kitchen table next to a list written on his yellow notepad, outlining the following day's goals and activities. Sometimes, there were five items on the list, and other times, there were twice as many to-dos to be done. Unconsciously, he handed me an invisible template for future boyfriends: fixer, dreamer, motivator. My father created a standard of measurement.

Was my father a good man? I believe he was. Later in life, he hurt the people he loved most and, of course, the victims and their families. He had a sickness that made him reach for a silent, violent control as often as he reached for love. I believe my father developed a sickness in his head based on the overwhelming pressure to be perfect, to be holy, to be successful. The man inside of him tried to fight off the mental illness by working harder and harder for control.

Like all of us, he had flaws, but his flaws were magnified during the last years of his life when light became dark. What a dramatic change from his early years of innocence and hope. What happened along the way? As I read his letters, I realized there is no straight line from birth to death.

CHAPTER 2

Caught between the Devil
and the Deep Blue Sea

*This hour I tell things in confidence, I may not
tell everybody but I will tell you.*

—Walt Whitman

I am now at the point where I am going to disclose the awful details of my father's crimes. This has been the hardest chapter for me to write. The title of this chapter includes the word devil. The phrase "Caught between the devil and the deep blue sea" is a way of saying that someone is in a predicament or a dangerous place with no easy way out. It originated from the nautical practice of sealing the seams between a ship's wooden planks with hot tar. The devil, in this context, is the name given to the ship's longest seam, which is typically the most prone to leaking. The devil for me was my father.

I've started, stopped, and started writing the content of this chapter several times, and thought about what I teach my composition students: writing is a process. Be patient. Be honest. Be brave. One of my favorite authors, Anne Lamott, shares her wisdom in "12 Truths I Learned from Writing and Life," a TED Talk I download and play in my classroom every semester. Two of my favorite truths she passes on are Truth No. 4: "Everyone is screwed up, broken, clingy, and scared, even the people who seem to have it most together. They are much more like you than you would believe, so try not to compare your insides to other people's outsides. It will only make you worse than you already are. Also, you can't save, fix, or rescue any of them." And Truth No. 6: "Every writer you know writes really terrible first drafts, but they keep their butt in the chair. That's the secret of life. That's probably the main difference between you and them. They just do it. They do it by prearrangement with themselves. They do it as a debt of honor. They tell stories that come through them one day at a time, little by little."

Even within ourselves, we can carry many versions of the past. Our relationship to the past can change, and stories we might have once told about our lives shift to more closely represent who we imagine ourselves to be. My father wrote mostly about his successes, accomplishments, and dreams fulfilled in the series of letters he sent me. He didn't reveal much about what may have led to his crime, his conviction, his confinement. But when your identity is threatened, you fight for your life—the life you imagined you would live. Being labeled as evil is antithetical to who my father thought he was and who many knew him to be—a trusted leader in the community, my softball coach in junior high school, a philanthropist, animal advocate, and churchgoer.

Shocking Secrets

I will never forget that day I found out the first big shameful secret. My father was on his knees, crouched down in our living room, cradling his face in his hands. It was as if he wanted to hide in the broad daylight, right in front of me. All the blood was drained from his face. He looked so lost and forlorn. He was scaring me. I had never seen him like this, shrunken and deflated. He usually carried himself with energy and confidence. It was supposed to be like any other low-key family weekend with a backyard barbecue dinner and maybe playing a board game. My father and stepmother had been married for seven years and were staying with us for the weekend after a short drive from their home in

Wisconsin, but I could tell when they arrived that something was amiss. They were both disconnected and acting awkwardly.

It was 1999, almost a decade after my mother had died. I was pregnant with our second daughter at the time, and our oldest daughter had recently turned two years old. I thought my father was about to tell me he was given a fatal cancer diagnosis or was filing for bankruptcy or going through a divorce from my step-mother or he had gotten into a car accident or was involved in a home foreclosure. These were the bad thoughts that swirled around in my head. I never ever imagined he would whisper, "I only touched her underpants. It was not on her skin. I wouldn't hurt her." The words hung in the air. I gasped. And for the first time, I had a hard time finding words. I had a hard time making meaning out of what my father had confessed out loud on the floor on his knees in our home.

Was he telling me he was a pedophile? This was absurdity. There must have been some mistake. This was *not* my dad. He would have to convince me that he was capable of actively seeking out children to abuse. What was his thought process? Where did this come from? Why did this happen? Was he abused as a child? Was it only once or multiple times? Were there multiple children? I could not believe his words. I felt ambushed. Shocked. I felt sick.

Finding out a family member is a pedophile is a brutal reality for all involved. "The family faced social ostracism and stigmatization from their community. And they felt their own feelings of shame. These repercussions often fall on the families of sex offenders. While acknowledging the seriousness of the crimes committed by these sexual predators, their families are confronted with the difficult task of trying to reconcile their good memories with the knowledge of the terrible act the relative committed. They are caught in the middle" (Muller 2018).

It was impossible to understand how our middle-class family of otherwise high-functioning, educated adults could be going through anything like this. When I was growing up, my father gave me the nickname "Boobah," a term of endearment he coined when

I was a baby. He told me he would walk into my bedroom and say "Boo!" and I would respond "Bah." The nickname originated from an element of surprise and astonishment on my face seeing my father's face. This was how I felt when my father confessed what he had done. It was completely unexpected, startling, and a sudden discovery of truth in terrifying proportions that I was not ready to believe.

Complex Definition

Not long after my father's admission of guilt, I started reading about pedophilia and trying to gather as much information as I could. I binged on articles, books, websites, pamphlets, statistics, and facts trying to regain a sense of certainty or control. Although I am not a counselor, psychiatrist, or lawyer, I decided that my father must have contracted a disease of the mind. It was the only possible explanation I could live with. I certainly didn't condone his behavior but felt the topic was worth exploring to try and understand how this lapse in judgment, this impulse, this horror could have occurred. I did not want to minimize or distort his actions, but I sought to figure out why and how he could act on these dark disgusting urges.

I was perplexed by the different terminology used to describe sex offenses. For example, what is the difference between a sex offender and sexual misconduct? And would these labels be considered within the same category of sex crimes? I was seeking information and found that *sex crime* is a catch-all term to describe illegal or coerced sexual conduct against another individual, including indecent exposure, prostitution, rape, sexual assault, solicitation, and statutory rape. Each state has its own statute of limitations to file charges against the alleged offender.

Sex offender is a legal term referring to a person convicted of a sexual offense such as rape, child molestation, sexual misconduct with a minor, sexual violation of human remains, incest, and/or communication with a minor for immoral purposes. Definitions vary by state and local laws would need to be consulted to determine what is applicable. There are levels or degrees of sexual offenses determined by the nature of the crime and possible risks to the public. In some states, sex offender laws apply to juveniles as well as adult sex offenders.

Sexual misconduct is a type of violence that uses power, control, and/or intimidation to harm another. It can include sexual harassment, sexual assault, domestic violence, dating violence, and stalking. The term sexual misconduct can be used as a more contemporary and perhaps humane approach to describe acts undertaken for sexual gratification against the will of another or without permission.

However, sexual misconduct fits within a broad category of sex crimes. The exact acts encompassed by the crime vary significantly by state and require a careful reading of state statutes. In some states, sexual misconduct refers to acts that do not fall within the precise definitions of rape or sexual assault, while other states may have sexual misconduct statutes that overlap significantly with other sex crimes.

The label sex offender can facilitate complex discussion. For example, in the advocacy group Women Against Registry (https://womenagainstregistry.org) or WAR, President Vicki Henry talks about how the sex offender label is unfair and can destroy families' lives. The stigma of being publicly branded a sex offender can result in job and housing discrimination. It is a blemish carried by the offender and the offender's family. Advocates like Henry support a more redemptive path back to society for those convicted of a sex crime. In addition, activist and public speaker, Matt Duhamel, (https://theoutspokenoffender.com) addresses this topic in one of his many videos, "Shedding the Sex Offender Label" available at https://youtu.be/vWgo8PAsIlM. Duhamel believes if sex offenders take full responsibility for their actions, have empathy for themselves and victims, forgive themselves and learn from their mistakes, the label can and should be changed.

Is the term sex offender difficult to say out loud? For me, yes. Is it shameful? For me, yes. In fact, the working title of this book was *Forgiving my Father, the Felon*, but after many rounds of editing, workshopping, and revising, I came to the conclusion that one of the best ways to find my voice was to include *sex offender* in the title. My publisher also advised that including sex offender in the title was most closely related to the authentic contents inside.

There was no debate about my father being labeled a sex offender. It took me a long time to forgive my father and accept who he was. The label did not define him but was a part of him. However, in someone else's case, they may not feel the label sex offender fits because it may be an injustice that was done or an investigation is still pending. Although my father was not convicted of pedophilia, he was convicted of a sex offense. In my father's case, I did not associate the term sex offender as derogatory or demeaning. Instead, it is an accurate legal term that contextualized his actions.

According to the World Health Organization, pedophilia is "sexual preference for children, boys or girls or both, usually of prepubertal or early pubertal age" (WHO 2010). A pedophile is defined as an adult who is sexually attracted to children. The word is derived from Greek *paîs* or *paidós*, meaning child and friendly love or friendship. Pedophile is exclusively used for individuals with a primary or exclusive sexual interest in prepubescent children aged thirteen or younger.

The American Psychiatric Association's publication of the *Diagnostic and Statistical Manual of Mental Disorders* (DSM-IV) outlines criteria for pedophilia (1994):

A. Over a period of at least six months, recurrent, intense sexually arousing fantasies, sexual urges, or behaviors involving a child generally thirteen years or younger

B. Fantasies, sexual urges, or behaviors cause clinically significant distress or impairment in social, occupational, or other important areas of functioning

C. Person is at least sixteen years of age and at least five years older than the child in Criterion A

Pedophilia was first formally recognized and named in the nineteenth century. Most documented pedophiles are men. What causes pedophilia? Is it physiological or psychological or both? I wanted a deeper understanding of my father's brain chemistry and the psychological underpinnings of his crime. Did his external circumstances and impulses provoke unconventional actions? According to a 2008 study published in *Neuroimage*, "The neuronal mechanisms underlying normal sexual motivation and function have recently been examined, the alterations in brain function in deviant sexual behaviors, such as pedophilia, are largely unknown" (Schiffer et al. 80).

Was my father abused as a child? Did he have multiple personalities? Is it genetic? What are the risk factors? Studies published between 1982 and 2001 conclude that child sexual abusers use irrational thoughts in order to meet their personal needs. They will justify the abuse by making excuses and redefining their actions as love and mutuality. Pedophiles also exploit the imbalance in adult-child relationships (Lawson 2003). Some studies of pedophilia in child sex offenders report that it co-occurs with low self-esteem, depression, anxiety, and personality problems (Marshall 1997).

Geriatric Sex Offenders

When my father went to prison, he was in his midsixties. According to a study of elderly sex offenders, "They are similar in most respects to sex offenders against children in other age groups, with regard to the seriousness of the abusive behaviors described, but they differ in terms of being of higher socioeconomic status, having stable backgrounds, and reporting low rates of personal sexual victimization. These factors may contribute to their apparent skill in avoiding detection. In common with younger child sex abusers, these elderly offenders demonstrate low levels of psychiatric illness and in particular of organic disorders" (Clark and Mezey, 360).

According to the Bureau of Justice figures from 2017, nearly two hundred thousand people fifty-five or older are incarcerated in America, including thousands arrested for sex offenses. While the vast majority of all sexual offenses are still committed by younger men, statistics show that nearly four percent of all persons arrested for sexual crimes in 2006 were age sixty and above (Hart 2008). Older sex offenders apparently engage in more passive sexual activity, such as fondling and improper touching rather than intercourse.

Some courts may treat elderly sex offenders as less of a risk because of their physical frailty. However, in "Elderly Sex Offenders: What Should be Done?" it is noted that although older adults have a myriad of special challenges tolerating the rigors of prison life, they still deserve punishment for their crimes. "Although compassionate in some circumstances, society generally hesitates before allowing freedom to those who inflict harm upon others, especially those that inflect harm upon children. Criminal responsibility and fair punishment require that criminals who commit such crimes, although elderly, be punished in accordance with the law. Some further topics needing investigation include considering the different treatment of elderly sex offenders during incarceration (e.g., the costs associated with housing these criminals, the special needs of sex offenders while in prison, and how those special needs are accounted for)" (429).

Should older sex offenders, the most-reviled class of citizens, be allowed to safely live as they enter their final stages of life? What happens to grandpa when he is not so grand? How do we take into consideration the long-term effects of caring for elderly felons? Older offenders often require more medical care and struggle to find help. But most states are not going to alter laws to accommodate an aging offender population. Vindictiveness is also a factor in the rallying cries, "Lock 'em up and throw away the key!" There is no empathy for a sex offender because a sex crime is still a sex crime, no matter if you're eighteen or ninety-eight years old.

Repulsed or Rehabilitated?

Unfortunately, there is no evidence that pedophilia can be cured and that is unlikely to change. This news was devastating as I was also told there was no cure for my mother who died from lung cancer. The lung cancer five-year survival rate is less than twenty percent. Despite our efforts to work with the benefits provided by our health care insurance to meet with a variety of oncologists, my mother died at forty-nine years old, only one year after her diagnosis.

My mother had access to a variety of treatment plans, including radiation, chemotherapy, and surgery. Unlike my mother's fatal physical illness diagnosis, my father's mental illness diagnosis appeared to be concealed or avoided as most prisons are not equipped to assess, manage, and treat predatory sexual behavior. There is a lack of suitable facilities for older offenders who require ongoing nursing care both physically and mentally.

Access to professional support and help is often limited for pedophiles. Treating sex offenders involves opening wounds that no one wants to open for either the victims or the perpetrators. Some treatments may include clinical castration as a "reasonable penalty" and solution in lieu of a rehabilitation program or lengthy incarceration. This barbaric form of punishment can appeal on an emotional level for victims and their families who may thirst for vengeance or a more severe punishment than time in prison. But chopping off body parts is not a "cure" to a problem that demands a long-term clinical approach.

Most psychotherapies used to treat pedophilia that incorporate the principles and techniques of cognitive behavioral therapy. The focus of therapy is to enable the patient to recognize and overcome rationalizations about his behavior. In addition, therapy may involve empathy training and techniques in sexual impulse control. The most common type of cognitive behavioral therapy used with sex offenders is relapse prevention and is based on addiction treatment. Relapse prevention is intended to help the patient anticipate situations that increase the risk of sexually abusing or assaulting a child and to find ways to avoid or more productively respond to them.

Can child sex offenders be rehabilitated? The most effective therapies to lower the recidivism risk focus on treatment that combines psychotherapy and medication. These methods help pedophiles refrain from acting on their desires, but therapy will not help to omit these desires entirely. In addition, treatment may yield positive results if a patient with pedophilia is motivated and committed to controlling his behavior.

My father's rehabilitation occurred outside of prison while on probation. I knew he was attending what he referred to as "counseling" sessions, but he never shared details with me while he was living. He would always change the subject if I asked about it. However, before he died, he verbally gave me permission on the phone that I could have access to all he "left behind" after he died. I wanted to make sure I was not breaching confidentiality from his therapy sessions. He did not object to me reading what he recorded in his therapy notebook that was mailed to me in the box of his belongings from prison. It was the first time I could excavate and try to understand some of his experiences during therapy.

I transcribed the notes that were shared with me in his Sexual Offender Treatment (SOT) classes. Attending weekly classes was a requirement during his probation period, 2001–2002. Participants were charged $26 per class.

SOT Meeting
October 18, 2002

Assignment: Categorize targets and write as many descriptor words as you can under each category.

Manipulation
Lie
Exaggerate
Sneaky
Cunning
Grooming
Enticement

Passive/Aggressive
Defiant
Frustration
Power
Envy
Defensive
Anger
Resentful
Inadequate

Self-Pity
Inadequate
Low Self-Esteem
Stupid
Failure
Worthless
Loneliness
Rejection
Self-destruct
Overwhelmed
Sabotage
Alcohol
Boredom
Hopelessness
Depression
Paranoia
Isolation
Unlovable
Acceptance

Deviant
My father left this section blank

Power/Control
Anger
Selfishness
Dominance
Perfection
Ownership
Revenge
Egotistic
Abusive
Aggressive
Gossip
Isolation
Obsessive/Compulsive

Entitlement
Favoritism
Envy
Selfish
Trust
Grooming

Reading the lists my father created using words to describe himself made me wince. Did he honestly associate these words with his identity? I noticed that the category "Self-Pity" contained the longest list of eighteen words, including derogatory adjectives, like stupid and unlovable. But the "Deviant" category was intentionally left blank. Did this category embarrass him or compound his shame? Was this form of list making helping him become more aligned with the truth? Did it help him communicate more freely without judgment? Or did these assignments in his therapy sessions trigger a range of messy emotions he didn't want to face? Would he rather not record the rawness and trauma? What lessons did he learn in these activities? And did other participants in the group have similar words on their lists?

I turned the page to read more notes for a specific chapter he was required to read in therapy from his Assignment Workbook in a chapter called "Victims." He had copied the words from this chapter in his notebook before completing the assignment connected to it.

Assignment Workbook: Chapter 9 Victims
(Page 58, Chapter 9, Victims)

Ultimately, there is one overriding reason for an individual to be in treatment. That is, you have harmed others, making them victims of your deviant behavior. Victims are also the final standard that must become very important in your future life. Having no more victims is also the measure of whether you are successful in your recovery or not. On the other hand, if you have more satisfying relationships, are successful in your career, and enjoy your life more but have even a single victim, then you have not made the slightest bit of real progress.

No matter how you feel as a sexual offender, you will never appreciate the full consequences of your deviant behavior on your victims. If, as a sexual offender, you are incarcerated and live a life behind bars for ten years, then you have paid a small price

DANICA HUBBARD

compared to what your victim will pay over a lifetime. The effects of abusive sexuality last long and go deep.

In a good treatment program, you will learn the detailed effects of your crimes. The final criteria of progress in therapy are not your level of satisfaction with yourself and your life. It is not how well you communicate. It is not your understanding. It is: Have you changed your deviant ways of thinking, acting, and feeling? Can you and society be sure that you will never victimize anyone again?

Assignment: Create a list of questions victims may ask and then answer those questions in essay form from their perspective.

Questions Victims May Ask

1. Why did you do those things to me?
2. Will you ever do those things to me again?
3. Why me, what did I do?
4. Why did I have to keep secrets?
5. Was Mom in on this with you?
6. How do you feel about telling as I did?
7. What if you were not turned in? What would happen?
8. Why do I feel badly about your offense?
9. Why did you seem the better friend than my parents?
10. What did you do to set up to control me?
11. How will I know if you are going to hurt me again?
12. What can I do to protect myself?
13. How will things be different at home?
14. Are my friends safe? Do I need to tell them?

And after the list of fourteen questions my father created, he followed up with a narrative he created from his victim's perspective. What would she say to him? Here is what he wrote:

> *I am so hurt that you broke our trust by touching me where you should not have. You scared me and made me feel dirty and that I*

was doing something wrong for you to pun-
ish me the way you did. I don't know why I
wanted you to be a better friend than my mom. I
thought you liked my mom. I thought you loved
me. I have horrible dreams at night wondering
if you are going to hurt me again. I don't want
to tell my friends so you can't molest them,
but how do I do that? Everybody must think I
asked you to touch me because I am a bad girl.
Everything is different at home now. Everyone
keeps asking me to tell them what you did. I am
so angry at you. I am so afraid. How can such
a close friend make me feel so much fear and
shame? Why me?

I'm not sure if these therapy sessions reduced or heightened his feelings of guilt. In his notebook, he appears to take some responsibility but not entirely. Perhaps, he thought he was part of some sort of twisted greater good? Was there a moral justification for his decision to behave badly because he had contributed to so much "good" in the community? Did he believe his good outweighed the bad? It is difficult to believe what our instincts tell us sometimes. I did not want to believe my father was a pedophile. I am still uncovering the truth of his crimes, and each truth is another shock to my system.

In March 2002, he wrote in his SOT notebook:

I was put on the hot seat in my SOT group.
They have lifelong histories of sexual offenses,
and they can't believe why I am not like them.
We even have a marathon (four-hour session)
in April which will cost $52 because they all
are convinced that without the SOT's leader,
they would have no life. The SOT leader told
the group that I haven't found a job yet and now
I want to leave the state to see my daughter.

*He said my daughter isn't ready to see me yet
and she will never accept me again as a father
or grandfather to her daughters. The parole
officer already called my daughter and knows I
will never ever be alone with my granddaughters. I have had counseling now though and
know I can do it. If I pass the lie detector test
and the SOT group all agrees, then I can visit
my daughter and granddaughters.*

Although I loved my father and desperately wanted him to give him a second chance in acknowledging progress he may be making in therapy, I was fiercely protective of our daughters. I could not trust him despite his promises that it would not happen again. I could not release my grip on our rules of no contact with our children or any children in our vicinity. He had to stay away.

The thought of him re-offending caused me to put up a fortress around our daughters. He was never allowed inside. I was so uneasy about my father trying to make plans with us that I had nightmares about him convincing me to get together with him. In my nightmare, he had manipulated and groomed me, telling me he made personal strides and changes and was ready for reintegration and reunion. I loved him because he was my father but made the permanent decision to keep him at a safe distance.

My father was granted a transfer from Wisconsin to live with his older brother, Bob, in Georgia in 2003. He was required to register as a sex offender in the state. Here is a summary from his Sexual Offender Treatment program leader upon my father's departure:

June 26, 2003
Discharge summary from Community Counseling, Ltd.

James attended adult, group sex offender group counseling eighteen sessions. He was an

*active participant in the group counseling ses-
sions. He followed through on all counseling
assignments that were given during the course
of his group participation.*

*Issues addressed included understand-
ing and managing triggers and urges related
to sexual offending, use of accountability to
negate opportunities to manipulate, understanding the impact of power differentials in
relationships, understanding relational aspects
within offense cycles, and use of planning and
preparation to intervene with offense poten-
tials. Recommendations regarding further
treatment will be provide upon request.*

Revered and Feared

I discovered my father had been living two types of lives,
presenting himself differently depending on the situation, like
Dr. Jekyll and Mr. Hyde. He was a man held in high regard in
the tight-knit town he moved to shortly after my mother died. He
made friends easily because of his extroverted personality. He was
reliable, a doer, and one to spontaneously offer help. I was proud
of my father's long list of accomplishments. I only knew him as
altruistic, a disciplined marathon runner, and faith leader in the
Catholic Church. Of course, I also had a built-in bias; after all, he
was my father.

I never saw anything overtly sexual or inappropriate in my
father's actions when he was with me or my friends. But looking
back, I now question all the times we enjoyed gathering for boat
rides, barbecues, outdoor summer concerts, and skiing vacations.
Was he really using that time to look provocatively at my friends?
I tried to retrace the memories and even asked my closest elementary school, high school, and college friends if he had ever made
unwanted advances. They insisted that he had been nothing but
kind and respectful toward them, but I kept asking and eventually

the answers I did not want to hear came to the surface after years of being buried in silence. The mask my father had been wearing was peeled back, slowly and painfully.

My father accrued a large network of friends wherever he went. From his daily lunch breaks ordering "the usual" tuna sandwich at the same local Subway restaurant to launching his boat every season in the harbor, he was pleasant and approachable. To his neighbors, my father presented a shiny and organized exterior: he was the guy who washed his car every weekend, kept an immaculate lawn, shoveled the driveway and sidewalks, and walked our dog nightly. He was known for his daily routines and predictability. I didn't see anything amiss growing up, but one of my relatives recently told me that she always thought my father was hiding something, that he was too good to be true. She never knew exactly what he was hiding but warned me, "All that glitters isn't gold." How could he be both the friendly guy and super predator at the same time? I never suspected the dreadful acts he secretly unleashed on young girls.

Was I oblivious? Caught up in my own world and not paying close enough attention to his? I was a young adult working and attending graduate school full time in a different state. Sometimes, I would see my father on weekends but not regularly. Was I too busy to notice? I thought back on the times I had called and my stepmother told me that my father was out on the boat with a young girl from a local family. Other times, he was not home because he was taking the same young girl out for ice cream or horseback riding. At the time, based on outward appearances, he may have been acting like a father figure or surrogate grandfather.

It appeared my father made himself valued and trusted to the family, showing interest in the young girl, spending more time with her. However, the harsh reality I later discovered was this young girl became one of his many victims of sexual abuse. Years later, he briefly confessed to me during one of my visits with him in prison, rationalizing his relationship with this young girl. He told me, "I never hurt her. I couldn't hurt her. We only had outercourse, not intercourse." I froze. What did *that* mean? He continued, "I only touched her on the outside, on her underpants." Shock waves. This sent shivers down my spine, conjuring up horrifying images of when I was also sexually abused around the same age, in first grade, by a man in our neighborhood in 1974. I will never forget that vulnerable, confused, and unsafe time. That feeling is imprinted forever.

I learned predators often groom parents to gain their trust before turning their attention to the child. When they groom the child, they often do so right under a parent's nose to give the impression of innocence. I've also learned that perpetrators count on parents being afraid to call out exactly what they are witnessing because they are worried about hurting feelings, offending, or being seen as wrongfully accusing someone. They will ignore their instincts and shy away from difficult conversations to avoid a falling out.

Were there more victims like her? How many secrets was my father keeping? After he confessed to me and the police, I reluctantly started asking my friends and family again. Did my father ever touch you? Did my father hurt you? Did my father make you feel uncomfortable? The majority of my friends and family initially responded "no" to all my questions, but recently, another victim emerged and disclosed her encounter to me.

We went to out lunch, and I brought our Catholic elementary school yearbooks; we reminisced about ice skating in the park district rink across from my grandparent's house, watching the freight trains from our backyard, and making brownies after school. She became a police officer like her father. During lunch that day, she told me how different our fathers were. Her father spent his career chasing people like my father. She revealed to me that my father took his one and only chance with her in a "safe and spiritual" place over forty years ago, in church. She told me it happened when we were together as an elementary school class, during our First Holy Communion, a religious celebration when a child receives the Holy Eucharist for the first time. She was seven years old, standing in the vestibule in her white dress. The vestibule of the church is a gathering spot for before and after Mass.

First Communion is an important moment for Catholic families and is celebrated with gatherings and gifts, just like a child's baptism. This ceremony has a conservative tone, so the girls' gowns are modest or not embellished too much. White or ivory dresses are worn with sleeves and simple cuts or patterns below the knee in length or calf length.

This ceremony is seen as a reenactment of the final meal of Jesus Christ, known as the Last Supper. The communicants receive bread, His Body, and wine, His Blood, in the memory of Jesus. The First Communicants are ushered to end of the pew near the aisle. I remember the day being crowded with family and friends. It would have been a rare moment to be alone on such a day.

But on this day, she was alone in the vestibule. My father walked by her. He brushed his hand under her dress. She thought maybe he was leaning in to give her a celebratory hug. But it quickly turned into an inappropriate invasion of her space. This was another gateway for his abuse to continue. What could she have possibly done in a crowded church? Scream? He clearly crossed the line in a split second. And she played it over and over again in her mind. Was it considered groping? A violation? Indecent?

Examples of sexual battery include:

- patting a person's buttocks
- grabbing or fondling a woman's breast
- touching the victim's genital area
- forcing the victim to touch an intimate part of the offender's body
- pressing a kiss on the mouth

When I told her that I was writing a book about my father, his conviction, and prison sentence, she told me it was a very painful memory. I respected her decision not to provide additional details, but if I had known this information about my father earlier, it would have illuminated his recurrent behavior toward prepubescent girls under ten years old. The secrets of him engaging in consistent contact were coming out, and the stories were only getting worse.

Pattern of Pedophilia

While writing this book, a family member called to divulge her story about my father that she had kept hidden for several years. As I recorded her narrative, I felt like dry heaving at the keyboard as the details spilled out onto the page. I cautiously asked her a series of questions and wanted to know the answers, but at the same time, I was aware that by asking, I was reopening a wound that had been closed for her. How could this have happened *again*? And how did I not know?

When she told me about my father's abuse, I was coincidentally watching a series on Netflix called *Broadchurch*, a British crime drama. One of the lead characters, Detective Sergeant Ellie Miller, is involved in investigating a murder of a young boy. As the fictional series unfolds, her husband is accused not only of murder in the seaside town but also being a sex offender. Combining modern socially conscious themes, her husband is on trial for engaging in sexually explicit acts with a minor prior to his murder. The townspeople began to turn against Sergeant Miller because they didn't believe her claims that she had no idea her husband was a pedophile. After all, he lived with her, he slept in their marital bed, and she was a trained police officer. Exasperated, she swore to her family and friends that she had no indication her husband was a pedophile. There are many scenes throughout the series where Sergeant Miller is crying, screaming, and frustrated in dealing with her husband's alleged secret sexually deviant behavior.

I can relate to Sergeant Miller's dramatic reaction when talking with my family member now about my father. I couldn't know what I didn't know. Was she being merciful to spare me this sensitive and sickening information until now? What depths of pain was she feeling keeping it locked away all these years? Is this one of the reasons our extended family became disconnected?

Getting back to my family member's story of abuse with my father, she began our initial phone conversation with "It's just unsettling," which was a dramatic understatement for what she was about to willingly and graciously unpack. She described my father as having a special aura and charismatic charm that filled the room. Everyone loved him, including her parents. He was the man who personalized every situation by knowing your name, asking open-ended questions, sounding intelligent and interested. "The person he presented to the world was so polished. I know now that he had to be some kind of a sociopath." He existed in two worlds and could switch from one to the other effortlessly. She described him as disarming with a keen ability to engage people in conversation. He was inclusive, humorous, and warm. She admired these qualities about him. But as a six-year-old girl, it was confusing to witness him change like a chameleon when he wanted something more from the relationship.

She said that the abuse started amidst the chaos of my mother being sick with lung cancer in 1989. Her mother, a registered nurse, often came to our house to give my mother sponge baths, make her dinner, brush her hair, and help with medications. Her mother made a noble effort to help care for my dying mother for hours while trying to entertain her two elementary schoolchildren at the same time. So my father would step in to relieve some of the stress by taking her and her brother out to the grocery store while her mother cared for my mother. It all seemed heroic as they appeared to be working together as a family through the challenging stages of my mother's illness.

"On the car ride to the store, he would touch my leg or casually wrap his arm around me in the front seat." She continued, "I thought he was just sad because his wife was dying, so I wanted to help him feel better. I felt so badly that she was sick."

At the grocery store, she said my father would let them have free reign running up and down the aisles, buying whatever they wanted—cookies, candy, pizza, and potato chips. And sometimes, he would even drive through McDonald's on the way back for extra treats. He continued to lavish gifts each time they arrived, like colorful-scented markers and expensive toys. But the gifts were a twisted bartering system for what he really wanted in return. During the next car ride with her, he would grope her leg a little higher, hug a little longer. His persistence in taking her away in the car became more frequent as my mother became more ill.

"I only remember seeing your mom being sick and wearing a scarf on her head. When she lost her hair from the chemo treatments, your dad started asking me to sit on his lap in the car. He told me I could drive home from our trips to the grocery store on his lap." Was he somehow displacing his need to control my mother's terminal illness to making threats and exerting physical force against a vulnerable child? Was his grief impairing his sense of judgment? Or was he manipulating the situation for his own self-serving sickening gratification?

Six weeks after my mother died of lung cancer in 1990, my father announced he was engaged to marry another woman who was seventeen years younger than him. I had no idea he was even dating another woman. Was this going on while my mother was sick? He told me he met her at the grocery store. When I met her, I had a hard time accepting her. It was too soon. Members of my family were also furious and confused. "Your wife's body is not even cold in the grave!" they said, sorting through emotions of how he could have moved on so quickly into a new relationship. Years later, she would abandon and divorce my father when he was sentenced to prison. She stopped any contact with my father. I did not understand their relationship and was disappointed when she came into our lives and dropped out of our lives, never looking back.

My father asked my relative, the girl he was abusing for the past year, to be the flower girl in his wedding to my stepmother. He took her to JCPenney to try on dresses and insisted he model for him. He promised she could ride in the limousine to the wedding reception, again, manipulating and exploiting his position of trust within the family.

She said there was a lull in his abuse for about two years, and then he started to call again. He had moved to Wisconsin and wanted to reestablish his connection with family to stay in touch even though my mother had died. He began taking her and her brother, now a few years older, to the movies. "We didn't have money to go to the movie theater, so when he called to take us, it was special to see a movie when it first came out instead of waiting for it to come out on video. The first movie was *101 Dalmatians* then it was *The Mighty Ducks* and more. He sat through kids' movies with us, but, of course, I was expected to sit on his lap on the way home. I remember one time I purposely wore a complicated jumpsuit for protection. I thought it would be too hard for him to get inside, but he found a way."

Sinister Sleepovers

Outings to the movies eventually led to extended time with him on weekends. But because he now lived out of state, he invited her and her brother to stay overnight. He appeared to carve out time for these special weekends, and no one thought anything of it. She told me that her parents never hired babysitters and really did not go out. They were very protective during her childhood and established many rules, including no slumber parties, a rite of passage for many young girls that often includes inviting a group of friends overnight for fun activities like painting nails, eating junk food, and braiding hair. So when my father picked up her and her brother to stay for a weekend, this was definitely out of their ordinary family expectations and routine.

During this time, my father was married to my stepmother. However, on the weekends when he arranged for the kids to sleep over, she was conveniently not around. She would make plans to visit her elderly mother who lived out of state. My father would say that my stepmother wasn't interested in babysitting and didn't like children. These excuses sounded reasonable, and his exclusive time with them was welcomed and encouraged. He was acting like a caring role model, the perfect family member to spend time with. When they arrived in Wisconsin with no other adult supervision, the first thing he asked them to do was take showers. She said, "He wanted me clean, which made me feel dirty."

At night, he would give her younger brother a shot glass of Nyquil, the cough and cold medicine that causes drowsiness, so he could have uninterrupted time to abuse her. He told her to keep it quiet and not to tell anyone. She didn't think anyone would believe her. The "worst" sleepover weekend was when she was eight years old. My father was becoming more aggressive each time. "He got me away from my brother during the day and brought me into the bedroom, shut the door, and forced me to watch lesbian pornography with him. I guess it was not 'ordinary' pornography, but hypersexual, double-ended dildo style pornography, and I did not understand this at all. He locked the door and made me watch until the end."

It was embarrassing to hear about my father's wrongdoings. No one should ever go through the abuse that she did. It makes me angry all over again. I felt helpless that I did not know what was going on.

When she was in fifth grade, the school held an "officer friendly" safety day, and a police officer came to her classroom to talk about the warning signs of sexual abuse. He advised students what steps to take if they were in an uncomfortable and inappropriate situation, reviewing the warning signs and encouraging them to communicate openly with concerns. He said it was important that they know their body is their own and reminded them that they have a right to say "no" if they do not want to be touched. He assured the class that it was never too late to start the conversation when something is wrong. He offered a straightforward scenario, "An adult man is forcing you to sit on his lap. What do you do? If something like this has happened to you, tell a police officer, parent, or teacher." This presentation immediately clicked with her, but she still did not tell anyone for fear they would be mad at her. Instead, she went home and wrote all her memories of the abuse down in a journal so she wouldn't forget. And she put the journal away in a dresser drawer.

In 1994, she was ten years old, and suddenly, the abuse stopped. Looking back, she thought maybe she aged out of his preferential range. She was partially relieved that he no longer reached for her but carried the heavy burden of tarnished physical intimacy he created with "a feeling that never went away."

My father died in 2017. She didn't come to the funeral and neither did her parents. I wasn't sure why, but now, of course, I know. She said, "I was relieved when your dad died. I told my parents there was no way we could go to a funeral mass celebrating his life. I told them they had to be on my side. He didn't deserve our mourning."

When she was fifteen years old, a sophomore in high school, she found out my father was formally charged as a sex offender. She took out the journal she had kept secret for years and shared it with her parents for the first time. She was sobbing. She was angry. She was shocked that he did this to another girl like her. And this time, he was caught. Her parents never pursued charges against my father. They told her they didn't want to put her through the arduous process of testifying. He had already taken too much of her innocence away.

In her midthirties now, she is a vibrant young woman with a beautiful family of her own and is very successful in her career and community. The entire time we were talking, I kept thinking it was like she was describing a case of tinnitus, the ringing in your ear is always there, but you move forward in life and try to ignore it. I am so grateful that she shared her story. I hope I have respectfully captured the depravity of what my father did to her as he wreaked havoc in her life. She concluded our conversation by saying, "I wondered if he would write me a letter from prison and apologize, but he never did because he didn't think he did anything wrong. The only memory of your dad is my abuser, but he is still your dad."

My Friend, His Fault

Another victim who came forward after my father had died was one of my childhood best friends. She did not tell me about an encounter with my dad until we were both over fifty years old. We spent almost every day together from junior high until we both graduated from high school. We also went on skiing vacations for a few days during spring break. My mother did not accompany us because she said she didn't like the cold and had no interest in downhill skiing, so as an only child, I enjoyed having a friend along, plus it gave my father the opportunity to be alone with us.

My father reserved a hotel room, and me and my friend would sleep in one bed and he would sleep in another, and I didn't think anything of it. We were in junior high school. She told me that when she slept over at my house and when we were on one of our skiing vacations, she would wake up in the middle of the night because she sensed someone was watching her. She initially thought she was dreaming, but it turned out that my father was sitting on the edge of the bed, watching her sleep. This sent shivers down my spine. She said he never touched her, but it was obviously uncomfortable and creepy to have your friend's father looking at you while you slept. We had known each other since we were eleven years old, and she had been internalizing it for over forty years. When he admitted to his sexual abuse crimes publicly, it brought her little comfort. She said, "He can't ever make it right because he should have never started."

In the months and years that have followed, I have learned a lot more about my father's crimes, but I still struggle with uncovering the truth. He could never make up for what he did. Why wasn't he honest in coming forward with his abuse of multiple victims? Did he have remorse for every individual he hurt over the years? It was as if we were all tugging on opposite ends of a rope, trying desperately not to fall into the dark massive abyss he created.

I'm not sure there will ever be closure for the victims' families, and I don't know if justice was fully achieved. The only thing

I can be thankful for is that my father is in a place where he can't hurt anyone again.

My Story of Sexual Assault by the Man Next Door

Learning about my father's crimes triggered memories of my own childhood sexual abuse. The nightmares came flooding back. To be clear, my father never touched me inappropriately, but a male neighbor did. It happened over forty years ago in 1974. I was in first grade, and we lived in a southwestern suburb of Chicago. At that time, it was a new neighborhood with single-family homes constructed in cozy cul-de-sacs. I remember riding home from school in my mother's aqua 1965 Ford mustang, turning off Cass Avenue, and seeing the subdivision entry sign welcoming us home to "Hinswood" in big white cursive lettering.

Mr. G was the man who touched me when I was six years old. He and his family lived a few doors from our house, and his children were part of our playgroup. We would roam the neighborhood on our bikes and play kick the can until sunset. Mr. G's house was popular for a variety of reasons. First, he had a refrigerator full of Coca-Cola. He would offer all the neighborhood kids a chilled bottle and a bowl of pretzels almost every time we were in his sunken living room. I vividly remember his living room because it was the same style and decor as the one of my mother's favorite television shows, *The Mary Tyler Moore Show*. When we stepped down into Mr. G's living room, we would sometimes pretend to be characters from the show, dancing and singing the theme song:

Who can turn the world on with her smile?
Who can take a nothing day and suddenly
make it all seem worthwhile?
Well, it's you girl, and you should know it
With each glance and every little movement, you show it
Love is all around, no need to waste it
You can have the town, why don't you take it
You're gonna make it after all!

Mr. G would hover around me and my friends. He would pull on our ponytails and tease, "I got your tail!" Or make odd observations like "It's too hot out today to wear those tight jeans." He would greet us with an enthusiastic "How ya doin', buttercup?" I used to tell my mother that Mr. G's house was the coolest since there were no rules, just television and treats, a place to hang out and escape the heat during summer days.

I got to Mr. G's before my friends arrived one afternoon. He answered the front door and told me his kids were finishing their chores but I could come in and wait in the living room. I had been in this same room many times before, so I didn't think it was strange to watch cartoons alone. Plus, he gave me a bottle of Coca-Cola, so I was content to bide my time before my friends could join me.

I had no reason to distrust him. And then things got strange. Mr. G was sweating. I could see yellow circular stains on his tank top. He told me he had been working outside. Then he turned around and left the room. A few minutes later, he returned, and I jumped. It was as if he snuck up behind me. I didn't hear him coming. I looked at him. He crouched down toward me and got a little louder, "I am going upstairs to take a shower." It was an announcement. A proclamation. I wasn't sure how to respond, so I remember saying something like, "Uh, okay." And he left the room again.

Trust Me, Touch Me

Something inside of me questioned why he would tell me he was going to the bathroom, but I turned my gaze back toward the television because an episode of *The Bugs Bunny Show* was on. A few minutes later, he called from upstairs, "Hey, Danica! I need you to come up here. I need your help!" My heart beat faster. Had Mr. G fallen in the shower? What if there was blood? What should I do? I had never been upstairs in Mr. G's house before. I scrambled to my feet and spilled Coca-Cola on the carpet. It frothed over the fibers, leaving a sticky mess on my sandals. I thought I would get in trouble for not cleaning it up, but I left the spill and ran upstairs. "Here, over here!" he shouted. I turned the corner and saw him standing naked, holding his penis in his hand. The water was off, but he was dripping wet. I froze. "It's okay," he purred. Long pause. "You're okay." Silence. "Touch it."

He lunged toward me. My eyes felt like they popped out of my head. I screamed and ran down the stairs. I was so thankful not to be wearing a ponytail that day because I replayed his aggressive grab toward me and thought how he could have gotten "my tail." I ran down the block. I ran home. When I got home, I didn't know how to process what happened. As a six-year-old, I had never seen male genitalia. I was scared. I thought I would get in trouble. I was a rule follower, and when an adult asked me to do something, I did it. I felt like I had broken the rules. My mother was home, but I didn't tell her right away. I remember reconstructing the time line; the first person I told about Mr. G's unwanted advancement was my father. I trusted my father to protect me, rescue me, and make things right.

In the mid-1970s, reporting and interviewing children about sexual abuse was different than it is today. It was not easy for a child to come forward to report predatory behavior. At that time, the standard forensic interview technique in a sexual abuse case often led to a child withholding or denying sexual abuse allegations. Kathleen Coulborn Faller, a principal investigator on the University of Michigan National Child Welfare Work Institute, has published extensively in the area of child welfare. She addresses how forensic interviewing practices have changed over the past forty years, pointing out how children used to be interrogated in the 1970s when asked about alleged encounters with sexual offenders.

Faller explains, "The initial professional response was to gather information about sexual abuse 'by any means necessary.' The means included interviewing the child multiple times, asking leading questions, and using other suggestive techniques" (35). The process needed to change to lead to increases in sex-crime reporting. As a child, speaking out and holding people accountable for bad behavior like sexual abuse was not encouraged or accepted like it is today. A lot has changed.

Faller notes in her longitudinal research:

> In the United States, the passage of the Child Abuse Prevention and Treatment Act in 1974 (CAPTA) had implications for child welfare policy and practice beyond what the US Congress could have anticipated. Among other provisions in CAPTA that transformed the child welfare system was mandated reporting of child maltreatment. This provision in federal law both expanded the professions who were mandated to report and the types of maltreatment to be reported. Subsequent to the passage of CAPTA, virtually every state amended or promulgated a state law to comply with CAPTA. States did this because there were federal discretionary funds tied to a state statute in compliance with CAPTA provisions. Mandated reporting resulted in an exponential increase in reports of suspected child maltreatment to local child protection agencies.
>
> In 1978, the first year of data collection under CAPTA, fewer than 700,000 cases, or 10.1 per 1,000 children, were reported. In 2012, the most recent year for which there are aggregated data, there were 3.4 million cases reported involving approximately 6.3 million children, 46.1 per 1,000 children (36).

This was decades before the #MeToo movement where more people newly felt empowered to share their stories. The terms "rape" and "sexual assault" have been used interchangeably in coverage of events leading to the #MeToo movement. In contrast to the specific criminal act of rape, the term sexual assault can describe a range of criminal acts that are sexual in nature, from unwanted touching and kissing, to rubbing, groping or forcing the victim to touch the perpetrator in sexual ways.

Child sexual abuse in the 1970s was a crime that often went undetected or was dismissed. It wasn't talked about and stayed hidden in the shadows with the perpetrators. Fast forward to the recent media coverage of Larry Nassar, the Michigan State University gymnastics coach who pled guilty to three counts of first-degree criminal sexual assault as part of a plea agreement with the Michigan Attorney General's Office. Nassar's young victims, many of whom were sexually violated for decades, didn't tell anyone about it and kept their secret until now. Nassar first began working with young girls in 1978 as an athletic trainer in high school. He joined the USA gymnastics national team medical staff as an athletic trainer in 1986 and went on to sexually abuse hundreds of girls over decades before being sentenced to life in prison in 2018.

In my case, my parents worked with a field investigator who came to our home and visited others in our neighborhood to interview kids regarding Mr. G's behavior in 1974. I remember pieces from the line of questioning, like "What were you wearing?" and "Did he touch you?" and "Are you sure?" This seemed to drag on and on. I squirmed in the chair. I felt like there was uncertainty as the investigator took notes and listened to my answers to his questions, which led to more questions. Was Mr. G's purpose to sexually degrade or humiliate me? Was he sexually aroused or gratified using words to elicit a future sexual encounter clothed or unclothed?

Mr. G instructed me to touch his body part, but I didn't. Did the investigator think I was lying? Was he looking for my story to change? I started to regret telling my parents about Mr. G. There was so much attention on me and my friends now, and I did not like it. In my six-year-old mind, what did I gain by telling on Mr. G? What were my friends saying? Were our stories the same?

I just wanted it to be over. Although I don't remember every question that was posed throughout the investigation, I can recall the investigator handing me a Dum Dum lollipop when he finished interrogating me. I got the same type of lollipop when I went to the doctor's office. Was this investigator man some type of doctor? I wasn't sure. I was in first grade, and all I knew was the lollipop he gave me wasn't the flavor I liked.

Ultimately, my parents did not move forward with formally charging Mr. G. I recently requested a record of Mr. G via the Freedom of Information Act (FOIA), a state statute that provides the public the right to access documents and records, but I found out no record exists. How would Mr. G be held accountable for what he did? How would he take responsibility? The "solution" in 1974 came in the form of a moving truck outside of Mr. G's house toward the end of the summer before school started again. Mr. G and his family moved away to another neighborhood, a different community. Even now I wonder if his abuse stopped or continued on.

Child abusers aren't strangers luring kids into white vans with tinted dark windows. They are usually known adults playing games kids like, giving kids things they value, working their way up from affection to things far more nefarious. It is the type of grooming relationship featured on the true crime Netflix documentary, *Abducted in Plain Sight* (2017), where next-door neighbor Robert Berchtold sexually abuses twelve-year-old Jan Broberg during the 1970s in a small Idaho town. In awkward and uncomfortable interviews, the Broberg family candidly share how they revered and trusted Berchtold with their young daughter. They had no idea he was sexually abusing her in the basement of their own home. It shattered their trust in him and one another as details of her kidnapping, brainwashing, and violations came to light. Eventually, their family relationships unraveled because of the sexual abuse, shame, and guilt. How could they not know? How could they believe in a man who was harming their daughter all along? How can the cycle be broken?

Researching and revisiting my father's sexual abuse crimes uncovered not only one young girl but allegedly multiple young girls since 1974, the same year I was abused by our neighbor. I created a graphic to visualize the hidden pattern and how it continued for decades until he was arrested, tried, convicted, and sentenced to prison. The time line of his sexual abuse is jarring.

**My Father's Alleged Sexual
Offenses Time Line**

James Colwell

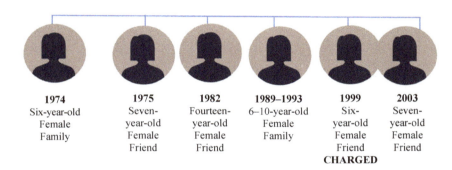

1974	**1975**	**1982**	**1989–1993**	**1999**	**2003**
Six-year-old	Seven-year-old	Fourteen-year-old	6–10-year-old	Six-year-old	Seven-year-old
Female	Female	Female	Female	Female	Female
Family	Friend	Friend	Family	Friend	Friend
				CHARGED	

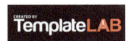

CHAPTER 3

Below Deck

*It is not what a lawyer tells me I may do but what
humanity, reason, and justice tell me I ought to do.*

—Edmund Burke

This chapter will chronicle what it was like for my father to secure legal counsel, appear in court, await sentencing, be placed on probation, released on parole, and register as a sex offender. Below deck is the nautical phrase that refers to what happens inside of a ship beneath the deck; the crew may be gathered below deck to work, sleep, and eat as they reside on board. In my father's case, it is a look inside at what types of legal responsibilities and expectations are involved when a parent goes to prison.

Though my father committed the crimes, our immediate family was also embroiled in the heat of an unrelenting pressure cooker. As each week passed, we were bombarded with making choices in this highly sensitive situation he put us in. Our challenges in handling his crimes may provide insights on how to find resilience along the way.

Slogging through the legal system can be confusing, emotionally draining, and costly. Between 1999 when my father was first arrested and 2000 until his first court hearing, we lived in a perpetual state of purgatory. I developed insomnia and panic attacks wondering and worrying. Would the case go to trial? Was my father going to jail? Or worse, was he going to prison? Jail and prison are often used interchangeably, but jail is a place for people awaiting trial, and prison is a place for convicted criminals. How long? Where? What are the legal fees going to be? Would his conviction be publicized? Would we be targeted by victims of his crimes?

Preamble to Prison

My armchair reference of a courtroom proceeding was watching the television show *The People's Court* in the mid-1980s. Watching Judge Wapner render a verdict from the bench alongside his trusted bailiff, Rusty, was the only litigation drama I had witnessed. It was my introduction to court, and I was fascinated by the discourse community with vocabulary, like plaintiff, defendant, and revocation, and hearing Latin words and phrases like mens rea (criminal intent), de jure (according to law), and prima facie (the way something looks at first glance). In high school, I explored the idea of becoming a lawyer and enjoyed taking classes that centered on research and persuasive writing. Law felt like a noble career I could count on, so I immersed myself in critical thinking skills, reading, and honing in on communication tools that promoted argument as a way to uncover the truth. I practiced pacing a pretend courtroom floor in my bedroom, arguing a case and impressing a makeshift jury of my childhood stuffed animals.

Despite my keen ability to engage in verbal sparring and confidence in making formal presentations, my daydreams of attending law school were not realized. Instead, I took a different but related path in earning a degree in Bachelor of Science in Communication, a degree in Master of Arts in Writing, and a Doctor of Philosophy degree with an emphasis in reading, writing, and literacy. I have been teaching composition, developmental reading, and service-learning courses for over twenty-five years at a community college and love reading students' essays just as much as creating my own. I have published travel blogs and academic articles centered on global perspectives and analyzing the writing process. Ultimately, my career led me to the classroom instead of the courtroom.

However, my problem-solving skills and passion for research did not fully equip me to handle my father's intensive investigation and multiple court proceedings. His ongoing criminal case challenged every intellectual resource I had. It's important to become familiar with legal terminology and definitions while going through the process because it can be overwhelming and confusing. Knowing some "lawyer talk" allowed me to partially participate and follow along as the conversation continued between the courtroom and corrections facilities. I included a glossary in the back of this book for first-timers.

Steps to incarceration often happen slowly over weeks, months, and sometimes years depending on the court's caseload. After an individual enters a guilty plea (like my father did), the vast majority of cases are resolved without trial, and defendants are arrested, charged, and sentenced.

It makes the most sense to protect victims of sexual abuse throughout the legal process, with the perpetrator having no contact with the victim. In my father's case, I thought he would be jailed immediately after his arrest. However, there is a process where the case is decided, and it takes time. This is a neutral time period where courts are protecting both the sexual abuser and the victim throughout the investigation.

It is a labyrinth of logistics before sentencing can finally occur. According to Ave Mince-Didier, a criminal defense attorney who has worked with the Georgia Court of Appeals, the California Supreme Court, and the San Francisco Superior Court, she writes about child molestation cases like the one my father faced, "Those convicted of child molestation face a dire reality. The laws governing child molestation vary from state to state, but most jurisdictions mandate long prison sentences and vigorously prosecute child sex abuse cases. When released from prison, those convicted must register as a sex offender. They must also report to a probation officer and may be ordered to undergo counseling. In some civil cases, offenders have been directed to pay restitution to their victims."

My father recorded a personal time line in a notebook while his attorney assisted in managing this high-stake case. Although a six-month gap appears in his notes, he kept many files of court papers and documents related to his case. Once he was taken into custody after being arrested, he went to jail to undergo the booking process which included getting fingerprinted and photographed.

Although no determination of guilt was made at that point in the process since his case was still pending, the evidence forwarded to the district attorney (DA or prosecutor) decided whether there was sufficient evidence to present to a judge. He confessed to sexually abusing one of his most recent victims at that time, but it was officially considered my father's first offense. He was first detained in jail then given probation with strict supervision, a required treatment program and long list of rules.

The following are his notes from his confession to police in 1999 to his only collect call to me from jail in 2002 before he was permitted to transfer to the state of Georgia following strict probation guidelines, including registration as a sex offender to live and work in the state of Georgia.

August 30, 1999

Went to police. Moved out of town to Whitewater. Resigned from church board and as trustee for Village of Fontana. Free on $10,000 signature bond.

September 1999

1:15 p.m. court call. First time in Walworth County Circuit Court. Criminal complaint charges formally read in front of Judge John Race with my attorney Frank Lettenberger. Assistant District Attorney Tara Schipper presented state's charges. Three felony charges. First charge alleged July 29 incident in Village of Walworth and two charges from alleged August 25 incident in Delavan. Victims and Witness Coordinator Evelyn Schulz together in court.

64

October 1999

   Motion to suppress. Videotaped testimony from victim's family used as evidence.

November 1999

   Judge Michael Gibbs—preliminary hearing.

May 2000

   Turned sixty years old last month. Sentenced to one year in Huber with thirty years probation.

Huber Facility is a county jail located in Waukesha County, Wisconsin. When assigned to the jail, the inmate will go through a process called "classification." According to the Waukesha County Sherriff Department County Jail Facility Inmate Rules, Regulations, and Information Packet, classification is the process to determine a housing assignment (restricted, medium, or direct supervision). During the initial ten days of confinement, the classification unit will gather information about criminal history, incarceration history, and past and current disciplinary record.

An interview will be conducted on or near the tenth day of confinement, and a determination regarding housing assignment will be made. Routine housing reviews will be conducted throughout incarceration to determine if the current level of supervision remains appropriate.

Classification determination is not arguable nor can it be grieved or appealed. The individual's status is reviewed on a regular basis. If the individuals are classified for a direct supervision housing assignment and refuse the assignment, they will automatically be recycled to a restricted housing unit. There are a number of factors used to determine a long-term housing assignment and classification. No one's factor is more important than the others; however, the ability and willingness to follow all facility rules and staff instructions and behavior during the initial ten days of incarceration will receive a high degree of scrutiny (2).

May 2001

Received no credit for 2,000 hours of kitchen work

State stayed ten-year prison sentence (a stayed sentence means the court gives the convicted person a more lenient sentence in return for his cooperation with certain conditions. If the conditions are not followed, harsher penalties will ensue).

May 2002

Released from Huber 5/15/02

Must report weekly to parole officer

Weekly SOT class (Sexual Offender Treatment) required, $26 per week, over $100 per month

June 2001

Sherriff received a call from a concerned citizen that people in my old neighborhood must be told about my offense. Parole officer sent a letter to victim's family informing them of my new address and vehicle type. A neighborhood meeting was held about me. There was a red X spray painted on the door of my trailer and a bag of dog shit left on my steps.

August 2001

Fired from Geneva National Golf Course where I was mowing lawns.

September 2001

Parole officer already made multiple home visits. I am required to see him weekly and write a report on where I am at all times. I can't have a computer, but I can't go to the library to use one.

October 2001

Received permission to go into the jail each Sunday morning to help Pastor Mike with church services. Parole officer putting pressure on me to get a job or I will go back to jail.

November 2001

Still don't have a job although I sold my Chem-Dry business and building, equipment, and assets. I don't know where to apply because I am overqualified for a lot of jobs in the area.

December 2001

Got a job as operations manager at Petco in Janesville. They did a background check. I worked for the general manager with the plan that after a year I would become a regional trainer to help train new managers in the Midwest. I can be alone around animals.

January 2002

Parole officer told me he was giving some of his clients to a new PO, a female understudy. He told me he was only giving up his good and well-behaved clients like me.

On January 3, I met with both parole officers and told them I got a job at Petco. They were both very upset because I was working in a pet store with kids. I explained my job responsibilities, but they were still upset and said, "When you come back here in two weeks, you must have told your immediate supervisor the details of your crime." When I returned two weeks later, the female parole officer asked if I had spoken to my boss. I said, "No, he had been off work for a few days, and I couldn't find the proper time to talk with him about it privately." She said I must tell him within the next few days. I told her I would tell him. But when I went to work that day, she had already called my boss and told him I could no longer work there. I then told my boss about my crime, and he said he still wanted me there and that I was supposed to call my parole officer immediately. I did and she told me to come straight to her office. When I arrived, she said I lied to her and have no option but to go to jail within the hour.

So on 1/17/02, I went to jail for five days. My punishment upon release was I must go back to a weekly schedule at the parole office and I must go to SOT every Saturday with "the tough group." These are offenders who have been in prison for ten years, and they will not let me lie. It turned out to be the same SOT leader in this group, and the SOT is required to be paid in cash for each class.

February 2002
Required to give parole officer a list of all job interviews, also any side jobs I have done for cash. She said I am too sneaky.

March 2002
Requested a travel pass to see my daughter. The parole officer initially said it would not be a problem but then told me I needed to bring her an updated list of my job search. While I waited, she verified several jobs I had attempted to get but then said she had to schedule a lie detector test for my sexual history, the same test I took while I was in Huber jail and passed. She said I am too vague in my answers. If I pass the test, they may give me a travel pass to see my daughter. In the meantime, I was put on the hot seat in my SOT group. They have lifelong histories of sexual offenses, and they can't believe why I am not like them. We even have a marathon (four-hour session) in April which will cost $52 because they all are convinced that without the SOT's leader, they would have no life. He told the group that I haven't found a corporate executive job yet based on my background and qualifications. He told the group I wanted to leave the state to see my daughter. He said my daughter isn't ready to see me yet. and she will never accept me again as a father or grandfather to her daughters. The parole officer already called my daughter and knows I will never be alone with my granddaughters. I have had counseling though and know I can do it. If I pass the lie detector test and the SOT group all agrees, then I can visit my daughter and granddaughters.

April 13, 2002
I showed up at a meeting at the parole office today at 3:00 p.m.

There were six people there, including the parole supervisor. At the end of the meeting, they handcuffed me in the office and *took me to jail. I paid $405 cashier's check at this meeting for the lie detector test. They said I had broken probation rules and lied.*

I called my daughter collect today from Huber 4:27 p.m.–4:42 p.m. I told her to get a hold of Frank. He can help me. He knows my case. He knows me. I have to get out of Wisconsin. I can't live here without being fired, threatened, or maybe even killed.

Call My Lawyer

My father initially retained Defense Attorney Frank Lettenberger, partner in a law firm located in Delavan, Wisconsin. His firm provides legal advice and representation in criminal law, traffic-related offenses, family law, and personal injury cases. I spoke with Mr. Lettenberger a handful of times over the eighteen years my father was in and out of prison. My father would constantly reference Frank in his letters.

I interviewed Mr. Lettenberger in February 2021. I asked him to review the chronology of my father's case, but he told me that attorney-client privilege still survives even after death, but I could look at the Circuit Course Access Program (CCAP) to read public records and court of appeals decisions. He told me he defended my father's case because he was part of a segment of society that was left without support and most often condemned.

He developed both a professional and personal relationship with my father throughout the course of events. "We will never know all the underpinnings of what happened, but I always thought what he had was similar to an addiction, like a drug. People like your father don't have to have pedophiliac tendencies, but they do have a need. They often need more in different degrees and potencies. Loving your father was an amazing gift you gave to him. No matter what his offense, there is still a human being in there."

Mr. Lettenberger represented my father on his original charge of sexual abuse but did not represent him in later years when he was extradited from Còsta Rica. James Martin, another defense attorney, represented my father when he returned from Costa Rica, but Mr. Martin has since died. Mr. Lettenberger tried to help my father toward the end of his life by fighting for a compassionate release but was unfortunately not successful. He told me he harbored a lot of anger toward the attorney general and judges in my father's case. "It was some of the most aggravated anger I have ever had. It was garbage. The system is broken and becomes more broken every day."

Mr. Lettenberger is no longer defending sex offenders and hasn't for many years. He told me that looking back, the only thing he would have done differently in handling my father's case is advising him not to move to Georgia. "This caused even more problems for him. There were more allegations. Further offenses. I felt I helped him the best I could, but it was up to him at that point."

Public or Private Attorney

If someone has been accused of, or charged with sexual child abuse, it is advised to consult with an experienced attorney as soon as possible. Most courts deal with this crime very seriously as a matter of social policy. Even if someone considers themselves innocent, they still need representation. My father was interested in finding a lawyer who had successfully defended those accused of child molestation.

A criminal defendant generally has two main options in the legal process: securing a public defender or hiring a private lawyer. There are pros and cons to either decision. A public defender is a governmental employee whom the court appoints to the case. Public defenders are familiar with a variety of criminal cases and work with prosecutors on a routine basis. Since many people are unable to afford a private lawyer for their criminal defense, public defenders often have large caseloads. Due to possibly juggling hundreds of cases at a time, a public defender may have limited amounts of time to actually meet with clients. Sometimes, the public defender may only meet with a client a few minutes before he or she enters a plea. A public defender may have difficulty finding the time, energy, and attention necessary to formulate a solid legal defense. If a client is not satisfied with their legal representation, he or she may find it difficult to get a new public defender.

The accused or convicted could select a private lawyer who appears to have more one-on-one time with clients and access to paralegals, staff, and associates to help work on the case. This time can also be used to get better acquainted with the defendant and to discover information to scaffold and build the case. Although my father turned himself in to the police and confessed to his sexual offenses, he still wanted to mount the strongest defense possible. Consequently, he hired a private attorney. But legal services and related costs were a high price to pay to aid in his defense.

Probation and Parole

Probation in criminal law is when a person has been convicted of a crime but is not sent to prison. Instead, it involves a period of supervision over an offender, ordered by the court. Probation officers are assigned to make sure they are abiding by the rules the judge has ordered. If an offender does not abide by the rules, the judge will revoke probation, and the offender can be sent to prison. The terms of probation, including how long it lasts, will be laid out in the order of probation, which describes what the offender is required to do.

The most basic terms of probation require:

- meeting regularly with probation officer by phone or in person
- appearing at all court hearings
- paying fines and restitution (money to victims)
- not traveling out of state without permission of the probation officer
- following all local, state, and federal laws
- avoiding illegal drug use or alcohol consumption

Parole is when a prisoner gets out early and serves some part of the remaining sentence under parole supervision. Parole is considered on the basis of reports from various people, such as prison officers, psychologists, offender managers, and others. These reports cover the nature of the offense, home circumstances, release plans, behavior in prison, and progress made in prison. The parole process begins months before the earliest date of release. Reports will be considered by the parole board, and the prisoner may have to attend a hearing. If a prisoner is granted parole, he will be given license conditions and supervised in the community. Parole can allow the offender to reside in the community rather than being sent to prison. The idea is to reintroduce the offender as a productive member of society while keeping the community safe.

Parole and probation regulations vary by state, but in the state of Wisconsin, according to legislation in the year 2000, there are several Wisconsin Statues pertaining to sex offenses:

- Wis. Stat. § 939.62 (2M), § 302.11 (1M), 939.62 (2M) creates a new category of persistent, repeat child sex offender and establishes mandatory sentence of life without parole. Defined as having second or subsequent conviction for a serious child sex offense, which includes child sexual assault, sexual exploitation, incest, enticement, soliciting for prostitution, other offenses.
- Wis. Stat. § 302.11 (1g), § 301.03 (11), 980.12 (2) denies release to a person sentenced to imprisonment for a serious child sex offense if the person refuses to participate in pharmacological treatment using an antiandrogen. Also authorizes such treatment as a condition of parole or probation. Requires in three years a report by the corrections department to legislature on use and effectiveness of the treatment.
- Wis. Stat. § 301.08 (1), § 972.13 (6), § 20.410 (1) allows lifetime supervision of persons found not guilty of certain sex offenses by reason of mental disease or defect,

following release from mental health commitment. Establishes hearing, examination process for termination of supervision, and allows temporary corrections custody of persons who violate conditions of lifetime supervision.

In my father's case that began in 1999, initially, he was sentenced to probation and sent to county jail. He was required to participate in a work-release program. The conditions of his probation included paying court costs and registering as a sex offender. Following a conviction for a sexual offense, a prisoner will be assessed to determine how much of a risk he is. The risk assessments are reviewed on an annual basis and also prior to release. My father was determined to be a risk based on the seriousness of the allegations; therefore, the long list of twenty-five parole rules were readily enforced. Additional restrictions were placed on him as part of the terms of his probation.

His defense attorney at the time, Frank Lettenberger, wrote this letter on my father's behalf:

April, 2002
Letter from Law offices of Danz, Lettenberger, and Glasbrenner to Probation and Parole

Under Wisconsin Administrative Code DOC Sec. 328.01, the purpose of probation is:
"To provide rules for community- and facility-based supervision, services, and programs for clients under control in order to ensure public safety, promote social integration…to provide opportunities for obtaining education, training, work experience, coping skills, and other programs and services to enable offenders to live constructive lives…"
The spirit and purpose of this provision is to help probationers adapt back into the community and help them have successful transitions so they will not re-offend and become involved

in the system again. One of the purposes of the Department of Corrections Code is to provide guidelines for coping skills as well as reintegration into the community. It is clear that while living in Walworth County, Mr. Colwell* is basically a man without a country.

At the time of sentencing, Mr. Colwell was a prominent member of the community as he was serving on the Village of Fontana Board as well as serving as a board member at St. Benedict's Catholic Church. It is a long fall from grace for Mr. Colwell, and no matter which way he turns within the community, he is haunted by the memories of these incidents as well as his inability to find employment. It has become an impossibility for Mr. Colwell to live within the community.

This coupled with the fact that Mr. Colwell has now met financial dire straits in that he is paying the highest supervision fee, he is paying for counseling in cash on a weekly basis, he is now going to be required to pay a $400 fee for maintenance and monitoring. Mr. Colwell has been a model probationer and has complied with all requests by his parole officer.

It is interesting that a carrot-and-stick approach is being used on Mr. Colwell despite the fact that he has already completed and successfully passed the first lie detector test. Therefore, the basis of this new condition from the agent undercuts the progress which Mr. Colwell is presently making and does not further the spirit or purpose of probation.

(*Mr. Colwell in this letter refers to my father.)

Sex Offender Probation/Parole Special Rules

1. You shall have no contact whatsoever with any victims of behavior for which you received a criminal conviction nor contact their families—whether in person, in writing, by telephone, by electronic devices, or through a third party without prior agent approval.
2. You shall have no contact with anyone under the age of eighteen years old.

3. You shall notify your agent of any involvement in a relationship and introduce this person to your agent to discuss past sexual behaviors. This shall be done prior to any sexual activity.

4. You shall fully cooperate with, participate in, and successfully complete all evaluations, counseling, and treatment as required by your agent, including, but not limited to, sex-offender programming.

5. You shall fully cooperate with all procedures required to undergo lie detector examinations.

6. You shall not reside or "stay" overnight in any residence other than your designated and approved residence without prior agent approval.

7. You shall permit no person, whether juvenile or adult, to reside or stay overnight in your designated residence at any time without prior approval from your agent.

8. You shall not possess, consume, or use any controlled substance or possess any drug paraphernalia without a current prescription from a physician from who you are receiving medical/psychiatric treatment.

9. You shall not possess, or consume any alcohol, unless given prior approval from your agent.

10. You shall not possess or have in your residence any sexually explicit material, whether visual of audio. This includes, but is not limited to, videotapes, movies, films, magazines, books, pictures, or computer-generated materials.

11. You shall not have in possession any toys, devices, or appliances used for sexual gratification.

12. You shall not purchase, possess, or use a home-based computer, software, hardware, or modem without prior agent approval. You shall not access the Internet without prior agent approval.

13. You shall not enter any establishment whose primary source of income is derived from the sale or display of sexually explicit materials. This includes, but is not lim-

ited to, adult bookstores, adult movie theaters, exotic dance clubs, topless bars, or massage parlors.

14. You shall not attempt to engage in any occupation, not participate in any volunteer activities that places you in direct contact with children under sixteen years of age.

15. You shall not purchase, own, or manage residential rental properties without prior agent approval.

16. You shall fully comply with all requirements of the sex offender registration law. You shall register in person with local law enforcement agencies as directed by your agent.

17. You shall fully comply to submit a biological specimen to the State Crime Lab or DNA testing as applicable and as directed by your agent.

18. You shall pay all court-ordered financial obligations and treatment co-payments as directed by your agent.

19. You shall not enter into any area frequented by persons under age eighteen, including, but not limited to schools, day care centers, playgrounds, parks, beaches, pools, shopping malls, theaters, or festivals without prior approval from your agent.

20. You shall fully cooperate with the electronic monitoring program as directed by your agent.

21. You shall not subscribe to or use any sexually explicit phone service whatsoever, including, but not limited to, 900 sex telephone lines.

22. You shall not hold or exercise any position of authority with the following categories of people: children, the elderly, the mentally/emotionally disabled, physically disabled, or the culturally different/disadvantaged without prior approval from your agent.

23. You shall fully cooperate with the in-house alcohol monitoring system as directed by your agent.

24. You shall maintain a daily written log of your whereabouts and activities as directed by your agent.

25. You shall comply fully with the Department of Corrections Program as directed by your agent. This includes appearing as scheduled to obtain your identification card, carrying the card on your person at all times, and voluntarily producing the identification card when you have any contact with law enforcement officials or Department of Corrections personnel.

Sex Offender Registration

Many states require the convicted person, upon release, to register with the national sex offender's database. They have to provide their name and residence as well as their fingerprints, DNA, criminal history, and photo and vehicle registration. Megan's Law, enacted May 17, 1996, mandates that a county be notified of child offenders residing there and residents have access to that information. Federal law requires adults and some juveniles convicted of specified crimes that involve sexual conduct to register with law enforcement. Megan's Law establishes public access to registry information, primarily by mandating the creation of online registries that provide a former offender's criminal history, current photograph, current address, and other information, such as place of employment.

In many states, everyone who is required to register is included on the online registry. A growing number of states and municipalities have also prohibited registered offenders from living within a designated distance (typically 500 to 2,500 feet) of places where children gather, such as schools, playgrounds, and day care centers.

Sex offender registration with the Wisconsin Department of Corrections, where my father was convicted, must occur once a year. The information required for sex offender registration includes:

- Name, including any aliases
- Personal identification information, including date of birth, gender, race, height, weight, and hair and eye color

- Detailed information about the offense committed
- Address of residence
- Supervising agency
- Vehicle description
- Name and address of employer or school

Any change in job, address, or any of the information above must be provided to the Wisconsin Department of Corrections within ten days. Registered sex offenders are not allowed to change their names.

Under certain circumstances, some or all this information is made available to the public. It may be available on the Internet or through notifications from local law enforcement. The registry is designed to help the public know if someone has been convicted of sexual assault or other sex-related crimes, like possession of child pornography. The aim is to give people information about past offenders and where they live.

The consequences of sex offender registration can be quite onerous. The US Department of Justice conducted a study of Wisconsin's sex offender community notification program, including interviews with sex offenders. Those interviewed reported loss of jobs, denial of housing, and the breakup of personal relationships as consequences of expanded notification and subsequent publicity.

Along with the sex offender registry, people convicted of sex crimes are likely to have a long period of supervision by the Wisconsin Department of Corrections, with restrictions on what a person can look at, who they can visit, and where they can be. They may be monitored by GPS and required to take regular lie detector tests in the way that someone on probation for a crime related to addiction may be required to take drug tests. Local law enforcement officials use the registry as a tool for the public and a way to keep offenders on the list accountable.

Although these laws are in place to protect victims, some believe that perpetrators' rights may be violated in the process. This can be an unpopular opinion on a lightning-rod subject. However, it does offer another perspective to add to a highly sensitive conversation. In an article published by Humans Rights Watch, an advocacy group of approximately 450 lawyers, journalists, and others who investigate and report abuse to bring justice to victims, reform for sex offender laws is discussed in "No Easy Answers: Sex Offender Laws in the US." The article acknowledges the need for public safety but also recommends reform in order to rethink sex offender laws.

The article states, "Protecting the community and limiting unnecessary harm to former offenders are not mutually incompatible goals. To the contrary, one enhances and reinforces the other."

The Human Rights Watch group believes the goal of increasing the effective protection of children and others from sexual violence while protecting former offenders turns into a long list of unnecessary, unjust, and even counterproductive laws. The group recommends changes in federal and state legislation, stating:

> Our research reveals that sex offender registration, community notification, and residency restriction laws are ill-considered, poorly crafted, and may cause more harm than good:
> - The registration laws are overbroad in scope and overlong in duration, requiring people to register who pose no safety risk.
> - Under community notification laws, anyone anywhere can access online sex offender registries for purposes that may have nothing to do with public safety. Harassment of and violence against registrants have been the predictable result.
> - In many cases, residency restrictions have the effect of banishing registrants from entire urban areas and forcing them to live far from their homes and families.

Love 'Em or Leave 'Em

Imploring society to treat sex offenders more humanely is one thing, but actually achieving that goal is another. They are still *humans*, many of whom need psychological help. I am not soliciting empathy for my father's heinous crimes, but he was immediately ostracized within the community where he previously made significant positive contributions. It went from one extreme to another.

When he was on probation, my father read me the list of places he was no longer allowed to go: shopping malls, schools, parks, arcades, playgrounds, bus stops, family functions, holiday festivities, or any other place where children are present. He had a curfew. He could not be in possession of computer programs, photographs, drawings, videotapes, audiotapes, magazines, or books without approval from his parole officer. His world became extremely small and limited, and doing routine tasks was arduous. My father was an avid long-distance runner, and he couldn't run outside without first establishing a route with his parole officer. He was prohibited from changing the approved route despite inclement weather, unexpected detours, or seasonal road construction. He could not have a dog because walking a dog would most likely lead to a place where children may congregate. It was as if he was on house arrest. There were so many rules.

Moving about "freely" became a cruel game of Whac-A-Mole as my father was constantly being struck down with a metaphorical mallet anytime he surfaced anywhere. All eyes were on my father, passing judgment. His efforts to return to any form of routine were futile. And I realized it was his fault. He must come to terms with what he did and accept the consequences of his actions. The saying "You made your bed, now lie in it" would apply here. Based on local newspaper reports, most people would not want him living in their community.

Where *can* sex offenders live and work when they have little choice? There is a unique remote community in South Florida called Miracle Village where sex offenders are welcome to live in clusters with one another. Offering sixty-one concrete bungalows on twenty-four acres, with 120 resident offenders at any given time, the village is operated by the nonprofit Matthews Ministries Inc. Potential residents must profess their belief in God and take responsibility for their crimes in order to be accepted here. There are rules about the types of crimes as well—no violent sex crimes or other convictions related to drugs or burglary. According to the article, "Welcome to Pariahville," "When you are a registered sex offender in America, you lose the right to choose where you want to live. By law. Your backstory doesn't matter. Nor does the nature of your crime or your excuse. You are exiled from society, and only a few places will welcome you. Here is exile that is also asylum from the larger, unforgiving world. Here is weirdly enough, real community. I mean the kind of community that would protect you from vigilantes' intent on dragging you out of bed in the middle of the night to take turns kicking your teeth down your throat."

In addition to the required legal parameters that now surrounded my father, I had to deal with my immediate family, friends, coworkers, relatives, and neighbors who I feared would change their relationships with me if they discovered what my father had done. I kept his crime a secret for fear that people closest to me would pull away and reject me and my family due to the disgrace he caused. I was worried that if anyone was aware my father was a sex offender that somehow, I would be tainted as well by having a criminal in the family. According to the article "Collateral Damage: Family Members of Registered Sex Offenders," being associated with a sex offender can raise a family member's profile in the community, resulting in a closer scrutiny into their lives that can affect the normalcy of their daily existence. This intensified surveillance can worsen the sense of stigmatization. It's like being secondarily imprisoned.

It took a couple of decades to work through my worries and realize my family and friends respected and loved me no matter what my father did. These were not my illegal acts. His crimes were not hereditary or genetic.

It's a confounding paradox. How do I support someone I love while not condoning their actions? Instead of reacting and attempting to do damage control, it was important for me to realize I could not edit out his actions. There is no backspace or delete button when it comes to a sexual offense. Being strong and decisive about the details of my father's case but caring and attentive about his emotional needs made the process even more stressful. I needed to maintain a balance between my personal needs and the needs of my convicted parent. My father completely ghosted his parental responsibilities and obligations because he was immersed in his own emotional, social, mental, physical, and financial well-being. He went into survival mode, and I went into a protective shell for my family. We both suffered in our own ways.

Sentencing Hearing

Before the sentencing hearing in my father's case, there were a lot of meetings scheduled, phone calls made, e-mails sent, documents prepared, reports filed, and character references requested. A judge heard arguments from the prosecutor and the defense attorney and sometimes the victim. Prior to the sentencing hearing, a presentence investigation report will result in sentencing guidelines, which are a range of possible jail or prison times. The court may also consider alternative programs like probation.

The judge evaluates several factors in order to decide on a sentence, including:

- Criminal history
- Family support
- Employment history
- Social history
- Circumstances of the case
- Risk of danger to others
- Risk of future alcohol or substance abuse

In sentencing a first-time offender, a shorter sentence may be considered with additional stipulations based on the crime. There are sentencing ranges based on several factors including the age of the perpetrator, age of the victim, age disparity, and relationship between the perpetrator and the victim. My father's case did not go to trial. The victim testified via videotape that was played before the court. I was relieved when a trial was avoided so the victim did not have to publicly recall every detail of the alleged abuse in a live courtroom setting.

It was difficult for me to determine what kind of sentence my father would receive. He had no criminal record, sterling employment history, reputable social history, and no indication of alcohol or substance abuse. He also had full support from me, his only child. My father asked for character references from family, friends, faith leaders, and coworkers. Several letters were written on his behalf.

His brother not only wrote him a letter but also traveled from out of state to be with us during the sentencing hearing. I will always appreciate his kindness and comfort during that incredibly stressful time. Not only was he sympathetic but supported my father emotionally when he needed it. "That's what family does," he said. His brother was convinced that it was all a terrible misunderstanding and thought the case would be thrown out of court. His assumptions and expectations were that his brother was innocent. He could not come to terms with my father's crime as a sex offender and denied it ever happened.

We went out to dinner at a local restaurant the night before the sentencing hearing. We all ordered spaghetti. I kept thinking how "normal" it felt to be at a restaurant with my father and uncle, but then my brain would switch into overdrive, worrying about his criminal case. Would this be his last dinner with us? Is there spaghetti for dinner in prison? I looked across the table at my uncle. He kept shaking his head and repeating, "This just isn't Jim. It just isn't." I could not sleep that night. I felt the kind of exhaustion that sleep doesn't cure.

I wrote my character reference letter to the judge on April 3, 2000, and kept a copy for my father. I hoped to provide context regarding my father's fortitude in caring for my mother while she was ravaged with terminal cancer, his integrity in the workplace, and dedication in practicing the Catholic faith. These virtues were how I defined my father while growing up. It was troublesome coming to terms with this new and shocking information that he was a sex offender.

Honorable James L. Carlson
Circuit Court Judge
Walworth County, WI 53121

I am writing this character reference on behalf of my dad, Jim Colwell. In 1968, my mom and dad welcomed me into their lives. Raising me as an only child, both of my parents were responsible for making long-lasting positive impressions not only on me, but family, friends, neighbors, teachers, coworkers, and the community.

I have fond memories of my parents. They were my best teachers, offering me a spiritual, moral, and ethical foundation. During their twenty-seven years of marriage, they exhibited a loving relationship, complete with trust, laughter, and honesty. My parents were friends and supported each other.

I witnessed their loving support throughout my life but especially when my mom was diagnosed with cancer. In less than a year, I saw my parents undergo one of the most dramatic transformations both physically and mentally as my mom quickly lost her battle with cancer.

My most vivid memory of their love and compassion was the night my mom died. I watched my dad as he whispered prayers, trying his best to comfort her throughout her pain. He crawled into the hospital bed with her, stroking her hair until 5:30 a.m. when she took her last breath.

In the tragic loss of my mom, my dad started looking for refuge without her. He tried to leave the sad memories behind by remarrying, moving to another state, starting a new business, and becoming involved in the community. My dad turned his anguish inward, burying his deep sorrow. My dad's attempt to carry all the grief on his shoulders translated into restless energy. He was trying to unsuccessfully fill a void in his life.

As his daughter, I ask you to recognize Jim Colwell as a widow, father, and grandfather. This is not the same man being presented to you as a predator. Instead, he is a gentleman who has suffered quietly for so long. Please provide him with an appropriate direction for healing, instead of one that will further devastate him and our family. Your judgment in this case is instrumental in his healing process.

I pray for my dad's healing. I pray he can find peace and forgiveness through continued therapy. I pray for the victims and their families that they will find healing. I pray that he is not incarcerated. I pray our family does not suffer another loss as the uncertainty of his fate hangs in the balance. I pray for your understanding in giving him a chance to survive.

Thank you for your thoughtful consideration.

Sincerely,
Danica Hubbard

I was asked to give an oral statement on behalf of my father in the courtroom. Three months pregnant at the time, I remember shaking and wiping away tears as I looked at the judge and pleaded for him to show mercy. There was a palpable anguish in the room. My father was being vilified as a dangerous sexual predator. It wasn't an unfair portrayal, after all, he did confess to the crimes. However, I had never witnessed people looking at my father with focused disdain like he was a target to hit. The glares and sneers during the reading of his criminal charges made me squirm. The barometric pressure reached a boiling point as I walked to the box beside the judge to sit down and read my statement.

I felt like I was speaking under water. My vocal cords were vibrating, but I wasn't sure what was coming out of my mouth. There were all sorts of unpleasant feelings running through the room that day, but as his daughter, I felt defeated, small, and helpless. Was my father expecting more from me than I could give? What side was I supposed to take? We had a two-year-old daughter, and I was pregnant with another daughter. My father was being accused of hurting a family's daughter.

What more could I do or say to come up with reasons why this should have never happened? I felt like a novice in the courtroom defending my father. Did the judge understand? Was I trying to convince the judge my father was remorseful? Was he really sorry for what he had done? Could the judge see my grief and despair? I was the only one who took the stand on behalf of my father. Was that my duty as a daughter? I stood by my promise to speak for him, listen to him, and continue to love him.

Lock Him Up

The year our second daughter was born, my father became a convicted felon, sentenced to one year in the county jail, a ten-year prison sentence, and thirty years probation. He was released in May 2001, but in 2002, it was revoked, and they sent him back to county jail for three months before prison for another three months. This began a revolving door of court, jail, and prison over the next decade. It was devastating for me. My goal was to live a productive and beneficial life, working toward a better future and trying not to succumb to self-pity. I was still scared for my father, scared for myself, and scared of people's perceptions.

According to the article "Facing Truths About Pedophilia Could Help Us Keep Kids Safer," "When it comes to pedophiles and other people with weird sexual urges, our society is all about punishment, not prevention. We don't want to help people who we think could mess with our kids. We want to pretend they don't exist until they *do* mess with our kids, and then we want to punish and make an example of them. Even saying the words *help* and *pedophile* in the same sentence pisses people off. But this is likely the best path to reducing child sex abuse."

I resisted knowing about pedophilia, especially thinking about sexual desires and deviance in connection to my father's outrageous scandal. I vacillated between anger and acceptance. It's important to carefully consider opening a dialogue according to your own comfort level. I will never feel qualified to pass judgment, but what worked for me was making a conscious effort to separate myself from my father's criminal behavior while still maintaining a relationship with him. It took me a long time to explore forgiveness. Coming to terms that my father would be away but not completely gone was a marathon in mental manipulation.

CHAPTER 4

Abandon Ship

What you can't run away from, you have to face.

—Lilith Saintcrow

This chapter, "Abandon Ship," talks about running from situations that were self-created and unfortunately self-destructive. In abandoning me and those closest to him, my father engaged in a different form of running—not the physical but emotional and psychological running. Eventually, he was caught. He could no longer run.

There's a line in one of my favorite movies, *Forrest Gump*, starring Tom Hanks, where his friend commands, "Run, Forrest, run!" My father regulated his emotions much in the same way. After his first release from prison, he ran from state to state and eventually ran from country to country.

He gravitated toward a controlled routine and repetition, setting a running goal and achieving it. In establishing intervals between easy runs which were up to five miles every morning to intensifying his training by running longer routes up to fifteen miles on weekends, my father would push himself to perform at his highest level of athletic capacity.

Running elevated his mood and temporarily satisfied his appetite to get up and go. One of his catch phrases after completing a run was "Never let grass grow under your feet," which meant keep moving. It was rare that he missed a run outside, but when he did, he would chastise himself for being lazy or sedentary. Being idle for any period of time was part of a negative feedback loop for my father as sitting still was a sign of weakness and apathy.

It was his desire to explore the best he could be and do while running. He kept track of pace and distance, calculating how these measurements would affect his predicted finish times for "fun runs" he entered during the summer and fall seasons. His running ego helped to measure success in his mind. It was an extrinsic motivator to earn a medal, ribbon, or plaque based on his running prowess. He kept these first-rate symbols all over the house: hanging in the hallway, neatly stacked in drawers, positioned on the front edge of his desk, and cataloged in scrapbooks. In his quest to strive for personal best and acquire more accolades, he ran several Chicago marathon races and logged thousands of miles over the years. He would often run with injuries and return home to rub topical Bengay pain reliever cream on his calves, fumigating our house with the pungent scent. He downplayed any injury, including sprains and pulled muscles, in order to keep putting one foot in front of the other, no matter what the cost.

I also started running during high school. I tried to keep up with my father's running regimen, but his early morning wake-up calls and fast pace were not appealing in my teenage years. I was not on the track or cross-country teams but rather chose to train with my dad. I wanted to make him proud by taking an interest in running. He ran beside me at a quick clip and boosted my motivation to eventually run longer and faster. If I complained of cramps or fatigue, he would dismiss me with a smile, "Are your legs barking at ya? Work through it, kid. Keep going." When I completed my first half marathon, he smiled and immediately asked, "When are you going to start working on finishing a full marathon? After all, if you run thirteen, you can run twenty-six. It's not much more when you think about it, right?" My dad's line of thinking was when you completed one accomplishment, it was quickly time to make a substantial commitment to start working toward the next goal. There was little satisfaction in enjoying the moment because it was more important to plan for the next occasion and opportunity.

Running from Wisconsin to Georgia

In the spring of 2013, my father received approval for a state transfer of supervision from Wisconsin to Georgia. According to the Interstate Commission for Adult Offender Supervision, there are several steps to apply for transfer, including these reporting instructions:

- all assessment information, completed by the sending state;
- victim information if distribution is not prohibited by law;
- additional documents necessary for supervision in the receiving state, including a narrative description of the initial offense in sufficient detail to describe the circumstances, type, and severity of offense and whether the charge was reduced at the time of imposition of sentence; and
- the sending state's current or recommended supervision and treatment plan.

My father was released to live with his older brother, Bob. This made a lot of sense to me because they had built a strong brotherly bond. Bob lived alone, and his adult children had already moved out of their family home. He was semiretired, financially independent, and enjoyed taking his sailboat out on the lake overlooking his backyard. The two single siblings would be together again under one roof, almost forty-five years later. They could help each other in maintaining the house, taking turns going to the grocery store, and sharing companionship.

However, becoming roommates presented some challenges. My father was a neat freak, and my uncle was more casual about tidiness. As a pair, they reminded me of the 1970 television series

The Odd Couple, where Neil Simon depicted two main characters: one narcissistically clean, the other a slob. But they also had a lot in common. They enjoyed watching movies together and taking walks each night. My father used to call me and brag about getting my uncle started on a heart healthy diet. I could hear my uncle in the background complaining about the salads being "too green" or sautéed chicken tasting like cardboard, but he ate every bite my father cooked. Now in their old age, the two brothers accepted their quirky habits, likes and dislikes. They loved each other with an endearing mutual closeness. "We have talked more now than we have in years. It's better than being alone," my uncle told me. And most importantly, they placed their trust in one another.

Living with my uncle offered a second chance for my father, a new start. My uncle accepted him with all his warts and bruises. As the respected patriarch of the family, my uncle would not allow anxiety in the same room as my father. He believed my father did not pose a high risk around our extended family. My father's felony was transparent but not expressed in everyday conversation, so when one of my cousins found out my father's criminal history, she was wide-eyed with surprise when he was invited to a traditional holiday family gathering. "Have they forgotten what he went to jail for?" My uncle assured our family that his brother had just made "some mistakes" along the way. He did not want him to be ostracized or ridiculed. He was in favor of new beginnings, leaving the past in the past.

He didn't completely dismiss my father's crimes, but he wasn't fully convinced that my father needed such severe blanket restrictions either. He thought exiling him was unnecessary and unfair, so he took him into his home and opened his heart. I don't think he ignored the risks he was taking, but he was willing to help my father, knowing the potential consequences. He opened the door and let my father in.

My father still had to comply with Georgia residency restrictions similar to the long list of sex offender probation/parole special rules. He was required to register as a sex offender and meet with a parole officer. He lived with my uncle for a few months before he started looking for a place of his own. I did not exchange letters with him during this time, but we talked on the phone. I remember the day he told me he was looking for a new place to live in Georgia. It had not been that long since he arrived and settled in with my uncle, but he was already running toward the next move, another new address. I had a barrage of questions about his new residence, but he didn't tell me much other than it was time to become independent again.

Embedding into a suburban neighborhood was not allowed according to the rules of my father's sex offender probation. I was surprised when he told me he had purchased a small house and was already starting to renovate it. He took pride in scrubbing the place from top to bottom for a squeaky-clean shine. Again, moving to a new address coincided with my father's manic cleaning and running. He liked packing, unpacking, organizing, and sanitizing a new environment. I believe he was never diagnosed with obsessive compulsive disorder, OCD, but certainly carried many of the classic characteristics. He cleaned constantly: car washing, floor waxing, and Windexing countertops. He wanted control and order. Maybe cleaning was a way to chase his obsessive thoughts away, but the relief didn't last because he immediately began starting a new cleaning project around the house. His cleaning never seemed good enough. His impulse was to clean even more. Was this a way of easing impurities he may have been feeling about himself or his actions?

To further illustrate his daily personal cleaning habits on a professional level, my father bought his own carpet-cleaning business. Cleaning carpets created a vibrant and rejuvenated image that my father truly enjoyed. He invested in a Chem-Dry franchise in Wisconsin after my mother died. He used to delight in telling me about cleaning the stains out of people's carpets. He took pride in removing bacteria, dust mites, and allergens, helping families to breathe easier and reduce health problems.

Looking back, his role as carpet cleaning technician was symbolic of what appears on the surface is not indicative of what lies beneath. Vacuuming carpets regularly only provides a superficial clean, but pollutants still lurk deeper and can create harm. Plus, this job, cleaning carpets, kept him literally running. Carpet cleaning was a physical job, and he would run from house to house with the bulky equipment, going inside for a few hours, and then onto to the next dirty job. The pace combined a frenetic schedule with an irresistible desire to shampoo, rinse, and repeat.

Recidivism Risk

My father moved out of my uncle's house after a few months of living together. *First red flag.*

He began to socialize with a group of children while washing his car in the driveway. *Second red flag.*

Within weeks of moving to his new neighborhood, he invited a ten-year old girl into his house to play with his dog. *Third red flag.*

And this is when it all went sideways *again*. Whispers and rumors in his new neighborhood took flight, and he could no longer participate in the charade he created of the friendly man with a gentle smile and manicured lawn. It had only been one year since my father moved to Georgia, and he was already being accused of grooming a young girl who lived in his neighborhood. The same sexually deviant behavior pattern emerged. He formed trust and shattered it by acting on his insatiable attraction to be uncomfortably close to prepubescent girls. There was no question in my mind that he was a repeat offender with identifiable grooming behaviors. Why couldn't he stop himself?

According to the American Bar Association, "Understanding Sexual Grooming in Child Abuse Cases," there is a list of grooming behaviors to be aware of in sexual abuse cases:

- An adult seems overly interested in a child.
- An adult frequently initiates or creates opportunities to be alone with a child (or multiple children).
- An adult becomes fixated on a child.

- An adult gives special privileges to a child (e.g., rides to and from practices, etc.).
- An adult befriends a family and shows more interest in building a relationship with the child than with the adults.
- An adult displays favoritism toward one child within a family.
- An adult finds opportunities to buy a child gifts.
- An adult caters to the interests of the child so a child or the parent may initiate contact with the offender.

My father's behavior was clearly in alignment with many items on the grooming list; however, he appeared genuinely surprised by his neighbor's visceral reaction. He told me that it hurt his feelings, and he was just trying to be a nice neighbor. Listening to him rationalize his behavior with such conviction was like trying to successfully nail Jell-O to a wall. He just couldn't wrap his brain around the reality of his wrongdoings or tried to convince me that he couldn't. Like Jell-O, his sensibility wriggled away into an alternative state. He formally defended his actions by documenting and sending a letter to his parole officer in Georgia.

January 22, 2004

When I moved here in April 2003, I lived with my brother. I began seeing a probation officer at that time and never missed an appointment. They approved the purchase of my home in July, then said in August I may have to move if I'm close to a school. I am not. The closest facility with children is a day care center located 2.5 miles from my home. Within a month, I met both neighbors on either side while I was getting the mail, walking the dog, or washing my car. Both neighbors had children under the age eighteen. I never told my neighbors I was a sex offender.

Now one neighbor has filed a three-page complaint saying:

1. *In August 2003, when I pulled into my driveway, I saw their daughter (ten years old) and a friend in their front yard. I called from the street to ask if she could get her mom to help me unload the doors I bought at a hardware store. I knew I could not get them out of the truck myself. At no time was I alone with the children or had them inside of my home.*
2. *Another time, I saw the mother, father, and daughter in front of their home while I was washing my car. A group of kids were across the street playing in a neighbor's yard. They called for me to come and play football, but I told them no and kept washing my car. At no time was I alone with the kids.*
3. *I often had to leave my dog outside while I was working ten hours a day. One day, the neighbor came over and told me the dog was barking all day. He asked me if I could put the dog inside because his wife was having a party and didn't want to listen to the barking dog. I decided to get another dog to keep my dog company and perhaps stop from barking. I did bring a flower over to my neighbors to apologize for the barking.*

The neighbor stated on her complaint that I was grooming her daughter. The last complaint that was filed concerned me knocking on the backsliding glass window of their home. I gave them a key to my house in case of emergency. I was there for maybe two minutes and not with any children.

When I called the probation office today, the supervisor said these were all perfect examples of grooming, and thankfully, the neighbor found me on the sex registry on the Internet. When I tried to answer the charge, they cut me off saying that the file will be sent back to Wisconsin and if asked they will fly to Wisconsin to testify that this was grooming.

Then they asked, "What do you think the judge will do...send you to prison?"

In his letter, he blatantly justified his behavior. He frequently minimized and normalized his interactions with children in the neighborhood. In displacing any blame, he believed he did nothing wrong. Although he broke several rules of his parole, he still thought he was doing the right thing. The disconnect was apparent to everyone around him except my father.

His distorted view of reality was difficult to come to terms with. It's as if he was on a hamster wheel that could not stop spinning. Could he ever be capable of curbing or completely stopping his urges? Or was he stuck in a continual downward spiral? There aren't consistent patterns of common psychological features associated with pedophilia, so it remains a mystery as to why offenders will repeat the same crimes of abuse. According to the Crime Victims Center, "Reported recidivism rates vary widely depending on the length of follow-up period employed, the methods used to calculate recidivism, and, perhaps, the sample size of the study. Of released sex offenders who allegedly committed another sex crime, 40 percent perpetrated the new offense within a year or less from their prison discharge."

Where in the World Are You Going?

The next chapter of my father's life was even more surreal and completely hidden from me. I had not seen my father since I testified on his behalf in 1999. It had been four years. We moved. He moved. Life continued to march forward, and I was immersed in taking care of our two young daughters now under the age of five years old. We were busy and wrapped up in our everyday lives. I did make efforts to reach out to my father during those years, but it was sporadic and difficult. Our relationship was frayed around the edges, and I felt like it needed repair.

After careful consideration, we decided I would fly solo to visit his new home in Georgia after Christmas in 2004. I had purchased a round-trip ticket and was looking forward to seeing my father and our extended family in the area. I wanted to tell them in person how much I appreciated their altruism in embracing my father after his felony conviction. I was looking forward to a reunion. The night before my trip to Georgia, my bag was packed, and I called my father's cell phone to confirm he would be picking me up at the airport. The phone rang and rang, but there was no answer. I thought this was odd since we had solidified the dates of my visit, and he told me he was excited to show me his new home and neighborhood. The next phone call I made was to my uncle. I told him I was looking for my father, and he fell silent before the words finally tumbled out, "He's not here." More silence. I was confused. I didn't understand what he was saying. Were the dates wrong on my itinerary? Was there a problem with my upcoming visit? Did my father no longer want me to come? I was in a daze when my uncle repeated, "He's not here. You can't come." I hung up the phone and sobbed. What could have possibly gone wrong? Where in the world was my father?

At that time, I was not privy to the events that unfolded in his neighborhood, the letter he wrote to his parole officer, the meetings he arranged with a lawyer, and his eventual swift and illegal disappearance to another country. I had no idea what was happening. But a few years later, after my father was extradited and returned to prison in Wisconsin, I found out that instead of facing the latest accusations of grooming a minor and taking responsibility as a sex offender in Georgia, my father made a choice to run away. And once again. he left his family and friends behind to sit in the pain he caused.

Cutting Off Contact

To people who run, leaving can be more comfortable than staying. Running can be easier than remaining. Packing up your life and flinging it into a state of perpetual chaos is a unique way of staying safe because as long as we're leaving, we have some sense of control. We choose the chaos. Admittedly, there's a certain rush that comes from running—it's the realization that not all problems can necessitate solutions. Running can give a false sense of security by ignoring the parts that desperately need attention.

When you are in a new physical place, the pain can be out of sight, out of mind because there are new things to focus on. But running can be exhausting, and in my father's case, he could no longer run from his criminal record or himself.

The way he tells the story, there was no other choice but to run and keep running. He was trapped and refused to go back to prison in Wisconsin. I'm not sure how he concocted this plan so quickly but knew my father was a seasoned international traveler and adept at blending in. Throughout his corporate career, he had been to far-reaching places, like China, Switzerland, and Taiwan. He made long-distance travel appear effortless. I wasn't sure if he had ever visited San José, Costa Rica, prior to landing there on the lam.

In his mind, the best place to escape was Central America. He hopped a four-hour flight from Georgia to Costa Rica with a valid passport. I'm also unsure how he could have possibly made it through customs as he would have had to show a sheath of documents, including proof of fingerprint registration issued by the Ministry of Public Safety, proof of consular registration issued by the corresponding consulate in Costa Rica, a birth certificate, and authorized certificate of a past criminal record from his country of origin. Somehow, he slid underneath the radar. It was like he was now part of an even more dangerous club alongside fugitives, like international spies or government whistleblowers finding themselves on the other side of the law. Was my father's confidence so inflated that he thought he could relocate to a popular vacation destination with beautiful coastlines in the Pacific and Caribbean without being caught?

To flee to somewhere tropical in a last-ditch effort to avoid the rules of probation was destructive and cavalier. At the same time, I speculate that my father chose Costa Rica for the sun, sand, and surf. One of his favorite musical artists was Jimmy Buffett and the Coral Reefer Band. He went to a few summer concerts and was a self-proclaimed Parrothead, part of the group of Buffett fans who dressed in tropical attire and had an affinity for tiki bars. Jimmy Buffett sang about how changing your location can change your outlook and your mood. It's an attitude adjustment. He talked about running and cunning—just laugh and forget about your troubles. Enjoy the sunshine, Caribbean, and umbrella drinks. Jimmy Buffett sang a particular song about disconnecting completely from home, embracing a new place and latitude. The song talked about bringing more freedom from obligations into our lives and going somewhere where no one knows you. The song is called "Changes in Latitudes, Changes in Attitudes."

Oh, yesterdays are over my shoulder,
So I can't look back for too long.
There's just too much to see waiting in front of me,
And I know that I just can't go wrong.

I imagine this was the soundtrack for my father's departure. He was happy until he was caught. His problems just followed him and grew larger because the more crimes are hidden, the bigger they become. My grandmother used to say, "You can put lipstick on a pig, but it's still a pig." Going rogue didn't solve any problems, it just exacerbated them.

Knock, Knock—Is Your Dad Here?

It was over a year later, 2005, and at this point, I felt officially abandoned by my father. He decided to have no contact with me in order to stay concealed, completely ignoring his only child. It was another grieving process to go through, another loss. I was angry that he not only left me but became estranged from my uncle who had helped him begin a new life in Georgia. His decisions were reckless and selfish. At this point, he forfeited his right to offer any type of logical explanation as to why he suddenly disappeared. His narcissistic decision to terminate our relationship and only look out for himself cast me further adrift.

I suppose if he had reached out during that year of dead air, I would have bombarded him with a myriad of tough questions and demanded answers. I was hurt and confused. My trust in him was long gone. So I didn't look for him. I didn't ask questions. I tried to stop thinking about him, but at times, it was like having a phantom limb. I was still attached to him because he was my father. His absence heightened my anxiety and caused nightmares. I hoped he was safe and well but had no way of knowing. He put himself at risk, and I sensed he was in danger, but I could not contact him because he was deliberately invisible to me, gone without a trace.

This was also a time when the Internet was really starting to transform how information was shared. The worldwide web was adding plenty of words and features to our lexicon. I don't think my father was aware of what Googling or blogging online meant. Broadband was changing rapidly, even stretching to his hiding place in Costa Rica. My father was old school. In his corporate executive life, he relied upon secretaries and administrative assistants, fax machines, and carbon copies. He was oblivious to the power and reach of the Internet. By 2005, television networks and news sources were increasing the types of content they could make available online. It changed the way people communicated and made it easier to identify and capture criminals. Social media platforms like MySpace were also launched, reaching millions of active users. With these modern-day tools, there were very few obscure corners of the globe where people could comfortably hide without being discovered.

I grew up watching the long-running television show *America's Most Wanted* in the late 1980s and 1990s with host John Walsh. His commanding, authoritative presence was mesmerizing in providing intricate details from victims and law enforcement. The show was dedicated to finding criminals and bringing them to justice. For a moment, I wondered if my father could possibly be featured in one of the episodes. What would it take to apprehend and arrest him? My father's unexpected departure was a mystery I could not attempt to solve on my own.

And then it happened. We woke up to a jarring bang on our front door around 3:00 a.m. Completely disoriented, I jostled my husband out of bed, and we both stumbled downstairs in the dark. My heart was thumping. Who was causing this unwelcome disruption in the middle of the night? Was I dreaming? What was the emergency? When we opened the door, two agents from the FBI, the Federal Bureau of Investigation, were standing in the shadows.

They displayed their credentials and asked to come inside. They did not tell us they had a search warrant, but we had nothing to hide. I still was not registering what was going on. My throat tightened, and my mouth felt dry. My kneecaps were convulsing. I felt like I would collapse in a heap at their feet. Our two elementary-school-age daughters were still sleeping in their beds upstairs. Would they hear the cacophony of footsteps and strange voices? How could I explain we invited strangers into our home? What if our dog started barking? Were there police cars parked outside? Nothing was making sense to me.

Dazed, we led them into our dining room and sat down at the table, the same table where we gathered to celebrate birthday parties and baptisms. Two strangers stared at me from across our family table where we ate charcuterie and drank wine with friends during special occasions. They slid the placemats aside and took out a notebook and pen. They instructed us to put our hands on the table where they could be visible. Their ability to intimidate worked. I was scared. What was their intention in showing up now? Why were they here? Was this a misunderstanding? How long would this take? Would our daughters wake up during their questioning? How could I protect them?

They told us they came to our home as part of an investigation and it was a typical practice following standard procedures. They were searching for my father and requested an interview with the two of us because we were relatives of the person they were looking for. They said there was an urgency to the case and they needed more information. The agents began asking a series of questions, ranging from open ended to more specific. When was the last time I had spoken with my father? Did my father leave his belongings with me? Was I giving money to my father? Did I have my father's address? Did my father ever visit me here? Did I know that my father left Georgia? Did I know where my father was living now? There was a steady aggressiveness to their questions that felt accusatory. Sometimes they would ask the same question but in different ways. Were they trying to catch any inconsistencies in my answers? Were we considered accomplices in the investigation of my father? I was clear and measured in telling them the truth. I had absolutely nothing to hide. I repeated the same answers. I had not seen or spoken with my father since he disappeared in 2004. There was no way to implicate myself or others because I had no idea where he was. I was living as an honest, ethical, decent, and law-abiding citizen.

When there was a lull in their peppering inquiry of me and my husband, I started asking the FBI agents some comprehensive questions of my own. I was seeking answers too. Did they have evidence as to where my father might be? Did they have a recent picture of my father? Was my father in good health? Was he working? Had he moved to multiple locations? Was he coming back to Wisconsin? Was he alive?

The intensity in their early-morning call was deliberate and a possible attempt to throw us off guard. Perhaps they would try to use something from their notes documenting our interview to add to my father's criminal prosecution. I wondered. Did I utter something that could be misunderstood or provide some nuance or unintentional detail? No, I was telling the truth, the whole truth and nothing but the truth. I did not know where my father was. But this invasion into our home was another instance that made me feel guilty by association. Even when I confirmed what I told was the truth, the agents generated an environment of intimidation. I was cornered in the middle of the night. The FBI agents seemed under no obligation to treat me politely during their investigation process even though I did nothing wrong. I wasn't the one they were after. It was my father.

The FBI has federal jurisdiction as an agency under the United States Department of Justice and reports to both the Office of the Attorney General and the Director of National Intelligence.

The FBI has the power to investigate all federal crimes, including:

- Terrorism
- White-Collar Crime
- Cybercrime
- Public Corruption
- Organized Crime
- Weapons of Mass Destruction
- Civil Rights Violations

After that sledgehammer approach to interviewing was conducted in our home, I wasn't sure if the agents walked away with the answers they were looking for. Although we willingly answered their questions with firm, detailed, and clear responses, the ultimate objective was to find my father. This was a complicated case and one that would progress step by step, stretching the long arm of the law from Wisconsin to Costa Rica, culminating in his international capture, arrest, and extradition process.

Caught in Costa Rica

The following year, 2006, I found out my father had orig-inally entered Costa Rica in January 2004 and was working in a real estate office, Emerald Shores Realty, on the northwest-ern coast of Guanacaste in the town of Playa Flamingo. He was hired as an office manager. His picture was posted on the real estate website, smiling in a group photo with his new cowork-ers. Costa Rican International Police (INTERPOL) agents and special agents within the Department of State arrested my father, then age sixty-five, as a fugitive considered a continuing danger to children. The agents in Costa Rica were sent a collateral lead by the Great Lakes Regional Fugitive Task Force (GLRFTF). Also taking part in the arrest were the Sección Aérea of the Ministerio de Gobernación, Policía y Seguridad Pública, and the Sección de Capturas of the Judicial Investigating Organization.

My father was brought to San José by a government airplane where he faced extradition. Extradition is when one country repa-triates an individual who is accused or convicted of a crime back to the country where it was committed. It usually involves a bilat-eral treaty though these treaties are not legally binding and are based upon the cooperation of law enforcement agencies of both countries. The United States has extradition treaties everywhere in the Western Hemisphere and much of Europe securing bilateral extradition agreements with over 107 countries. Extradition can be a long and murky process.

On May 10, 2006, he called me from a jail in Costa Rica. It was the first time I had heard his voice in over two years. His self-imposed, no-contact period was hurtful to me, but he expected to pick up where he left off. He did not acknowledge his abrupt departure, parental neglect, or illegal desertion. On the contrary, he appeared optimistic and eager to reconnect. I thought I had come to terms with his absence and moved on. I was able to take a break from all the drama he created and developed coping mecha-nisms to compartmentalize his disappearance. He was out of sight and out of mind.

His unforeseen reappearance struck a bolt of lightning into our lives. Completely oblivious, he was ready to defend his actions with irrational thoughts. He was plotting to maintain our father-daughter relationship by pressing my buttons of empathy and worry. He spoke hastily, soliciting an emotional reaction to his arrest, "My boss got me a great attorney, and they are fighting the extradition. I heard they can send you back for a crime but not a parole violation. So it will all work out. I've got to tell you though, in Latin America, the conditions are miserable here in jail. But don't worry, I am tolerating it. And I have money, so you don't need to send me anything. I have a lot of commissions from selling real estate here. I wanted to let you know I have to go before a tribunal in Costa Rica. And I put my house in my boss's name so he can hold onto it for me. So that's all. I have to go now. They are telling me to go now." The phone clicked, and I heard a low-pitched buzzing noise then silence. It was hard to avoid the invasion of his long-distance phone call, causing a tornado of lies and manipulation to swirl around me, leaving a devastating trail of debris in his wake. I hesitated to emerge again because I realized the storm wasn't over yet. I loved my father, but I had to let him go.

How did extradition work in my father's case? Would Costa Rica grant him asylum? It did not appear that he was living in a regional safe haven for wanted criminals. When these types of individuals—sex offenders—come to the country, they act forcefully to get them out. Under orders of the of the Dirección General de Migración y Extranjería (immigration service), he was to be extradited. His request for asylum was denied. He was caught under extensive surveillance and an abundant exchange of information within the framework of INTERPOL which played an important role in determining his whereabouts, identifying him, and booking his subsequent arrest. In December 2005, he was taken to San Sebastián Prison which was notoriously overcrowded in its maximum capacity of 664 inmates but often held well over 1,000. It had been reported that more than fifty people were assigned to a cell block room with only eight beds, requiring inmates to sleep on a piece of foam while crammed in the crawl space under a bed. Here, my father awaited extradition proceedings, which took months.

My father was taken into custody and faced justice, pending a one-way ticket back to the United States. He would eventually be expelled from the country of Costa Rica and flown to Wisconsin under the escort of FBI agents assigned to the US Embassy in San José. Once in Wisconsin, my father was turned over to the custody of the Walworth County Sherriff Services to face the allegations of his parole violation. The victims' family told the court they never lost hope and would have spent the rest of their lives trying to find him so he would be captured and brought to justice. The scars he created in the community ran deep. He made his initial court appearance, and the legal process dragged on before he was finally transferred to Fox Lake Correctional Institution, a medium-security state prison for men in Dodge County, Wisconsin. His probation was revoked, and he was ordered to serve the entirety of the original thirty-year sentence.

First Letter from Prison

After two years as a fugitive running from the law, my father was in prison once again. I had taken a break from reaching out to my father after his only phone call to me from the prison in Costa Rica in 2006. I needed to reestablish boundaries and redefine our father-daughter relationship based on what I knew at that time. The separation provided some healing and perspective on this complicated and painful situation. I decided to find my father's new address and send him a letter in prison. He had time to read. He had time to write. He had time to repent. He would be behind bars in prison for the rest of his life.

His first letter in response to my letter started a consistent exchange between us totaling five hundred letters over the next decade. He documents his version of what transpired before fleeing to Costa Rica. His words gave me insight into how contorted his view of reality was in his actions and reactions during that time. He really believed in himself. He was only responsible for building his own psychological brick wall and hiding behind it.

Dodge Correctional Institution
May 22, 2007

Dear Danica,

> *I have prayed every day for the last three years that one day we would be able to be father and daughter again as we were for more than thirty years. I know your mom had a hand in your writing to me at this time.*
>
> *When I left Atlanta, it was because I was falsely charged by a neighbor who found out I was a sex offender and wanted me out of the neighborhood. She called the probation officer in Atlanta, and they told her to write a letter saying I was grooming her ten-year-old daughter. They lived right next door, and they were the only people in the entire neighborhood that I met and waved to as I pulled into the driveway coming home from work. After living with Uncle Bob for three months, I took a job selling boats. It was great because I did very well, my boss was really cool, and I wanted to be close to Uncle Bob and not live in Wisconsin. I worked from 8:00 a.m. 'til 8:00 p.m. six days a week and many weeks all seven days. They gave me the keys to the boatyard so I opened each morning and closed each day. This was a fresh start, and I felt for the first time that God had blessed me with a new start. With God's help, I was blessed to be able to see Uncle Bob almost every night when I got home.*

I would take my dog and walk to his house, and then I would walk down to the marina and back then get something to eat and go home. I worked hard because I wanted to have my own home again, which took saving a down payment and showing the bank that I could make the monthly mortgage payments. Fortunately, interest rates were low, so God's timing was perfect. I bought a modest home and spent my days off tearing down walls and fixing the place up. Just before you were to come to see me, I had everything done and painted and new carpet throughout the house. I even bought a bedroom set for one extra bedroom so you would have a nice room to use on your visit.

I had not one problem with Atlanta probation for the year and a half in my new home. They approved of the house and neighborhood, and I attended classes every two weeks as part of my agreement to be able to transfer to Georgia. I purposely did not want to socialize or become known in my neighborhood.

I want very much to restore our relationship even if it's only to exchange letters as you are and always will be my daughter. I am so proud to be your father.

So I was shocked when my probation officer called me at work one day and asked that I come in to see her as soon as possible. That night on my walk with Uncle Bob, I told him about the call, and he said, "Don't worry, it's probably something they want you to sign or something." The next morning, I went to the probation office, and my probation officer said she wanted me to see her supervisor. We went to his office, and he said the neighbor had sent

*a letter saying that I was grooming his daugh-
ter. I started to answer this false charge, and
he said, "Get out and return to Wisconsin. We
don't want you in Georgia anymore!" I asked
if I could respond to the charge, and he said,
"No! Get out!"*

*I went to Bob's house, and we talked the
rest of the day and into the night. We agreed
to see an attorney, who used to be a judge,
the next morning. Obviously, I didn't sleep all
night. When we saw the attorney, he said, "Get
out of the country because Wisconsin will send
you to prison." I asked, "Where should I go?"
He said, "Costa Rica." So Bob and I stayed up
to talk about the situation, and by midnight, we
decided and agreed it would be best for me to
get out of the country so I would not have to
spend years in prison.*

*The very next day, I signed power of attor-
ney papers so Bob had control to sell my car
and house. I packed two suitcases, and Bob
took me to the airport. I really felt in my heart
that Wisconsin would be happy to get rid of
me and I would be able to open another new
door before I died. However, this time, I was
really scared because my whole life (including
pictures of you and my granddaughters) was in
two suitcases, and I had no idea where to go
once I got to Costa Rica and could not speak
Spanish. Financially, I had enough cash on
me to live for a month or so before I would be
totally broke.*

*But once again, God listened to my prayers
(and I'm sure yours as well) and helped me.
I got to Costa Rica at night and had no idea
where to stay, so I walked out to the curb and*

saw a Marriot Bus, got on it, and thought eventually I'll get to a hotel. I stayed that night at the Marriot. The next day, I spoke to one of the managers (who spoke English, thank God), and he suggested I travel to the West Coast of Costa Rica because there were some Americans who had retirement and second homes in that area. I rented a car and drove six hours with a road map in Spanish to the West Coast.

I just kept praying because I thought I would probably sleep that night in the rental car. I got to a small (about 1,200 people) town on the ocean called Flamingo before dark so I could find a hotel to stay in that night. It was January and the hotel industries' high season, so rooms were very expensive, but I found one.

Within a week, I found a small off-the-beach condo to rent cheap by the month. Two days later, I went into Emerald Shores Real Estate Office in Flamingo and met the owner's wife. She took care of the inside, and her husband took care of the outside sales. They had been in Costa Rica for ten years. The next day, the three of us had lunch together, and before lunch was over, they offered me a job selling real estate in that area. Well, it took a little time, but after I became familiar with the area (which is beautiful), I started to make sales. I never changed my name or passport or tried to hide. I met several Americans who were retired there and quickly had a group of solid friends who spoke English. My business there was selling to Americans and Canadian clients who wanted to invest in Costa Rica real estate.

After about four months, my American friends asked me to help them start a nonde-

*nominational church in that area. It was around
that time that I called you, and Brian answered
the phone. When I asked for you, he said you
did not want to talk to me, and it would be best
if I respected your wishes. I felt like I had been
hit by a cement truck. I couldn't believe my
ears. Brian's voice was the firmest I had ever
heard from him, and I'm sure it was filled with
anger. I cried and cried. Went home and laid in
bed for the rest of that day, night and all day the
next. Finally, my new boss came to my condo to
see what was wrong and to tell me that his wife
was just told she had cancer and had a year or
less to live. I couldn't believe what was going
on. My daughter did not want to talk to me, and
my boss just got news that his wife, just like
mine, was going to be taken away from him.*

*God used me for the next year to help
him get through what I had gone through, and
we became very close friends. He knows a lot
about you as I bragged and told him about your
life and how proud you made your mom and I
and what happened to tear us apart. I missed
our relationship and love so much that God
put him and the sorrow of his wife's cancer in
my path so I would have someone to talk to. I
was at his house on Easter morning when his
wife passed on. I know Mom welcomed her to
eternity.*

*While all of the was going on, I bought
a very small house from a native at a bargain
basement price. It was absolutely a mess. Small,
old, and dirty, but I could see the potential, and
it was all I could afford at $400 per month on
the mortgage. Over the months, I completely
remodeled it and made it very livable.*

Then I answered my friends' call to help start a new church. We hired a pastor; I was made president of the new church council, and I worked with the government in San José to get a tax-free status and be recognized as a church. When I left, we had seventy-five members that met each Sunday for a service and singing. They are currently in the process of getting $50,000 together to buy a piece of property and then build a church. We did a lot for the very poor Costa Ricans, especially working with their schools to build computer labs and get computers donated. All students go to very overcrowded schools, who do not have enough textbooks, must wear uniforms. Many families cannot afford uniforms, so their children stay home. So we got a list of families, sizes, and bought one hundred uniforms for three schools in the area so those kids could come to school. The schools are so overcrowded that they have two shifts each day, and the teachers work for less than three hundred American dollars a month from 6:30 a.m. until 5:30 p.m.

It will be two years ago this December that I was arrested in my office and thrown into a prison for eight months. Wow. That was an experience. They had guns, drugs, and knives, but I was helped by a young (about thirty-five years old) man who could put together a few English words as he was a native of Costa Rica. Thank God he was put in my path to help me get through that journey.

I went through two Costa Rican lawyers that cost me $25,000 and $12,000, a total of $37,000 of which Uncle Bob put in $6,000 while my boss put up $25,000, and I had to sell *my car and house to get the rest. Both attorneys took me down a garden path. By law, Costa Rica does not send people back for probation violations. But the US Embassy put a lot of pressure on the tribunal court, and the lawyers said I had won (without ever appearing before a judge) my lower court and appeal court cases when in fact I had lost. I only found that out when the US Embassy notified me that the US Marshals would be there in one week to extradite me.*

Yes, I had violated my probation by not going back to Wisconsin, but where they got me was I did not register for two years and now in Wisconsin that's a felony offense. Walworth County Jail may have told you I got three years in prison, which was for not registering as a sex offender for two years (while I was gone), which is a felony. What they did not tell you is I was sentenced for leaving and not reporting, and for that, they gave me thirty years in prison. Yes, thirty years!

When in court, I could not afford a private attorney, so they appointed a public defender. He said a total of five words. The same district attorney I had eight years ago and the "family" who were there in court got what they wanted eight years ago.

So here I am in Dodge Correctional Institution (prison) which is a classified prison to decide where I will go permanently. I've been encouraged to appeal my thirty years. So now I'll be getting another public defender that will file my appeal. Unfortunately, with no money and no private attorney to help me to get the time reduced, they will no doubt keep me for the rest of my life.

I may be moved any day now, and I will not know where or when until the night before. They said six to eight weeks, and I've been here seven weeks now. So do not plan to come here until June as I will not be here. Soon as I get my new location, I'll send you my new address.

I have read and reread your letter five times since I got it about an hour ago and began immediately to write this one. My heart is so heavy right now. I've asked and thanked God for your letter. What a beautiful blessing.

Thank you for not giving up on me. I love and miss you more than you'll ever know. But I also love and respect Brian. If he feels that you should not talk or see me again, I can understand that. He is your husband and the very best one you could ever have. Thank you for reaching out to your dad.

We are locked down here twenty-two hours per day and get out two hours a day to eat, shower, and walk outside. I have had plenty of time to run and rerun all the beautiful times we had together. I pray for you every day. God has given me time to read the Bible, study his word, and pray.

One thing you and others can do immediately is please pray and pray and pray. Pray for my appeal so I may not have to spend the rest of my life in prison. I know that your mom is on her knees in heaven talking to our Creator and asking him for mercy.

May God continue to lay His hands upon your head every day. Please look in your Bible and read Ephesians chapter 6 verses 10 through

18. Also Psalm 91. I pray these each morning.
I know in my heart that God is holding you in
His arms and Mom is reminding Him each day
that there is only one Danica and she is very
special. God be with you. I love and miss you.
Christ's peace.

Love,
Dad

If my family and friends would have known I was corresponding with my father, would they have wanted him to stay away from me? Should I have made an effort to maintain contact and communication with him after all he had done? It wasn't like I had an excessive curiosity about prison life, but I was interested in *his* life. Intellectually, it made sense to cut him off, but emotionally, I still wished for some sort of involvement with my only living parent. Ultimately exchanging letters kept his spirit alive for both of us.

CHAPTER 5

Man Overboard!

There is only one thing in the world worse than being talked about, and that is not being talked about.

—Oscar Wilde

When someone falls out of a boat, they can slip, lose their footing, and potentially drown. The exclamation "Man overboard!" indicates distress and is a call for immediate rescue, a traumatic call for help. My father figuratively fell overboard when he committed sexual abuse. When he violated probation and fled the country, he was eventually identified, captured, and arrested in Costa Rica. His arrest in Central America made headlines nationally and internationally.

My father's extradition process returning to the United States generated a lot of media attention. Determined that this story was newsworthy and the public had a need and right to the information, local reporters wrote a David and Goliath story: the headlines featured the county sheriff's department in southeastern Wisconsin working together with US Marshals in the Department of Justice to bring my father, the fugitive, back into the country to face justice. The story provoked and inflamed readers who were not only reminded of my father's sex offender status, but made aware of his dramatic escape to a tropical paradise. The wound was reopened, with unsurprising calls to tar and feather my father.

Through this publicity, my father's secrets became exposed. Although the media portrayed him in a negative light, I believe he deserved every unfavorable report of who he was and what he did. However, on the other end of the spectrum, there are advocates who specifically support sex offenders in attempts to protect their reputation. For me, this viewpoint is difficult to understand. For example, in the article "Ideal Victims and Monstrous Offenders: How the News Media Represent Sexual Predators," Rebecca DiBennardo discusses how offenders can be dehumanized in the media. She claims that sex offenders are frequently portrayed unfairly. "Much news media research focuses on victim framing only, without examining how it may shape representations of offenders. When news media do discuss sex offenders, they tend to conflate violence and pedophilia and perpetuate the 'boogeyman fallacy' that those who commit sex crimes have unique, unknown, and monstrous identities." In contrast, I support shining a light on crimes that were previously hidden. Each news story could possibly give another victim courage to come forward and receive help.

My father bristled when each article was published about his crimes, but I could not feel sorry for him. He no longer had agency over the narrative, and the truth came out. He finally needed to deal with the problems he had caused. In hindsight, I think my father never considered his former small-town neighborhood law enforcement agency capable of assembling the resources needed to successfully apprehend him internationally. There were several officers actively working on his case, trying to track him down. He underestimated their interest in pursuing him. Although he somehow slipped through border patrol in Costa Rica and was on the run, he certainly didn't plan on his criminal database being constantly updated and circulated all over the Internet.

He could not stay under the radar for long. The spotlight intensified in drawing attention to his whereabouts. There was a serious manhunt going on with an outstanding warrant for his arrest. His case was a high priority. As a convicted felon fleeing the country, my father's mug shot picture appeared on a US Marshals' most-wanted poster. A complex integrated effort to take him into custody was finally achieved, and the small town triumphed, the arm of the law reached Costa Rica.

The publicized events of his capture in Costa Rica further agitated an already fractured circle of friends he had formed within the Fontana, Wisconsin, community he left behind. Shortly after my father's original move to Fontana, he was looking to make new friends and a fresh start. Settling in a small town was a change from the bigger cities he had grown accustomed to. There were many adjustments in rapid succession: a new marriage, a new address, and a new business. On the outside, he appeared to handle these changes in stride, but the stress caught up with him.

Within the first few years of living in Fontana, he told me he felt like an interloper; he didn't feel like he belonged. He had a difficult time making friends in a town entrenched in their own social circles and families spanning multiple generations living in the same area. He wasn't part of a clique. People in town put their guard up. But gradually, he was able to carefully select and connect with acquaintances that eventually became close companions and good friends. These relationships empowered him, and his confidence seemed to return.

He strengthened his status in the community by taking on leadership positions, volunteering, and continuing to network with high-profile civic and faith groups. By the time he was accused of a first-degree sex offense, he had served as president of the Village Board of Trustees and a church board official, solidifying a stellar image of being responsible, trusted, and valued. He was no longer anonymous but recognized and well-known. However, when reports of his crimes surfaced, he ran out of strategies to hide from the unwanted notoriety. Remaining anonymous or undetected was no longer an option.

Fleeting Fame

In the 1940s, local talent shows were the norm. The Sachs program was considered the granddaddy of all amateur hours. The amateur hour was the modern-day version of shows like *America's*

Got Talent and *The Voice*. Musicians, jugglers, acrobats, singers, and comedians took the stage. Some were hoping to go to Hollywood. My father told me he was there for the thrill of being on the radio and an opportunity to win a prize. He remembered feeling worshipped and liked getting adulation from adults on a large scale.

My father was no stranger to publicity. He grew up in the public eye but wasn't fully aware of the future risks and rewards. When my father was in elementary school, he started singing and tap dancing professionally. As a child radio star, he was bombarded with both praise and criticism from the media. He appeared on the *Morris B. Sachs Amateur Hour* on WGN radio and WGN TV in Chicago. He would sing songs like "Down by the Ole Swimming Hole" standing on a box in order to reach the microphone. His picture was published in the local newspapers, advertising the next performance. My grandmother collected and read his fan mail, but what seemed glamorous was in reality very taxing for a kid to suddenly give up his childhood to work full-time spending hours practicing, performing, and most importantly maintaining a perfect image. He cut his first record when he was seven years old. He sang cover songs like Roy Acuff's "Night Train to Memphis" and the Mills Brother's "Lulu's Back in Town" produced on forty-five vinyl records that my grandmother used to hand out to talent agents in the industry.

As a kid, he was already a confident, positive role model. Compliments inflated his ego. Each time he received praise for his talents, he would work harder to earn awards and prizes. Winners of the talent show went home with watches, jewelry, and cash. Every few months, there was a large prize presented to one of the lucky semifinalists in the talent competition: a car.

From 1947 to 1952, my father sang on WMBD radio in his hometown of Peoria every Saturday morning and continued to make headlines for his talent. He tried to manage high expectations from his parents, producers, and fans. He traveled with a young tour group to local hospitals, schools, pubs, and diners to dance and sing. The pressure to perform and win at an early age ushered in new complications. Once he hit puberty and his body made changes he could not control, he was no longer seen as the adorable, charming kid who captivated an audience. The effects were detrimental because he thought he was destined for fame to help financially support his family and himself. Instead, he was easily replaced and quickly forgotten. Were these early experiences in the entertainment industry where he first learned to put on a mask when he faced rejection? Was he able to create a better character than his true self?

I believe my father's performance solidified how he measured his self-worth. He was driven by extrinsic motivation, participating in activities because he wanted to earn a reward or avoid punishment. He completed tasks in anticipation of a return on his investment. It wasn't necessarily satisfying, but he was motivated to chase external rewards. He aimed to project a certain image of success by buying a big house, fancy car, or deluxe vacation to strut his peacock feathers. He had a zest to impress with the best. However, the perfect exterior veneer would one day wear off.

Death of a Salesman

In his five hundred letters, my father wrote about his escalating and prominent career in marketing and sales. Over the years, he honed critical communication skills to close substantial deals domestically and internationally. His polished, gregarious personality helped him achieve enormous success and a hefty paycheck. With every promotion, he displayed the hallmarks of a successful life. Accolades were published in internal company newsletters, sales convention announcements, and award banquets. He accumulated plaques, crystal trophies, and medals honoring his excellence in sales and marketing. My father welcomed the publicity and always had an appetite for more. Did this insatiable hunger begin years earlier when he professionally sang on the radio? Was he practicing his performance since childhood?

Before there was an official "Take Your Daughter to Work Day," my father occasionally let me tag along to his office or shadow him at off-site sales calls with clients. I was struck by how much his customers genuinely liked him professionally and personally. He knew everyone's name in the company from the CEO to the custodial staff. He was a popular everyman. Walking the hallways like a superstar, he would flash his signature smile to coworkers, reach out to shake hands, ask about their families, and schedule time for future lunch meetings. I was often told how my father went out of his way to help fellow employees by looking at their resumes, practicing interviews, and how to make connections within the industry.

My father was influential in shaping my early views of what sales was all about: serving people. Most salespeople are trained to believe their job is to take a product to prospective customers and explain why it would be a valuable solution to a given problem. The assumption many of them make is that if they do a reasonable job articulating great product features, they will have a high probability of closing the sale. But my father's definition of sales was based on his attitude to serve someone who needed help solving an issue. He wasn't on the sales call to convince but to assist. He made an impression that led clients to admire and appreciate his innovation and creativity in selling products. I enjoyed watching his artistry in deal making.

My father's personality was linked to commercial publicity, advertising, and showmanship. Like entertaining on the radio, my father's career in sales involved a formula to reach his primary objective: keep score and win. Winning or losing involves making constant adjustments to improve performance. Achieving results mattered, but it wasn't enough to achieve. Kudos like "Salesman of the Year" would tell people what a good worker my father was. The goal was to be recognized and validated for the achievements. This steady diet of recognition and accomplishment became part of an elaborate and emotionally exhausting scoring system. Although winning signaled public success, my father experienced private failure in not feeling good enough in maintaining genuine relationships with family and friends.

Bad Publicity

A reporter's job is to tell a story that is well-rounded, informative, and objective. As an English Professor, I often teach the 5Ws, or reporter's rubric, in my composition courses, guiding students to answer questions who, what, where, when, and why to help focus and organize during their prewriting process. I teach students that ethical journalists strive to ensure information is accurate and thorough, but sometimes, reporters participate in excessive coverage of tragic events, evoking a feeding frenzy that can lead to exploitation of personal lives.

As a consequence of extensive media coverage, my father's publicized arrest evoked responses and actions to protect children within the community. News stories covering the events that led to my father's extradition placed my family's tragedy in the public eye, and we were living through a never-ending nightmare. With splashy headlines, like "Sexual Predator Worked Real Estate in Flamingo," "Walworth County Sex Offender Who Disappeared Two Years Ago Turns Up in Costa Rica," and "Captured Fugitive Endeared Himself to Coworkers," the media amplified his sexual perversion in newspapers, radio, television, and websites. Sometimes, it appeared like reading pages from a tabloid. It is important to show compassion for all who are affected by news coverage, using particular sensitivity when dealing with minors and victims of sex crimes. Although my father's behavior was clearly devastating, journalists should work to minimize harm when publishing a story, balancing the public's need for information against causing further damage.

Watching the latest breaking news covering my father's crimes was like being an unwanted guest on *The Jerry Springer Show*, the tabloid style talk show that first aired in the 1990s, where family trauma and dehumanization were the norm. Viewers couldn't get enough of it. I felt like our lives were hijacked for the public to debate and judge. Some may ask "Who cares?" or "What about the victims?" Certainly, the victims suffer the deepest wounds, but it is also worth discussing how it changed our family life by using this tabloid news approach. As a secondary victim myself, I often thought, *Were people talking about this story at the dinner table or office water cooler? How would this harm my children? How would this effect my marriage?* I was afraid my father would be verbally or physically attacked as people scrambled to seek revenge on a man they viewed as one of humanity's worst. In column after column describing my father's felony, I wondered if readers understood the pain these public revelations caused both victims and extended families. Did the media create a disconnect between the headline and the family behind it?

Ripped from the Headlines

A cadre of journalists both domestically and internationally reported on my father. Here is a small sample of some of the articles, pictures, and artifacts that were published after his arrest.

Green Bay Gazette Newspaper
September 10, 1999, by Kendra Mott, Staff Writer
"Colwell Could Face 40 Years for Each of Three Counts Against Him"

A very subdued James Colwell appeared before Judge John Race in Walworth County Circuit Thursday, September 9.

Assistant District Attorney Tara Schipper presented the state's charges against Colwell: three counts of first-degree sexual assault against a child. The first charge stemmed from an alleged July 29 incident in the Village of Walworth and the other two from an alleged August 25 incident in the Town of Delavan.

Colwell's attorney, Frank Lettenberger of Delavan, acknowledged that Colwell understood the three felony charges against him.

Judge Race advised Colwell that if convicted, each charge carried a maximum of forty years in prison.

Prior to the 1:15 p.m. court call, Victims and Witness Coordinator Evelyn Schulz ushered members of the six-year-old victim's family into court. Schulz admonished media person-nel not to approach the victim's family as they did not wish to make any public comments. The victim's mother had been one of Colwell's employees.

Colwell is slated to appear again in court for a motion hearing on October 14 at 10:00 a.m. to introduce videotaped testimony as evidence. Colwell will also appear before Judge Michael Gibbs on November 1 at 3:00 p.m. for a preliminary hearing.

Lettenberger also informed the court that Colwell had moved out of his Fontana home to Whitewater.

Colwell voluntarily turned himself in to court authorities on August 30. He immediately began resigning his numerous board positions with local church and civic organization, most recently his position as trustee for the Village of Fontana.

Colwell, owner of Geneva Lakes Chem Dry in Williams Bay, is free on a $10,000 signature bond.

*****

A.M. Costa Rica
December 22, 2005, by the A.M. Costa Rica Staff
"Sexual Predator Worked Real Estate in Flamingo"

A convicted sexual predator fleeing a thir-ty-year prison sentence has been working in Flamingo as a real estate salesman, according to agents who arrested him Wednesday.

The man is James A. Colwell, sixty-five, who entered Costa Rica in January 2004, according to a summary provided by the International Police Agency (INTERPOL).

Colwell was affiliated while in Flamingo with Emerald Shores real estate firm, the agents said. The man was located there in October, but the paperwork permitting his arrest did not come through until Tuesday, they said. He was arrested in Flamingo.

Colwell is well-known on the Internet, and his mug shot is easily available, including on the website of the US Marshal's Service of the US Department of Justice.

US authorities considered Colwell a continuing danger to children, agents said. Also taking part in the arrest were the Sección Aérea of the Ministerio de Gobernación, Policía y Seguridad Pública, and the Sección de Capturas of the Judicial Investigating Organization. Colwell was brought to San José by a government airplane where he will face extradition in the Tribunal Penal de San José.

Colwell was convicted of two counts of having sexual contact with a minor under the age of thirteen, May 12, 2000, in Walworth Country, Wisconsin. He was sentenced to thirty years in prison, but a judge suspended the sentence and gave him conditional liberty, a form of probation, said agents. Among other things, he had to register as a sex offender.

In 2003, his parole was transferred to the State of Georgia at his request, agents said. There authorities found in early 2004 that he had contact with other minors, and the Wisconsin Department of Corrections ordered him to return to that state to face the allegation of parole violation, agents said.

*****

Inside Costa Rica
December 23, 2005
"Captured Fugitive Endeared Himself to Coworkers"

About two years ago, Colwell applied for a job at Emerald Shores Reality in the Costa Rica in Playa Flamingo and was hired as the office manager and quickly endeared himself to his coworkers.

He had retired from running a business in the United States, Colwell told his new colleagues. He had lost his wife to cancer, he said, and he thought life on the island would be a good way to get away from his memories.

"This was actually the guy next door, the father figure you would want if you didn't know the truth about him," said real estate agent Michael Cromwell, who had worked with Colwell in Costa Rica for about a year and a half. "I'm just in shock, really."

Colwell, a former village official in Fontana, in Walworth County, Wisconsin, and convicted sex offender, was arrested late Wednesday at the real estate office, where, despite being wanted, was using his real name. He also appeared in a staff photo, posing on the beach, on the realty company's website.

A tip about the site alerted US Marshals to Colwell's location in August. After working through bureaucratic red tape for several months, officials from the Walworth County district attorney's office, the US attorney's office, the State Department, and INTERPOL this week secured an international arrest warrant for Colwell. On Thursday afternoon, he was in custody in San José, awaiting extradition to Wisconsin.

Authorities say Colwell's story about his wife was a lie. His tale about his business was partially true—he ran a carpet cleaning company in Williams Bay, but he left it after pleading guilty to two counts of first-degree sexual assault of a child.

Colwell, who was appointed to the Fontana Village Board in 1997 and elected to a two-year term in 1998, was serving as a trustee when the allegations came to light. He resigned on September 1, 1999, a few days after his arrest.

At a hearing in February 2000, Colwell admitted indecently touching a six-year old girl—a family friend—on two different occasions. As part of a plea agreement, a third count was dismissed. Despite a maximum possible penalty of eighty years in prison and tearful pleas from the victim's mother, Colwell was sentenced to a year in the Walworth County Jail and thirty years probation.

"I was looking for more maximum security, maximum sentence," the girl's father said Thursday. "We basically felt it was a slap on the hand. What they did give him (showed that) obviously they didn't take it serious."

In 2003, Colwell had his probation transferred, and he moved to Georgia, where his brother lived. When authorities there began investigating allegations that Colwell was trying to lure children to his new Georgia home, he disappeared, said Deputy US Marshal Paul Koenig.

Authorities now know Colwell went to Playa Flamingo, an upscale resort area on the Pacific Coast populated by wealthy American and European expatriates and retirees.

There he built a house in Surf Side Estates and was an active member of Beach Community Church, former coworker Crowell said.

"He was a very upstanding citizen in the community," Crowell said. "He was one of the nice guys. Nobody that I know of ever had anything bad to say about him."

Walworth County District Attorney Phillip Koss said he hopes Colwell will now have his probation revoked and serve thirty years in custody.

The victim's family hopes so, too, her father said. That's the only way to be sure he won't hurt another child.

The father said the family was grateful to the Walworth County Sheriff's Department, the Marshals' service, and everyone else who had a hand in Colwell's capture.

"We tried to have hope all the way through that they were going to find him," the victim's father said. "There couldn't be a better Christmas present."

CORRECTION: Sex Offender Wanted by Marshals and Not the FBI

In Thursday's edition, we erroneously reported that James Allen Colwell as being wanted by the United States Federal Bureau of Investigation (FBI), when in fact Colwell was wanted by the US Marshals Service.

Mr. Douglas Bachert of the United States Department of Justice was kind to send us a note correcting our mistake.

Mr. Bachert, his note, also pointed out that Colwell had been convicted of first-degree sexual assault of a child (rather than just assault) and that he was also suspected of being involved with the same activity in the state of Georgia before he fled the country.

"We hope that he was not involved in the same activity in Costa Rica. We're hoping the extradition process goes fairly quickly so that we can get him back here. We put a good deal of time into this one and are very grateful to the authorities in Costa Rica," wrote Mr. Bachert.

The US Marshals' wanted poster was included in a link to the .gov site but has since been removed.

*****

The Tico Times
December 23, 2005
"West Coast Realtor Arrested on US Charges"

A US fugitive who operated a real estate office on the northwestern coast of Guanacaste was arrested this week on charges related to sex crimes in the United States. It was the second such arrest in a month.

Costa Rican and International Police (INTERPOL) agents arrested James Colwell, sixty-five, Wednesday in Playa Flamingo, according to the daily *Al Día*.

Colwell pled guilty to sex crimes involving a minor in the US state of Wisconsin in

2000 and was sentenced to thirty years. He fled while on conditional parole and arrived in Costa Rica two years ago, the daily *La Nación* reported.

Following his arrest, Colwell was taken to San Sebastián prison to await extradition proceedings, which could take two to three months.

*****

Inside Costa Rica
January 3, 2006
"Trio a Force at Finding Fugitives"

When Walworth County fugitive James A. Colwell was selling real estate in Costa Rica, he probably didn't realize there was a task force of deputies looking for him.

Sheriff's deputies Tim Ruszkiewicz and Gibby Maas said they spent an untold number of hours and days seeking Colwell, who for nearly two years eluded authorities by living in Costa Rica. Deputy Tim Rumer also assisted in the search for the convicted sex offender.

Colwell, sixty-five, was wanted for probation violations. The former Fontana village trustee sexually assaulted a then six-year-old girl in 1999 and was sentenced to one year in jail and thirty years probation.

"It's pretty satisfying after how much hard work was put in," Rumer said of Colwell's apprehension Dec. 21.

"He was the no. 1 guy we were looking for," Ruszkiewicz said. "He was the guy that we were spending the most time on. Our biggest target."

The three deputies are assigned to a special Fugitive Task Force within the department. All three are deputized as US Marshals, which gives them the authority to cross county and state boundaries to apprehend wanted individuals.

Ruszkiewicz and Maas were the first officers with the task force when it started about two years ago. Rumer was deputized as a marshal last spring.

By cooperating with the US Marshals' Office, the task of finding fugitives became easier.

"They have some resources that we just don't have," Ruszkiewicz said, "such as nationwide contacts and enhanced computer network databases."

On the flip side, the local deputies have more knowledge of the area whenever the marshal's office needs assistance finding someone closer to home.

"There's always cooperation, and we've always worked well with them," Walworth County Sheriff David Graves said. "Whenever we call, we get good cooperation."

All three deputies work regular patrol beats, but they focus on finding fugitives as time allows.

"For our most serious warrants, one of us usually takes it and runs with it, working on different leads," Maas said. "We work on smaller ones at the same time, but when we get a serious warrant, we work on it as much as we can."

There are thousands of outstanding warrants to keep them busy. Talking to friends, family, and acquaintances usually yields the best results. "Ex-wives and ex-girlfriends tell us a lot," Maas said. "They are the best resources for us."

Officers suspect Colwell was in contact with people he knew back in the states, but they were not always forthcoming.

That's why it's important to pursue anonymous tips even though most are often dead ends.

Not in Colwell's case.

The task force received a tip that Colwell might have been working at a realty company in Costa Rica. The tipster led the officers to a website where Colwell was pictured with coworkers.

International warrants were issued, and Colwell was arrested. He is awaiting extradition back to Wisconsin.

"I interviewed a lot of people on it," Ruszkiewicz said. "A lot of them told me he liked to travel and of the various places he might have been. I'm not surprised he ended up there. Not that anyone mentioned (Costa Rica) specifically."

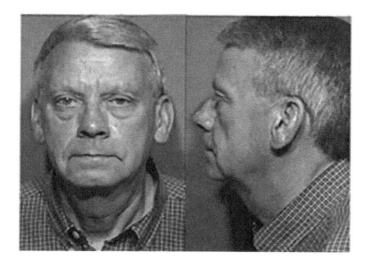

Most Wanted List and More

My father's name and story went beyond the headlines into a variety of places, like official police announcements, online mug shot databases, Village Board of Trustees official meeting minutes, and he even appeared in a John Hopkins University report on child sex tourism in Costa Rica. It was cringeworthy and difficult for me to read about him featured in this way. He was a criminal, but he was still my father. My world changed as I examined each document, trying to make sense of it all.

Biggest Mugshots Directory, Mugshots.com
Sex Offenders Mug Shots Added 10/24/2004

This sleaze bag is one James Allen Colwell, seen here in a mug shot taken by Wisconsin authorities in 2003 after they busted him on sexual assault on a child charges. He was convicted on those charges and is on a thirty-year probation from Wisconsin, but he's since moved to Georgia and hasn't registered as a sex offender, so cops want to pick him up again. Like a lot of sexual predators, cops say he may be using a dog or other small pet to entice his next victims. If you know where this worthless piece of garbage is hiding, drop a dime on him and send him back to the lockup where he belongs. Updated 12/26/2005—Not only is this guy a sleaze, he's pretty stupid as well. After running from the cops in Wisconsin and Georgia, he turns up in Costa Rica and gets a job as an office manager in a real estate company. Next thing you know, his photo (he used his real name by the way) turns up on their website. Someone spots him, recognizes him, now he's awaiting extradition back to the States. His victim's family hopes he gets the full thirty-year sentence. So do we.

Great Lakes Regional Fugitive Task Force
December 12, 2005
James Colwell: Wanted for Failure to Register as a Sex Offender and Probation Violation

On December 21, 2005, James Colwell, age sixty-five, was arrested in Play Flamingo, Costa Rica, by Costa Rican INTERPOL agents and special agents with the Department of State, via a collateral lead sent by the Great Lakes Regional Fugitive Task Force (GLRFTF). Colwell was wanted by Wisconsin authorities for probation violation (first-degree sexual assault of a child) and for failure to register as a sex offender. He also had outstanding warrants in the Eastern District of Wisconsin for unlawful flight to avoid prosecution and by Georgia authorities for failure to register as a sex offender. In 1999, Colwell pled guilty to two counts of first-degree sexual assault of a child, for which he received probation and a thirty-year stayed sentence—which he is facing upon revocation of his probation. Colwell had his supervision transferred to Georgia from Wisconsin due to family reasons.

In early 2004, Colwell fled Georgia when authorities began investigating him for continued inappropriate conduct with young children. Colwell allegedly was luring young children into his home to pet and feed his dogs and was also observed peering into neighbors' windows and playing tackle football with young children. In May 2005, the GLRFTF initiated a fugitive investigation. Leads were worked by the US Marshals in Wisconsin, Illinois, Washington, Nevada, Michigan, and Georgia and by the US Marshals' Financial Surveillance Unit (FSU), which led investigators to a realty company in Costa Rica, where Colwell was working. Coordination between the US Marshals International Investigations Branch and the Regional Security Officer in Costa Rica confirmed Colwell's address and employment. A provisional arrest warrant was issued, and Colwell was arrested at his realty office. Colwell will face extradition proceedings in Costa Rica.

*****

Village Board of Trustees Meeting Minutes,
Fontana, Wisconsin
December 4, 2006
State Legislature/Village of Fontana
Recognition of Walworth County
Sheriff's Department Officers and US Deputy
Marshals for James Colwell Arrest in Costa
Rica

President Whowell presented background information on the conviction and attempt to flee justice by former Village of Fontana and church official James Colwell and then introduced Walworth County Sheriff David Graves. Sheriff Graves stated Colwell was tracked down in Costa Rica and extradited thanks to the cooperative efforts of the Walworth County and Waukesha County Sherriff's Departments and the US Marshals Office. Graves stated that the officers kept working together for more than a year before they were able to locate Colwell in Costa Rica. Deputy US Marshal Paul Koenig stated that it took about one year to complete the extradition process after they located Colwell.

Coping with Press Coverage

While the flurry of press coverage continued for several months, I had to learn how to prepare for the likelihood of newspaper articles, television news clips, and website links reaching into our home, school, and workplace. I felt like a breach could occur at any moment, with a flood of unwanted information forcing us into conversations with our daughters, neighbors, and coworkers that I was not yet ready to have. What would happen if someone asked about my father based on something they read or heard? Could I stay silent? Would they make assumptions if I didn't reply?

As a parent, it was my number one responsibility to protect our daughters from harm. If anything were to happen to them, it would be a dagger to my heart. I was so worried about our young daughters coming home from piano practice, a playdate, or dance recital asking about their grandfather who they may have heard about in the news. Would one of their friends find out and tell them first? Would they be teased or bullied because of what their grandfather had done? Would an article appear on their computer screen or pop up on a cell phone? If parents in our carpool or on the swim team or school board knew about my father, it could certainly cause concern. Would they be shaken up by the thought that their children could be in harm's way? Would they opt to keep away from our children just in case?

My husband and I made a difficult but firm decision not to tell our daughters about their grandfather. It became part of my life that I kept very secret. We had several conversations about our decision and even sought counsel with my cousin, a Catholic priest, who advised us that if his name came up in conversation or they asked about him, we could tell our daughters that he had died. After all, the good memories of who we thought he was had already perished. We were able to keep that promise of not telling our daughters until one year before my father died.

Avoiding talking about my father caused tremendous stress as no Band-Aid was large enough to cover the festering wound. I could not imagine what people thought my father did, adding their own interpretive lens in reading about his crimes. In dealing with the aftermath of his destruction, I kept busy—really, really busy. I turned my pain into productivity and overscheduled activities to avoid feeling the pain.

Every moment was accounted for. I was craving order in the midst of chaos. I organized cabinets, color-coded clothes, and labeled folders. I poured myself into work, developing new curriculum, creating online courses, editing textbooks, presenting at conferences, workshops, and seminars. I transformed into a visually meticulous merchandise designer for each holiday, decorating our entire house with the same diligence in creating an attractive retail shop window display, spending hours arranging knick-knacks, picture frames, and novelty items. I became obsessed with scrapbooking, archiving pictures, and documenting positive memories. I invited friends over for elaborate dinner parties, making five course meals from scratch, cleaning the house from top to bottom. I created a cookbook with family recipes and made several copies to share. We also moved multiple times, and I busied myself with packing, unpacking, sorting, and purging. It was a frenetic pace to try to escape from the news outlets that were covering my father's story.

At one point, a concerned friend gave me a book called *Crazy Busy* by Kevin DeYung, a cautionary tale to slow down and be mindful of operating in a hectic, all-consuming culture. Looking at me on the outside, she clearly understood I was flailing and thought I needed to read this book to turn off, rest, and restart. DeYung writes about also recognizing his overly busy schedule and working hard to allow himself to take a breath and pause. "I want to grow in this area. I don't want to keep up this same pace for the rest of my life. Frankly, I probably can't." I had to do some soul searching about how to find grace and learn to deal with the complex situation my father created. I had to stop being busy and start being still to begin healing.

The relationship with my father had changed and needed to keep changing in order to live with the truth. Our father-daughter relationship was in exile, unable to return to what it was. How do I move forward to maintain this relationship? The answers aren't always clear as the story continues.

CHAPTER 6

Capsized

Going to prison is like dying with your eyes open.

—Bernard Kerik

I never imagined prison would be the last address my father would call home before he died. My family moved across municipal and state boundaries eight times before I began high school, and these frequent transitions became a normative part of our experience. We enjoyed the anticipation of making new friends, upgrading into a bigger home, and exploring activities within a new area. Moving created space for personal growth. Although my father was used to moving and adapting to new places, nothing could prepare him for moving to Fox Lake Correctional Institution, a medium-security state prison for men located in Dodge County, Wisconsin.

As my father began writing letters to me about his prison life, he described feeling like a caged animal. His descriptions of prison reminded me of the time we took our daughters to see the polar bear exhibit at the zoo. A typical zoo enclosure for a polar bear is significantly smaller than the size of its home range in the wild, and many scientists say that captive polar bears may engage in stereotypic pacing as a result of their confinement. At the zoo, we observed the polar bear's lumbering gait, his large front paws swinging outward onto the artificial snow bank. He was restricted with each step. Pacing back and forth, the polar bear seemed spiritless, his eyes lost and vacant. Clearly, there was a lack of mental stimulation and enrichment for this marine mammal who belonged on the sea ice of the Arctic Ocean. My father was trapped like him.

In 2008, during the time my father was incarcerated at Fox Lake, the prison had a maximum capacity of 691 inmates, but an actual population of 1,033. The facility has six housing units with ninety-six single cells each. To increase the holding capacity, fifty-two of the cells are double bunked. In addition to cells, Fox Lake Correctional Institution has two large dormitories to house inmates. My father's fellow inmates were murderers, rapists, thieves, drug dealers, and addicts. Many were diagnosed with severe mental illnesses and put on antipsychotic medication, mood-stabilizing drugs, or antidepressants to assist in their sporadic mental health treatment while incarcerated. He frequently mentioned that more mental health screening and rehabilitation tools were needed and necessary but often overlooked or completely dismissed.

As a first timer, my father described prison as a noisy, crowded, dehumanizing hellhole where he was stripped of self-confidence and hope. While serving time in prison, his narrative had power to destroy or redeem him. Prisoners are still *people*. The outcome depends not just on who's writing it but also on who's carefully reading and listening.

It's hard to find positive things to say about prison, but exchanging letters was one of them. In this robust chapter, I included the most salient snapshots of my father's life in prison. While cataloging his five hundred letters, I transcribed over 1,500 pages of repeated ideas about raw events he mentioned most frequently. From lack of hygiene, wearing the same clothes every day, to no privacy on the toilet and consuming a poor diet, I discovered patterns in his experience of prison life which included scarcity, deprivation, loneliness, hope, hardship, religion, work, and a limited but welcome outdoor recreation area.

New Sights, Sounds, and Smells

Like in the movie *The Shawshank Redemption* (1994), new inmates are often referred to as "fish." They swim in the "tank" with other fish while they are being processed on the first day during prison intake. Sorting and recording a new school of fish involves many steps. First, fish fill out several forms and are required to surrender their clothing and personal items. Next, fish are stripped, searched, and given prison-issued clothes and shoes. Finally, they are assigned housing and taken to a cell block. It can be a lengthy and nerve-wracking process to swim in an entirely new pond. The best advice my father learned was to keep his mouth shut, observe, and do not talk about a potential release date.

The other fish know instantly if you have returned to their pond or if you are brand-new, essentially a fish out of water. Consequently, you need to watch out for predators in order to protect yourself. My father learned that many of the fish are already accustomed to being part of the group, rotating in and out of prison for years. They have established a tight formation swimming together in prison and formed their own groups. There is no welcome for new residents. In his letters, my father writes about inmates who yell, taunt, and tease, especially aiming their insults at newcomers. On his first day in prison, he describes being shackled from the waist down, escorted by two guards on either side of him, shuffling down a long hallway. He said he looked straight ahead and clenched his teeth. He was terrified. How could he ever adapt or swim in this toxic pond without drowning?

Most prison cells measure approximately eight by six feet with a metal bed either bolted to the wall or free-standing on metal legs. Prison overcrowding has forced most prisons to keep two prisoners in each cell, and for many years, my father slept on the top of a metal bunk bed with rotating cellmates on the bottom bunk. He never had a cellmate for more than a few months before they were transferred out, and most of his cellmates were under thirty years old. My father was twice their age. He describes his mattress as plastic and paper thin with one itchy wool blanket and no pillow. Most nights, he was jolted awake by his cellmate's screaming, a guard shining a light in his face, or a count announced over the loudspeaker.

There are various counts by the corrections officers throughout the day. During a count, all prisoners must stand in front of their cells while the corrections officers do a head count to make sure no one is missing or in a place where they aren't supposed to be. If a prisoner is in the wrong place and doesn't make it to his cell for the count on time, he faces disciplinary action. Mandatory counts are conducted at regular intervals at the same time every day. There are counts in the middle of the night as well, but prisoners can usually stay in their beds while the corrections officers count them from outside the cell.

In his letters, he talked about forming a routine of getting up at 4:30 a.m. every day to avoid being harassed or sexually assaulted in the shower. He quickly got out of bed and often skipped breakfast or chow to go running on the outdoor track as part of his daily exercise routine. After exercise, there was another standing count to mark the beginning of the day, and then he would either go to class or a work assignment depending on availability.

He avoided socializing in the dayroom or recreation yard because he didn't want anyone to know who he was or, worse, his offense. Sex offenders try to hide because they can easily be found out. Inmates will quickly gossip about each other. Stigmas stick. He would never tell another inmate why he was sent to prison. But being older, he said fellow inmates automatically assumed he was a chomo (child molester). Sex offenders are labeled in the prison hierarchy as the lowest of the low. They are branded and can be the most vulnerable, targeted with violent punching, stabbing, or even rape. Although it is difficult to pity men like my father who are incarcerated for sex-related acts, prison is extra horrible for them. It's like a minnow in a shark tank feeling all the time. He was fearful of fights and kept to himself.

What is prison like? It is like living on a different planet day after day. Reading my father's letters introduced me to a cultural collision within the walls of prison as he tried to create a new

142

identity in order to survive. He revealed the nuances and complexities of reluctantly forming shallow relationships with guards, his coworkers, and cellmates. His five hundred letters taught me that compassion can lead to understanding as I read what it was like to be exiled.

Nesting Instinct

These excerpts are from my father's letters as he first settled into prison life in 2007 up to the year 2015, right before he was diagnosed with cancer. In these clips, he vacillated between trying to adapt and scan the landscape of living in prison to a constant turnover in cellmates and how this affected his outlook on future expectations of freedom. Getting used to being monitored 24-7 and grasping at any sliver of privacy is an ongoing experience in prison.

July 9, 2007

Praise the Lord, I'm finally out of Dodge. I have been assigned to Fox Lake Correctional Institution. If you want to send me money, they will only allow it at the PO Box issued. I am learning each day what I can and cannot do here, but so far, I've been told I'll be able to go to the library at least once a week. Also, I can go outside on the patio (an area about 20' by 20') to sit on a picnic table in the morning and afternoons.

I have a cellmate who is twenty-three years old. He has tried to commit suicide twice already before I got here. Hopefully with the help of the Holy Spirit, I can be of help to him. Once I get accustomed to the rules, I will obtain visitors' forms and send them to you. They tell me they have a large field with a track around it, so once I save up (I get paid $2 per week), I'll buy some running shoes and get back to my running again.

What do I use money for in here? For now, the basics of toothpaste (the stuff the state gives you tastes like sawdust), toothbrushes, soap, Q-tips, deodorant and shampoo. Once in a while when I have money, I buy envelopes for my letters to all my sup-

porters from our church in Costa Rica and letters to you. The church there continues to do great things for the poor people.

I want to purchase running shoes, a T-shirt, shorts, and running socks. We can only buy what is available through an authorized catalog, so you can't send anything to me. Sometimes, I really get carried away and buy a bag of peanuts through the authorized canteen which costs $3. That's a treat!

I want to go to the library and check out some good religious books. Also, I'm saving money to pay for a college-level correspondence course from the University of Wisconsin. That will be expensive! But if I can get a tutoring job here, I'll make twenty cents an hour, which is big money in prison.

Remember Isaiah said in chapter 41 in the Bible, "For I am Lord, your God, who takes hold of your right hand and says to you, do not fear, I will help you."

July 23, 2007

I have no idea where I am in Wisconsin as they brought me here in chains with no windows on the bus to look out. However, I believe the prison website has a map and visiting instructions. They tell me the process for you to be approved takes about three weeks. They will notify me when you are added to my visitor's list. Everything here has a way to be followed. I do not want you to drive all the way up here and not be able to see you.

I can't wait until I save enough to get a decent pair of running shoes. I will not run until I have the proper shoes. But in the meantime, I walk alongside of the track for at least 3 miles each time we have recreation to keep my body in shape.

July 31, 2007

By mistake, you sent your letter to the wrong PO Box. I was called up by property where the mail comes in, and I said my daughter made a small mistake. No! That was not acceptable. They threw one of your letters away. But the other money order you sent was deposited into my account. It went to the right PO Box. Thank you ever so much, that will go a long way toward my new running shoes. When I get them and start running again, I'll think of you and the pain that comes with training for a marathon.

Although I truly enjoy and read your letters several days in a row after receiving them, you do not have to write me every week. I can imagine how full your daily schedule is with work, the girls, and activities with your husband. My request is that you write only when it's easy to do so because you don't have to. Remember, I have time, a whole lot of it, and you don't. I would love a letter every day, but that's extremely selfish. So only write when you can. I'll always welcome your letters. We cannot live yesterday, it is gone, and tomorrow is yet to come, but we are here today to praise the Lord and thank him for all the many blessings we have received.

January 10, 2008

There is so much bitterness and hatred here and name calling—all examples of the work of Satan and his fallen angels. God gives me a break from all of it, and it is a true blessing. Unfortunately, things are now "back to normal" after the holiday stress, if you can begin to call this place normal.

February 3, 2008

It's been snowing every week since the time you were here. The ground still has about a foot of snow on it, and they are forecasting more next week. At my age, I really miss the beach and 85-degree weather. I walk outside and refuse to get old and fat, so I'm keeping my walking each day to maintain my energy. I find it really helps in this environment where you spend your waking hours sitting. It makes me laugh inside each morning when I put on the long underwear, sweatshirt, wool stocking hat, and the coat they give us so I can go out and walk. Without your gift of money to buy the underwear and sweatshirt, I would be sitting inside all day long. Your money, letters, and visits help me to survive here.

I'm on chapter 15 of my Learning Spanish *book, but it's getting pretty complex now with all the grammar changes that we don't have in English. But I'm determined to learn Spanish. Lately,*

I've been treating it like the preparation for my first marathon. There is no room for giving up, just keep working to learn and win.

February 12, 2008

Thank you for the Valentine's Day card. I laughed so hard my sides were hurting. But they frown on that behavior around here. They have no sense of humor. Actually, that's what this depressing place needs, which is why I enjoyed your card so much. I still can't get used to all the horrible language with all the swear words and hip-hop junk here.

April 27, 2008

You asked me about reading books. I do read some from the library here, but the selection is not the greatest. I'm almost through my Spanish book and still would like to learn more. Perhaps, you can locate a teacher's edition high school Spanish book that would help me expand my vocabulary. I am finding learning a new language at my age is not impossible but probably more difficult than a young college student. My mind isn't totally dead yet, but it does process slower than it used to. I don't want you to spend a lot on another book for me as you have already been more than generous sending me money each month.

Unfortunately, we can't have books on tape or CD as they are a security risk. Why? I have no idea, but I know they took the CD out of the Spanish book you sent and threw it in the waste basket in front of me, and I know they enjoyed doing it. As you can imagine, this is not living in here, it's simply existing. And I am not good at only existing, I'd rather live.

If the family of the victim knew we got more than bread and water, I'm sure they would ask to have that taken away as well. Although I have found that those who have the least are the ones who have the strongest faith in God. No matter how poor their station is in life, they still keep a smile on their face and love their families and know the heart of Christ. I ask God every day to show me what I must do to have joy in my life again before he calls me home.

June 20, 2008

Sorry your dad is behind bars. Just saying that makes me feel sick to my stomach. There is so much hollering here all the time. I will never get used to the horrible language they use. They call women bitches and everyone else motherfuckers. So much anger and hate. Obviously, I stay as far away as possible, but it's hard not to hear their voices when they scream at each other constantly. What a way to live. When they start to scream, I start praying loud in my head. I pray for the day when I am out of here. That's the only way I can deal with outrageous behavior. I pray inside of me.

I have finished at least five of the books you sent. I'll pack them up and send them back to you. We can't give the books to another inmate or donate them to the library here. We must always have hope. Prayer leads us to hope, and hope is Jesus. So our hope has to be in Jesus, not this crazy system that I am involved in. Prayer will take me out of here.

November 11, 2008

Today we are totally locked in our cells all day and night (except to go to the bathroom). This is the second day of the lock-down. Yesterday morning, at 8:30 a.m., an inmate attacked two officers with a hammer. One officer is still in the hospital today, the other was treated and released. The inmate that did this was from our cell block. He has been in prison for the last twenty-one years, serving two life sentences for killing two policemen.

He was working in an area where he had access to tools. He went crazy and tried to kill these two guards. We may be locked down for several more days, so I'm not sure when this letter will reach you. You never know in here if an inmate next to you is serving a life sentence for murder or if he is here because he wasn't paying child support. So I am always careful to be aware of everything around me. When I go out of my cell, I have to be ready and alert. This is such a horrible place to be. Please continue your prayers for my safety, and if something does happen, please let God take me quickly and suffer no pain. They took the inmate out of here and sent him to a maximum prison where he must stay in his cell all day and night. I pray for his forgiveness and that God will bring him peace.

I'm sorry I am here. I know it hurts you. Please pray for my appeal and the restoration from death of being here. All this reminds me of what a disappointment I have been to you as a father. I tried to be the best Dad. Mom is missed. She gave me the centering that I needed. She was my rock. She was the rock that the Bible talks about when Jesus told Peter "You are my rock and upon this you will build a church."

Tears are running down my face as I write this. I love you. God has blessed you, and I'm sorry to have let you down. I have caused this life-changing event in your life, and you did not in any way deserve what I did. I can't reach back and make it go away. I would give anything to fill the void I have created in your heart. Only God can heal. I ask him every day to heal you not for my sake but for yours. I'm sorry you can no longer talk to friends about your dad because I know how ashamed you must be.

I'm sorry because you have been the morning star in my life since you were born. My heart is sad because I can no longer brag about you as I love to do. This is not the place for that. This is a place of death, not life. The holidays will come and go again without me there. Thank you for making plans to see me on December 27. We may still be on lock down, but I talked to our officer, and he said visits are still allowed. But if a Christmastime visit saddens you, please do not come. I have caused enough damage and don't want to cause more. But I miss you. God bless you.

January 4, 2009

In no way would I ask you for help beyond your prayers and support. But if I do get out, I would ask if you can pick me up and take me to the airport. This is the help I have in mind. As you know, I have no money. They stopped my Social Security retirement checks while I was still in prison in Costa Rica. That was $1,150 per month, not much, but that plus my real estate job was more than enough to live on. All the money I had before they brought me *back was spent on attorneys. So today I have nothing. This is my fault and no one else's, so I am not crying.*

If I receive a favorable appeal decision, I'm told it's about a one in a hundred chance, I will hopefully be able to have a friend fly in from Costa Rica to testify for me. You went through enough emotionally nine years ago at my trial in that courtroom. You will not be asked to testify again. So far, my friends and church members in Costa Rica have raised close to $2,000 to fly my friend to the US.

I have tried to be very responsible with the money you have been so generous in sending me. I have and will not purchase a TV or radio and many treats from the canteen. I have not spent a dime foolishly. In fact, I have saved $500 out of what you have sent me so far and will put it toward a plane ticket out of here. If I can't get out, I will have the prison send you a check in the amount that I have saved. I am sorry if at times I can't remain positive, but facing the fact that I could easily die here makes it impossible to comprehend. Then my mind goes to how much I have hurt you through all this and realize that you can no longer be proud of your dad.

May 6, 2009

Thank you for sending pictures of your family and their activities. I should be there with you, but instead, I am rotting away in this hellhole for what I did almost nine years ago. I did the wrong and deserve the punishment. In the meantime, you are doing so well in everything and have so much energy. I love and miss you, and I'm so sorry that you have to have a dad in prison.

All people talk about in here is how they are innocent and the police are out to get them. So much bitterness. Thanks for taking me out of that negative environment and allowing my mind to concentrate on you and your family. I worry about my safety and try to stay alert during the day and night, always remembering where I am.

Sorry about my letters sounding sad recently. I'll pray to remain positive. It's so hard. I've been behind bars for over three years now, and it never gets easier. To be sixty-nine years old and

149

have to live with so many bitter and angry people is very hard for me. Your prayers and letters are a big help. I'm so sad you have to experience this journey with me. I know it's very hard for you.

August 1, 2009

Now that I'm "in the system," it's hard to understand what's behind some of the judgments that our judges make. I must wonder if my sentence will be a deterrent to others who may contemplate leaving probation and moving out of the US. I feel very strongly about unjust long sentences given when new crimes have not been committed. It seems the system works best when people can afford a high-priced or private lawyer who has the motivation to get someone out of this hellhole. My cellmate is a good example. He has been in prison for a fifteen-year sentence and served ten years so far. They moved him here from another prison so he could take a drug-abuse classes. But the classes never started. So his mom hired a private attorney, and within a week, he was called up to the PRC (Program Review Committee) and told within the next two weeks he would be transferred to another prison to start a six-month program to be sent home for early release. So he will be home. He will get out of this place.

February 27, 2010

My new celli (what prisoners call cellmates) is not working out. He just sits in the cell all day and watches his $295 flat-screen TV while I work in tutoring and helping people. He buys boxes of donuts, candy bars, and other junk food and eats out of frustration. I have softly suggested that he may want to borrow my Bible and read it to pass his time better. He said nothing.

There is so much about being here that I find hard. The tremendous loneliness should never be forced upon a person who has lived sixty years of his life in freedom. The only way I can relate to this loneliness is to say that everything we love in life, especially freedom, is totally taken away. You can never understand the feeling, and I pray each day that you never ever have to. There are probably some people who can adapt to this loneliness, but I have failed from the start. I'm just not good at being lonely. It's so hard to be here, and it's so hard to know it will last for the rest of my life.

March 14, 2010

When I was in the office supply business, I presented the specs for a paper shredder at a conference I facilitated in Germany. In fact, made several trips to Germany in order to set up the manufacturing agreement. Your recent trip there brought back so many memories. I wish I could have been there with you and my granddaughters.

I am so sorry that I have put you through so much over the last eleven years. I am not much of an example of what a dad should be. Thank God for a little part of my seventy years I think I had it together. I pray you will be able to keep those times in mind when I am no longer living on this earth. Each morning when I wake up at 4:00 a.m., the reality of spending the rest of my life here becomes more and more apparent. Any hope is taken away from my heart and mind. However, two things that I will always have in my heart are the thirty-two years with your mom, which twenty-eight were in the sacrament of marriage. The second is my love for you, the most beautiful, wonderful, caring, talented, and so much more daughter that I am so very proud of.

I'm enclosing a letter from the Inter-American Commission on Human Rights. One more turn down. Because I can't take anymore rejections from people who could help me, no more letters.

March 21, 2010
Dear Sir,

On behalf of the Inter-American Commission on Human Rights, I acknowledge receipt of your communication, received in this Executive Secretariat on November 4, 2009, in which you make certain requests to the Inter-American Commission on Human Rights.

In response, I wish to inform you that said requests do not correspond to the mandate or functions of the Inter-American Commission on Human Rights.

Before I forget, please do not put (as much as I enjoy them) any stickers on the outside of your letters to me. It's yet another rule and ends up holding your letter for an extra day to call me up to the mail room and be told that the letters cannot have stickers on the envelope. Just a stamp. They think you are sending me gang signals! Crazy.

Thank you is not part of anyone's vocabulary in this hellhole. Guards never say thank you, and no else in this place can find a way to say thank you with the exception of your visits, the balance of my life is a total waste. I am being warehoused to die, devoid of any hope to ever have a life outside these walls ever again.

July 10, 2010

Being this lonely is not what God had planned for me, but I messed up his plan. I liked the pictures from your garden. I must assume the cucumbers are from your harvest. They look really good. We don't get cucumbers here.

You will not have to worry about your dad getting too old and needing special and expensive living arraignments. First, if I ever get out of here at seventy-six, seventy-seven, seventy-eight, or more, I will return to Costa Rica where I can receive government health insurance and medical help. So there will be no burden on you. I've given you enough of a burden by just being here.

Secondly, I will no doubt pass away in this hellhole where I get fed each day and sleep on a half-inch foam pad on a steel bed. My three-hundred-pound cellmate sleeps above me, and each night when he turns over, it's like being in the middle of a thunderstorm.

September 3, 2010

My cellmate continues to listen to the radio with his earphones, so he's quiet. But I kind of miss my old cellmate because he had a TV set, and we watched the news together every night to keep up with what is going on in the world. Maybe, I can start

152

saving money for my own TV. We can only buy TVs from a catalog they have here, and they are expensive. The prices go up depending on the model. The TVs are a 12-inch screen and a clear case so you can see inside to prevent inmates from hiding contraband inside the set. The cheapest one is $230, which makes absolutely no sense. You could probably buy one at Best Buy for $100 or less. The TV in the dayroom is taken over, and all they watch is rap music videos and sexy shows and yell out "bitches" when women appear on the television. So I stay away from the dayroom TV.

September 26, 2010

Thank you for your letter, pictures, and early Christmas gift of a TV set. I also need a headset so I can watch without disturbing my cellmate. Although I hate to spend your money on what I call a luxury, please know that I will thank you each time I turn it on for the news or mass on a Sunday morning. And I'll thank God for having such a wonderful and caring daughter.

I'm enclosing an article from the newspaper Tico Times *I received this week. This year's television show* Survivor *is being filmed in Nicaragua. On my last trip before they arrested me in Costa Rica, I went to Granada in Nicaragua. On the way back to Costa Rica, I drove to San Juan del Sur, which is right on the ocean. It is located on the southwestern side of Nicaragua, just north of the boarder of Costa Rica. My boss and I were talking about opening another real estate office in San Juan del Sur, and he would remain in Costa Rica and I would move to Nicaragua to run the new office and hire a sales force. I walked upon the same beach where they are now filming the TV show* Survivor, *and ironically, I feel like I am not surviving in this place called prison.*

October 16, 2010

A new rule is you have to know the inmate's number to get in for your next visit. My number is 389188. I never forget it because it is sewn into all my clothes and the guards will scream the sequence of numbers at me almost every day. Wish I had something good to share with you, but I don't. Things are exactly the same here as I try to stay positive. This by far is the most difficult time of my life.

I really took for granted the little things every day that are not available in prison, like free access to washers and dryers. Laundering my own clothes would make things a little more bearable. But when you are stripped of everyday utilities, things can get more desperate. My cellmate started washing his T-shirt in the toilet the other day. Not the most hygienic, right? But then he hung the dripping T-shirt on the edge of our bunk, and it just made the room smell like moldy bananas.

February 6, 2011

Thanks for sharing about your friend's father who is also celebrating his seventy-fifth birthday. It made me cry because of a terrible mistake I made twelve years ago. I cannot be a grandfather to your daughters, and they will never be able to celebrate any of my birthdays. I so miss the times when we were together. At least once a day when my cellmate is out of our cell, I break down and cry for all I am missing. I cry for you and how you have been so hurt by your father.

February 9, 2011

This week, we missed two days of school because we were locked down. A gas explosion early Monday morning burned down a warehouse just outside the fence around the prison. The week before, the snowstorm closed everything down for two days. So my biweekly pay is minus four days. I am saving to buy a new sweatshirt for $21, and with the reduced check, I now have $16 saved. So I'll have to wait for my next check in two more weeks to order a new sweatshirt. In the meantime, I will pray this bitter cold lets up.

February 23, 2011

Thank you for your letter and money order. I ordered the new sweatshirt. Thank you! It's so hard for me to ask you for money. Almost all my life since your birth, I have been able to give you everything. It was not a problem for Mom and me. So after all these years of trying to help you financially, it is hard for me to ask you even though I am no longer able because of where I am to be financially independent. I will never forget your kindness.

This week, I was asked to help two inmates in filling out their release papers. The document is about ten pages in length, filled with questions about what they will be doing when they get out. For many, they are difficult questions, and they need clarification and encouragement to complete. I was excited to be able to help them and know they will be going home soon. But the next day, it hit me that I will never have the opportunity to fill out these types of papers for myself. I sent a note to my social worker to call me to his office, and he did. We reviewed my situation again, and he confirmed again that this institution cannot change my sentence. Even when I see the parole board one day, they will say I am a high risk because of my long-sentence structure. The only time I will come down off of the high-risk status is when I have served one half of my sentence, which is fifteen years. So in eleven more years, at age eighty-two, parole will consider my case but will probably say no for the first four years until I am eighty-six to recommend parole.

I'm going to stop going to my social worker because he doesn't help, and I know there is nothing he can do. He said the only way to get out of here is to go back to court for a sentence adjustment. That's not going to happen. Please pray that God takes me home now. This is not a life here, this is existence. I try to make it a life, but it's impossible. I just want to go home. Everybody would be better off with me in the grave.

April 9, 2011

Things here are negative, and I pray one day God will show me good. It's been very long ago that I have had a good, peaceful, and joy-filled day. I am grateful for the many I had before these four years in hell.

Thank you for depositing another check into my account. The prison takes 10 percent of any money that's sent from the outside. That money goes into a release account for my release that will never happen, so you'll get that money back when I join Mom in heaven. It won't be much, but it's a small repayment of all the money you have sent me over the past four years.

I also enclosed a bill for my tax preparation this year as I do not want to get in trouble with the IRS about not filing. I usually send out my taxes, but you can only send out $25 at a time to pay for the service to anyone on the outside. So I saved for almost six months to pay the bill for taxes, but this year, I don't have enough money saved. I spent the money on a book for my computer class to help me better understand Excel and PowerPoint. So my birthday money is gone. You know I hate asking you for money. All the years, Mom and I took care of you; there was nothing too good for our daughter. The results speak for themselves as you have had so much success in your life. I am now asking you to pay my accountant and mail it to the address I enclosed for $150.

April 23, 2011

My days here are out of my control. I start at 4:00 a.m. when I awake without an alarm. The guards count us four times a day, and we must stand at the door of our cell as an officer walks by to make sure we haven't escaped. The fourth and final count is at 9:15 p.m. And then the cycle begins again. I go to recreation to run 3 miles within the fifty minutes we are allowed. When I get up at 4:00 a.m., I cannot use the shower until 5:15 a.m., so I read my Bible and pray. It's the weekends that really drag. I stay in my cell reading and writing letters. My cellmate leaves next month, so I'll get another one soon.

Not all, but many of the guards here treat us like caged animals and show little respect. I work at staying out of their way although once in a while one of the more humane ones will say, "How are you?" But that's the extent of an intelligent conversation.

Life as I knew and loved it for sixty years is not a part of where I am now. Being a burden on you with asking for money and visits is a heavy burden for me. Since I left home at eighteen years of age, I have always found a way to take care of myself while still reaching out to others in love and care. Here I am living in a box with a roommate with virtually no money and no one to talk to and share my life with.

This place is much like me. It's tired (built in 1960, over fifty years ago), worn down, and not a place any normal human would want to be in. Your letters, pictures, prayers, and most of all your love is the bright light in my day.

May 26, 2011

Yesterday was a training day for the officers. So mass was cancelled, and we were locked down for the day. It happens once a month. Today is a furlough day, so again we are locked down because of the shortage of staff. No school, no recreation, no nothing. And the weekend we'll be without activity as usual because Monday is a holiday, and we are once again locked down. You would think that after four years of this place, I would be able to handle it mentally and emotionally, but I'm not.

July 24, 2011

Last weekend was hot. We do not have air conditioning, and for three days, we were under a severe heat index, which means the entire place was locked down. No school, no recreation, no air conditioning. Just sitting in front of my 6-inch fan in the cell and letting hot air blow over my overheated body. The humidity is so bad it's hard to take a normal breath. They took a few inmates to the hospital because of what they thought was heatstroke. I just kept drinking water constantly and going to pee about every thirty minutes.

I think about being on the boat during this time. I really loved the water. I had so many business friends who also shared my love for boating. When I climbed the corporate ladder, I met fantastic, successful, very intelligent, yet humble men who I had such great respect for. Too many people today hear about the few who have taken advantage of their companies and were selfish. Most in my lifetime were really great people in their business and home life. Many years ago, I was asked to chair the Young Executives Forum, an association of executives for two hundred companies *in the Office Products field. It was such an honor, and I really learned a lot in how to become a better executive. Fortunately, I was part of that group from age thirty-four to forty.*

Unfortunately, on this lap of life, I am not even allowed to drive the race car. All I can be is a bystander and try as I do; it's a part of life I cannot accept. To ever think that one day they will carry me out of here in a body bag is so hard to imagine, but in reality, it's more than likely to happen. Although I try to keep busy as many hours a day as possible, there are still the long nights when my mind tells me that there is no light at the end of this tunnel.

September 17, 2011

The young are taking over this prison. They are disrespectful, dope sellers, and treat this place like a summer camp. Their vocabulary is limited to "fuck" about every other word and continue to call women bitches. Most belong to a gang, and they shout about their bitches with total disregard, identifying them as strictly objects, not human beings. I try to see Christ in them, and when I'm not in school or running, I stay in my cell. At times, it can be intimidating when I am surrounded by eight or ten of them on the way to school or on the track where I run. I have never had to live like this my entire life. You will never know how difficult it is in prison. I just want to get out of here before they carry me out in a body bag. Please pray that somehow, someway, in God's grace, I will be able to get back to court to stop this punishment. I love and miss you.

January 12, 2012

I have always been clean and orderly in my life. Clean cars, spick-and-span. I liked to get up and wash my car every Saturday at 5:30 a.m. after my run. I couldn't stand dust on the car, and being in the sales business, I believed a clean car inside and out elevated my customer base and confidence. That's another reason why I really enjoyed being an entrepreneur in my carpet-cleaning business. I could give customers exactly what they dreamed of—a fresh-smelling, spotless carpet in their homes. It's so dirty here. I don't think the walls have ever been cleaned, and the floors are just mopped with the same rancid water over and over, just pushing debris around the surface.

March 11, 2012

I guess we never know what's around the next corner. I would have gladly taken Mom's place so she would not have had to suffer. That journey was hell. But it parallels, and some days surpasses how I am treated in here. The guards punish me more than I deserve. I know that fear of some is what I deserve, and the fact that society wants me to live here for the rest of my life because I am not fit to live among noncriminal people is depressing. I try not to get too negative, otherwise I will end up in the funny farm mentally.

I prefer to focus my daily life here on the positive. Here's a list that gets me through the day:

- *My faith*
- *Your love, letters, and prayers*
- *Mom as guardian angel*
- *Tutoring job*
- *Letters from friends who miss me and accept me for who I am for what I did thirteen years ago*

I feel as your dad, I have an obligation and serious responsibility to pass on my faith to you. During this journey, I never want you to lose your love that you give freely and unconditionally to me. Without you and your mom, I am nothing. In addition, I really do not want you sitting out there in freedom thinking about how terrible life in prison must be. I will get through this even if I am called home to heaven before my time here in this place is completed. Being positive does not mean dreaming unrealistic things or not realizing terrible negative vibes that this place gives off. Is it the answer to be positive? No, but it helps me focus on the blessings I have been given in this life. These are the blessings that remain in my soul for eternity.

April 19, 2012
Big news here today. We are changing toilet paper. Can you believe it? They installed special two-roll paper holders in each bathroom stall, and we no longer get the regular-sized rolls. The roll itself is very big in roundness, but the width of the paper is about 1/2 inch the width of a normal sheet of toilet paper. There have been a lot of complaints already. We can't do anything about it, but it is now the big news at Fox Lake.

July 6, 2012
In the five years (it seems like fifty-five) I've been here, I can't remember being so hot and not sleeping for two nights and then in and out of sleep for the balance of this heat wave. My sheets were soaked. It feels like a furnace. They say that excess heat is hard on older people, and they are right. Your fun in the sun sounds like it going by like a flash. I don't think my slow time here will ever approach that speed. I am so very tired of being here but remain positive if I even hope to get out of here at eighty-four. If I can make it, I'll probably only be running only one block a day.

Are You There, God?

My father talks a lot about faith in his letters. We were both raised Roman Catholic. I spent most of my childhood on the southwest side of Chicago attending Catholic school where the nuns and priests introduced me to the seven sacraments: baptism, communion, confirmation, penance, matrimony, anointing of the sick, and holy orders. Church was the center of my upbringing. We even had a hallway table or "altar" with a crucifix, holy water, and candles in our house. We never missed a Sunday mass. Even on vacation, the first thing my father would do was look for the phone book to find the nearest church and current mass schedule. Faith came first.

Within our immediate family, Father J, my cousin the priest was available at family gatherings; he blessed the food, blessed our home, and blessed our babies. Father J created one of our many family traditions of taking the baby Jesus figurine out of the crèche, the nativity scene, passing the baby around the circle of relatives and friends, kissing baby Jesus on the forehead, and sharing a prayer aloud during the Christmas season. His charismatic way of spreading the word of God with sensitivity and care was celebrated at our wedding ceremony, baptism of our two daughters, last rites for both my mother and father, and celebrating funeral mass with music, prayers, and hymns.

Before he went to prison, my father was an active member in the church council within his community. He was omnipresent as a church community builder, taking on leadership roles in outreach ministry. He organized fundraisers and pancake breakfasts at the church rectory. He assisted the priest in generating parishioner interest and attendance, uniting people who shared a desire to worship. My father took responsibility and initiative for spreading the word of God to believers and nonbelievers. He projected the image of a hospitable godly man.

In prison, his dedication to the Catholic faith was amplified. He made great efforts to befriend the prison chaplain, joined a Bible-study group, steadily aimed to convert fellow inmates to know Jesus, and wrote me several letters copying chapters and verses from the New Testament. In one letter, he wrote about his crimes. "God won't judge me as harshly as people do because God understands why I did it, and he forgives." It's like my father hid behind a "God shield" to justify his actions. How do my father's actions follow the Ten Commandments? What are the spiritual consequences of telling a lie? Although I believe we all commit sins in various forms, how are my father's crimes of sexual abuse seen in the eyes of God? How could I maintain my religious faith based on my father's religious falsehoods? This was a convoluted mixture of combining our faith with his felony conviction. I prayed my father would not harm my relationship with God.

My father writes about a loving, present, and nurturing God who believes in redemption and forgives human limitations. He frequently calls out to God to help and heal, relying on God to relieve his pain in prison.

July 22, 2007

Now that I can go to the library here (it's not bad but obviously not like the one at home), I can get religious or motivational books to read. I am currently reading Battlefield of the Mind *by Joyce Meyer. It's a powerful book about worry, doubt, confusion, depression, anger, or condemnation. Overcoming negative faults (remember me saying when you were young, "Think positive"). It's still great to think positive, but today, I know from my experience, we need Jesus to help us in thinking and following his word.*

Although the chapel here has been closed for remodeling, soon I'll be able to go to mass each Thursday. We have nothing on Sunday for Catholics, so I'll go to the Baptist or Protestant service at 8:00 a.m. on Sunday morning. No, I haven't given up the Catholic faith, in fact I am reading the Complete Idiot's Guide to Understanding Catholicism: Third Edition. *It's a good book because it talks about all the changes in our church since the Vatican II conference in the 1960s.*

Speaking of church, will you keep all the members of my beach community church in your prayers? As you know, I helped to plant that new church in Costa Rica three years ago as president of their first church council. For the first two years, I was able to help shape the mission statement and purpose for this church. They have been very supportive since I left Costa Rica, and they are all wonderful God-fearing people. They are in the process of gathering money from sister churches here in the US to build a church and one day a Christian school there. They continue to help so many poor people.

I'll close for now because I don't want this letter to be over the weight limit on the prestamped envelope. May Jesus bless you and your family to walk hand in hand in peace and love.

September 18, 2007

Next Thursday at 2:30 p.m., we will have mass. We only have it about every two weeks and only during the week. I will be offering that mass for you and your marathon run. Wish I could be there at the finish when the announcer reads your number. You're running in your dad's footsteps! The only final advice I have is to remember to pray as you run. Prayer will help you take every step along with Mom who I know is praying, and you know I will be. Just run and pray and pace yourself. Two of my very close Spanish friends were recently baptized in the ocean in Costa Rica. Praise the Lord!

God has put a Mexican man in my path recently who needs Jesus in his life. I have been working with him on his homework and took him to Bible study last week. The Holy Spirit is guiding me on this situation, and I've asked him to use me to help others know Jesus better. I would not want to face this time without my strong faith in Jesus.

December 17, 2007

We have a Spanish priest who comes here from Milwaukee to say mass at least once per month and sometimes twice. Well, today he came and had a Christmas mass in Spanish. And since I've been studying, I can share:

Padre Bueno, reconocemos tu grandeza, todas tus acciones muestran tu sabiduria y amor. Jú creaste a cada uno de nosotros a tu imagen y semejanza. Nos parecemos a ti, y te reconocemus en la presencia de nuestros hermanos y hermanas. Nos amas tanto, que nunca nos abandunas, y es por eso, que enviaste a tu hijo Jesús, nuestro hermano mayor, para que nus enseñara a vivir una vida plena y feliz.

As we approach Christmas, the bitterness and anger here has reached a new level. Many people here have little if any faith because of the way they were raised. Once in a while, the Holy Spirit helps me to reach out and try to calm some of their anger. Each day, I pray that Jesus will capture their hearts and put aside the hatred and bitterness for their families, others here, and even themselves. The words that come out of their mouths at this holy time of the year are unbelievable. Please pray for them. I will miss all of you at Christmas, more than you will ever know. But I will be with you in spirit and prayer. Have a beautiful Christmas.

February 3, 2008
This week is Ash Wednesday. No priest will be here to give ashes, but I will fast and then not eat meat all Fridays of Lent. That's the least I can do to show God how much I love him and thank him for all the blessings he gives me.

April 2, 2009
I pray for all the young people here who have hate in their heart and have chosen to walk away from God, not with him. The devil has a perfect playground here. But they can't take away the faith in my heart for our Creator and the love in my heart for you and your family. Please pray for my appeal. It can be different if I get out. In life, we become careless when we do the same things over and over.

They have taken everything else, but they can't take you and my family out of my heart and my love for Almighty God. Praying keeps me connected to you. My father used to tell me that he only wanted me and my brothers to have more in this life than he did—a better education, a better job, a chance to travel, and a beautiful marriage. And he worked hard so we could have those things. Now all I want is for my only daughter and her family to have more than I ever thought of having, along with a very strong love for the Lord. Please keep praying for my appeal. I don't want to die here.

December 11, 2010
I pray I will never become a burden to you because of failing health. I have already given you more than your share of hurt and heartbreak; you do not need more, that's for sure.

With Christmas almost here, the last few days I've been thinking about the Prince of Peace. We hear songs that repeat the angels' proclamation, "Glory to God in the highest, and on earth peace among men with whom he is pleased" (Luke 2:14). If God promised, why do we see so little of it in our world? Why don't we see more of it in so many families, workplaces, neighborhoods, and even churches? How much inner peace are we experiencing this Christmas season? Either God has let us down, or we haven't understood what he meant. He commits himself to transform every area of our lives. He can heal us, eliminate hurt, anger, and keep us loving each other.

December 22, 2010

Jesus does not give us more than we can carry in this life. At the end of the day as I lay on my steel bunk with a paper-thin vinyl cover to sleep on, I take stock of what was not a day to remember. It's been very hard to recognize sometimes.

The start of the new year is a time to reflect and set goals. You were raised in a results-oriented family and have lived up to that measure of success in terms of what you have accomplished. You have not engaged in idleness or apathy but rather a determined and motivated enthusiasm and energy.

When we wait for God's clear direction, we keep in step with him. He uses this time to prepare us for his will, strengthen our faith, and examine our motives. Waiting is absolutely essential in living and walking in obedience to God and receiving his blessing.

October 9, 2011

The priest who comes in every two weeks to say mass here told us the farmers markets had a great growing season because of all the rain and hot weather. I would love to feel the rain on my face again. I miss nature and smelling the earth in any type of outdoor setting. My heart cries out to God because of being in this lonely and isolated place. I thank him each day for your love and support. This time is so slow and hard.

Recently, I have focused on the difference between loneliness and solitude. Loneliness for me is that anxious feeling of longing for a personal connection that isn't presently possible or avail-

able. But I realize solitude is a deliberate choice to spending time with God and give him my undivided attention. From this perspective, solitude becomes something I look forward to. I'm spending time with the Father, the joy of his friendship overcomes loneliness. This is how Jesus met challenges on a daily basis. Before he ministered to a group of people, he would spend focused time alone with the Father.

A big challenge for me continues to be finding a silent place that's free from distraction and the people here. When I do, I try to make myself available to our Lord. I simply invite him to meet with me in stillness and listen to what he wants me to hear. Sometimes, I hear nothing, but I feel him surrounding me with his love.

With a deeper awareness of God, I find what was previously overwhelming is now more manageable. Solitude helps me develop a sense that he's there with me every step of the way, guiding my activities. Whatever the task, we can always turn it over to our Lord to receive strength. Nothing in the world compares to knowing him deeply.

January 29, 2012

Today, I got out of bed quietly to read my Bible. I had to get close up to the bars to receive light and looked up the beatitudes in Matthew where the persecuted are given ownership in the kingdom. The mournful are given God's special comfort. Those who hunger for righteousness are filled. The merciful will obtain mercy, the pure in heart will see God, and the peacemakers are identified in God's children. The longings of our souls and characters are all met by God.

In all my travels around the world, I always found a way to go to mass. I remember being in Taiwan for three weeks, and one of my first trips there was to mass on Sunday in Taipei. The church I found was located about 15 blocks from my hotel and in a conference room on the second floor of a multistory office building. When I arrived, there were fifteen people in folding chairs facing an altar which was the front part of the conference room table.

Although I couldn't understand a word the priest was saying, I knew I was at mass.

February 5, 2012

God help me. Although I never completely developed the power of patience, waiting for me has been difficult. But we're not born with patience because I believe it's a spiritual fruit which is developed over time. God wants us to respond with a calm acceptance to the seasons of waiting. He beat the devil for forty days. Good takes time and patience.

I'm fasting each Friday of Lent as my small sacrifice compared to the one our Lord gave us on the cross. It's hard at times, but very spiritually rewarding.

I have enclosed a will with this letter. Because my birthday is within weeks, it's time to have a simple will because I really have so little. I want you to have instructions on what to do with my body. To hold down funeral costs, I want to be cremated and only have a visitation at the church before my funeral mass. Obviously, you can bury my ashes next to Mom. I need to prepare now because the odds aren't good that I will walk out of here. I want you to get anything I have left. I'm sorry it won't be a million dollars. God blessed you with family, not my money.

March 25, 2015

Anything good and perfect is a gift from God. It's a beautiful truth. Every good thing in our lives comes from God. Promotion and pancakes. Rain showers and relationships. Songs and sunsets. The astounding blessings God gives and also the things he does so faithfully that we take them for granted. As I grow older, I see every good thing for the gift it truly is.

I would enjoy if you sent me another book. It's called Catechism of the Catholic Church. *It's a book for adults with all the Catholic rules, theory, and practices. I would like to know my faith better. It's the same book the deacon brings in each Monday night for our Catholic Bible study.*

July 15, 2015

Thank you for your inspirational card which tells a story of success. For me though, it reminded me of feeling discouraged because of a feeling of worthlessness. Discouragement is a tool Satan uses because he knows it hinders our fruitfulness and witness. The last thing he wants is for us to catch a glimpse of God's perspective. But that's exactly what we need to do in order to see the silver lining on our dark cloud. Prison is devil's playground, making it hard to overcome discouragement or lack of success.

Peter wrote a letter to a group of people who were discouraged because of persecution. He reminded them that they were "a chosen race, a royal priesthood, a holy nation." We need to remember how precious we are to the Lord. Not only did he choose us but he also tells us we are his own cherished possession.

By the way, I put a blank sheet of paper in every envelope with my letters to protect my letter from anyone trying to read it through the envelope. In this place, it's better to be safe than sorry. The devil's playground is full of people who would like to do others harm in many ways.

November 15, 2015

Without knowing it, your daughters give me something to pray for each day. Praying for their many accomplishments in high school keeps my mind off this tiring journey I am currently involved in. I am thankful God helps us to bring out good from the bad.

My lawyer filed the motion to the court to ask for a release based on my old age and health. He said it would take about 30–60 days to receive notice about a court date. I pray for following prayer for healing each morning: "Most merciful God, look upon me, with eyes of compassion. Let your healing hand rest upon me. Let your life-giving power flow throughout my body and into the depths of my being. Cleanse, purify, and restore me to wholeness. Empower me for service in your name."

May 30, 2016

I have been asked to be a sponsor in June for an inmate's confirmation. What an honor, even without the fancy outfits, but with a true blessing of confirmation at forty years of age. I was also asked to read a poem at the Veteran's Day celebration at the chapel. I did the same thing last year, and people really enjoyed it. Please put this poem in your memorial box for Dad's death. Hopefully, it won't be until a long time from now. When the day of my death comes, your mom and I will be watching you from the upper seats (way upper) in heaven. And please do not cry. Instead, open champagne and toast the great life I once had.

July 3, 2016

My father had a way to deal with a stress-filled life. He remained calm while my mom expressed her stress. They had a wonderful partnership and were a positive influence on us three boys.

I know many times my dad was thinking, Why do we rush around when the best gifts come not from endless action with its stress and strain but from the generous hand of God? *I really feel there must be a balance in life, but this is a goal that I have failed at miserably.*

Think of the things we value most. The love of God, the love of a marriage partner, our family gathered around the dinner table, the companionship of a friend, a good night's sleep, a sun-filled day. Sometimes, we just need to back up and also ask a question, "Do any of these things come from our work or business, or are they gifts from the hand of God?"

April 9, 2017

I have a terrible time trying to see Jesus in the eyes of inmates here. Jesus reminds me that he created all people equally, and if for any reason we cannot see his light in them, maybe it's because they have turned it off. But one thing we can always do is to be respectful to everyone and realize they are on a different part of their journey.

Life brings us challenges that bring us even closer to God. I have been talking to him and today to his Son and the Holy Spirit for strength to relive traditions through memories and pictures.

The priest was here to say Palm Sunday Mass. I was honored to be asked to be the narrator for the reading of the long gospel. It's a powerful way to start Holy Week. We did not actually have any palms (they won't allow it) but still it was a moving experience. I read recently that Pope Francis has over a million people following his Twitter account. It looks like I have a lot of catching up to do when I get out and get a cell phone.

CHAPTER 7

Stem the Tide

*Having a holiday weekend without a family member is
like putting on a sweater that had an extra arm.*

—Pamela Ribon

In this chapter, my father writes letters about his absence, his
empty chair at our dinner table, and long-lasting vacancy. Prison
is a difficult place to be but is especially difficult knowing holidays, birthdays, and family celebrations are happening outside
of the gates. Family traditions are remembered but can't ever be
replaced in prison.

For my father, Christmas was one of the most depressing
times in prison. He told me he missed hearing and singing his
favorite songs by Perry Como, Bing Crosby, and the Carpenters.
He missed comfort food, like turkey, pumpkin pie with whipped
cream, and his favorite, mashed potatoes dripping in gravy. He
missed driving around the neighborhood to see the twinkling
lights. He missed going to midnight mass. It was an overwhelming sense of loss.

To stem the tide means trying to prevent a situation from
becoming worse than it already is. When it comes to holidays,
having a parent in prison can easily go from bad to worse. While
many families look forward to traditions, like decorating a
Christmas tree, shopping for presents, or making festive cookies,

every holiday spent behind bars can be devastatingly boring and lonely. Dwelling on the fact that a parent will never spend another holiday surrounded by family is heartbreaking. What could I do to make the season meaningful in this unique situation?

Not Home for the Holidays

My father's absence was out of my control, so I focused on a creating a holiday-letter drive, asking close friends and family to send him Christmas cards, reminding him that he was not forgotten. I also planned a few weeks ahead before Halloween, Thanksgiving, Christmas, Valentine's Day, St. Patrick's Day, and Easter to send a few funny holiday cards to my dad. One year, I got overzealous and sent him thirty-one Halloween cards for each day of the month. He told me that even some of the guards started counting the orange envelopes and went out of their way to look for them in the mail room. During the holidays, I decided to make deadlines for my disappointment. I chose to surround myself with the love of my family and tried to highlight positive memories my parents had created during every holiday. I needed to prepare myself that my father would no longer be with us and his chair would remain empty at the table.

March 23, 2008
Did you get together for Easter dinner? I am sure it was special, complete with all the trimmings. I have to be an embarrassment to you and your family and friends. How do you talk about your dad when he is spending the rest of his life in prison? I pray that others will not come against you because of me, and I'm sure many will be happy when I am gone for good.

I cannot be with you and your family. I tried to live close to my brother, which was great until a neighbor wanted me out of the neighborhood. So my options are very few, in fact, only one, and it doesn't look like that has a chance without a miracle from God to ever happen.

By this time, you have celebrated your fortieth birthday. I want you to enjoy each day of your life as if it is your birthday. I pray that God continues to bless you and give you the strength to face the shame you must have when others ask about me. Find time to listen to what God wants to tell you.

December 12, 2008

Open our hearts on Christmas so we may receive the wisdom of the birth and bring him glory. Although I am alive and torn away from my family, please join me in spirit to say Happy Birthday, Jesus. Please make a paper ornament for me to hang on your tree this year.

And praise the Lord, the lockdown is finally over! I went back to work as a tutor yesterday. What a relief. Thank you again for all the books you have sent. Each one has been better than the last. No word yet on my appeal. I feel the system is in no big hurry since they gave me thirty years. Please continue to pray. God knows how tough it will be to spend another Christmas in prison.

April 9, 2009

Thank you for the birthday card and money. I will buy a new pair of running shoes with your generous gift. That is really spoiling myself in here. I was born in 1940, so the big seventy will have to wait if I can make it that far.

I enjoyed the painting of boats on the card. As you know, boats have always been a part of my life. I remember hosting all your friends on our boat. All your friends always treated me with great respect. I wonder what horrible things they think of me now. Or do they even know I'm here? What do you tell them?

April 16, 2009

Happy Easter! Today is the day the Lord has given us, let us rejoice and be glad in it. It's Easter. The only "extra" we had for Easter dinner here was two colored eggs with our regular serving of what they call food. But it was nice to see the eggs. In my heart,

I celebrate the risen Christ. I bet out in the world the churches were decorated on the altar area with beautiful white lilies.

May 23, 2009

It's Memorial Day, a holiday weekend, so that means everything is closed down and we are forced to be in our cell block for three days. Tempers get tested, and many who have bitterness problems start raising their voices, talking with words that I really don't want to hear. Their respect for life and themselves is totally lacking. One day, I pray to be able to live out what little life I have in an atmosphere of God-loving people who love life and each other. It's hard for me to practice patience now. There's nothing I can do but wait.

For now, this hellhole remains the same, and in times like this, long weekends make it worse. Please pray for my appeal. Wish I could be there to barbecue with you and welcome summertime on this Memorial Day weekend. Oh, how I miss that privilege and choices.

June 23, 2009

Thank you for your Father's Day card and loving words. As you father, I have been a great disappointment to you, and yet you still love me. I will always be grateful for you standing tall for your dad ever since this nightmare began. You chose to help.

November 22, 2009

Thanks for your Thanksgiving Day card. I wish I could show it to others, but I don't want to involve you in this place. It is so hard not to be able to brag about you, but I don't trust people here, so I just keep thoughts about you and my family to myself. To survive mentally, it helps to be able to smile, even if is to myself.

My Thanksgiving dinner left a bit to be desired. We had microchip pieces of turkey in a heavy gravy poured over a mound of instant, grainy artificially mashed potatoes. And we got an orange. I will tell you again not to come here for the holidays. Any holiday visit is confined to only two hours, and the visiting room will be packed. I want you to visit here when you want to, not for something you have to do.

December 10, 2009

You sent me my first Christmas card. It will most likely be my only one this year. I can only conclude that others have said, "Well, he'll never see us again, so why bother sending a card?" Here is my card to you. Merry Christmas, and may God bless your beautiful new home. If I was with you, we would break out the Jimmy Buffet CD and play it. But here, there is no music. No tree. No special dinner. Just prison. I need to focus on the real meaning of Christ's birth.

April 11, 2010

Thank you for the beautiful birthday card. I'm not sure I even deserve those kind words as your father as I know I have been such a disappointment to you and not a grandfather for your daughters. I will always remember your daughters in my prayers, but they will never know me. This part of my life is filled with suffering that does not stop. Yours was the only card I received to mark the milestone of seventy years. I am looking forward to your visit. It's the only time I have here where it feels like I am sitting in your living room, talking about family and friends.

My birthday was quiet. I kept looking at your birthday card and the pictures of your family celebrating Easter. By 7:00 p.m., I took out my scissors and cut up all the pictures and the card. I thanked God for my seventieth, for your visit, and for putting up with your father who has let you down.

June 14, 2010

Please tell your husband I send him best wishes on Father's Day. He is more than deserving as the best father I know. He has done so much for you and the girls. Thank God for your husband. He is the greatest. Thank you for the fantastic Father's Day card, letter, and money in my account. It made my month. I miss the box of Fannie May turtles you used to get me every Father's Day. To this day, they are still my favorite candy. This is not a place to cel-ebrate. At 3:00 a.m., an ambulance came to pick up a fifty-three-year-old inmate who hung himself with a sheet from the upper bunk in his cell. His cellmate was given a few days on a medical trip so he was alone in his cell. I wonder if he was a father.

December 3, 2010

Christmas always brings back very strong memories of grow-ing up. Your grandma and grandpa were very simple people who had a love for God and unconditional love for family. Grandma was much more religious than Grandpa, but Grandpa always sup-ported Grandma's faith and beliefs. Although he was not Catholic, he would attend at least Easter and Christmas mass with us as a family. I can never remember your grandpa teaching anything that was not Christ based or against the commandments. He made little, but we had more than we could ask for. We lived in a modest 600-square foot home on Indiana Street in Peoria, Illinois. This Christmas, as you give gifts to those you love, think of the love that was given to you that first Christmas. Though we do not deserve his love, God gives it freely and without regrets. Life's greatest gift is not contained in all those beautifully wrapped gifts under your Christmas tree but in the humble clothes of a baby who came to earth more than 2,000 years ago.

I read your Christmas letter and cried because for the past ten years I have been eliminated in your story. I understand why because of my actions, but it still hurts because I remember the days when I was included in your Christmas story. But I am still glad you write your annual Christmas letter and share the story about what happened during the year.

November 8, 2011

Many inmates are receiving fruitcake catalogs and placing orders for $30 to $35 each to receive in time for Christmas. Thank goodness I don't like fruitcake. It never ceases to amaze me that some of the inmates always have money to buy canteen and holi-day items. I overhear them when I walk by, begging their bitches *on the phone for money. Sure enough, their bitches send them another hundred to blow on "essential" items. It reinforces their belief in themselves, not God. I call it the "me" generation. What's in it for me?*

November 17, 2011

With the Christmas season starting again, I know your family will be busier than ever with all the decorating, shopping, attending and giving parties, and travelling with no shortage of things to do. In here, time stands still. It's a paralysis of the soul that has a spotlight on misery during the holidays.

My cellmate got some Christmas candy early this week that he ordered from canteen. He offered me some of the chocolate-covered peanuts. He left the bag on the desk and told me to help myself. I took one piece and no more. If that had been my bag, I would have emptied it in one sitting. But I'd rather be running in my new shoes in January than eating Christmas candy that will not last until the new year.

Christmas 2011

My Christmas began at 3:00 a.m. when I woke up crying. I prayed asking Jesus to get me through this very emotional day in celebration of his birth two thousand years ago. But I guess my computer in my brain would not go on sleep mode because all the beautiful Christmases I have been blessed with over the last sixty-plus years from the time I was old enough to know what Christmas was went through my mind. It's always been the most joyful time of the entire year. I have been taken out of Christmas forever. There is a huge hole in my heart that only family can ever fill.

I'm glad you liked my card. I used dental floss for the decorative rope around the tree. I only have so much to work with in here, and two other inmates were generous in letting me use their paint markers and card stock.

Thank you for the Christmas bonus money. If I had a Christmas tree, I would put the money order receipt under it. Now

I can order some Christmas goodies from canteen this week. I'm glad you received the Silent Night snow globe I ordered from the catalog for you. I know you'll think of Mom every time you wind it up to hear her favorite song.

Please stand tall for the small family we have left. The values we have as a family can't be lost. Although over the years times will change, the love of family, like the love of Jesus, will only grow stronger.

December 16, 2012

It sounds like you have a wonderful Christmas dinner planned. Prime rib! Wow, I can only dream of that in comparison to what we will have here. We will be served a very basic meal on Christmas. I know every year your Christmas season is ultra busy, and I pray you will lean on God when the holiday pressure seems to be just a bit too much. Remember, Christ is Christmas. The truth will carry us through the holidays and into the New Year. I enjoyed your Christmas picture and traditional letter. I read it several times, and one time, I read it out loud while no one else was in my cell so your mom could hear it in heaven. I am so proud of you and your beautiful family. Our daily moments can be treasures, like Christmas gifts under the tree for our lives. Our loving presence in the lives of others can be like Christmas lights shining into the hearts of those who dwell in darkness. I miss you so much during Christmastime. God bless you.

January 1, 2013

This year, I received four Christmas cards—one from you, one from an aunt, and one from your college friend and her mother. I was so overjoyed to receive cards in this place. Who wants to write someone in prison? I am thankful to share the memories of times we were together on the outside and having fun. These letters are so important to my mental health and preserving the connections that are so vital. Thank you for going to Mom's grave with the annual mini-Christmas tree and paper ornament wishes. I loved your daughter's response, "I know she gets the messages in heaven because when we visit her grave again, the messages are faded."

February 15, 2013

I now have my own cell, thank goodness because when I received your Valentine's Day card, I laughed so hard. I don't have the opportunity to laugh very often in this place, so your card was refreshing and so damn funny.

And a few days after I received your Valentine's Day card, I received notice that my bank account went from $5 to $105. Thank you for sending yet another money order. Many daughters would say "To heck with him. He got there, and he should handle it alone" if they had fathers in prison. God sees your letters, pictures, encouragement, visits, and money orders.

October 14, 2015

Yesterday, I got four Halloween cards in orange envelopes from you. The cards made me laugh so hard I had tears running down my face. Thank you for keeping a smile on my face.

The orange Halloween envelopes keep coming daily! My gosh, how many Halloween cards did you buy this month? The cards bring me laughs and tears of joy. Thank you for all you are doing to help me. Obviously, you have told many of your friends and family about my cancer because I am getting more cards and letters. Please tell all of them I am far from dead.

October 25, 2015

Last night, I couldn't fall asleep and was thinking about the thirty-one orange Halloween envelopes you have sent this month, and I would like to tape all the envelopes to the walls of my cell, turning it into the orange Halloween cell. I would like to do this especially before a cell inspection from the guards. But then I thought this was not a good idea after all.

March 12, 2016

For Easter Sunday, we'll probably have a paper-thin slice of turkey ham (not real ham) with potatoes and mixed frozen vegetables. I am sure the chow line won't be extra long.

April 9, 2017

Today is Palm Sunday, but we have our mass on Thursday, so I am praying alone in my cell, this small boxlike room. Unfortunately, today and next Easter Sunday will be lonesome at best. If it's God's will, I will be able to celebrate Easter in a real church with a choir and the smell of incense in the air.

I remember when you were two years old and we went on an Easter egg hunt. Mom brought a basket with a handle almost as tall as you. I watched while she ran with you to pick up eggs for your basket. You were thrilled with the different colors. When we came home, Mom went through the basket on the kitchen table to be sure no eggs were broken and the candy was properly sealed in its package. You got really excited with a hollow chocolate bunny, and we broke off a piece for you to eat. You stuffed the entire piece into your mouth, much of it spilling out all over your face and hands. But you were smiling, and Mom and I finished the rest of the chocolate.

June 22, 2017

I got your Father's Day pop-up card, my favorite. But this time, the guards called me up to property and told me I had to remove the front of the card because it had two small springs that are metal and considered contraband. So I took the little springs off and took my card. I walked and read it at the same time because I couldn't wait. Thank you!

Christmas Day 2016

I remember taking you for a ride when you were about four years old to look for Santa. Of course, Mom couldn't come because she had to put all the beautifully wrapped gifts for you from Santa around the Christmas tree. You pressed your little nose so hard against the car window that I thought you might break it! Then you would run into the house screaming to Mom that you didn't see Santa. And it was if you had air brakes, you stopped cold when you saw all the gifts under the tree. You were so excited that you didn't know which one to open first. You were a Christmas angel who spread the joy and love for Christmas with everyone who came to our home for the holidays. What a blessing you were and still are for me and Mom.

Missing You

Staying connected with family and friends while being locked away in a long-term detention facility is challenging. Missing someone who is no longer in your everyday life can unearth feelings of total helplessness and despair. My father's letters were often a combination of persevering in prison and yearning for his former "normal" life. It was a mixture of describing current hardships while remembering sixty years of freedom. He missed the ordinary rhythms of mornings, afternoons, and evenings.

The dynamic of our father-daughter relationship naturally shifted because of distance and time and, of course, the recognition of my father's imperfections. His memories of the things we used to do together were difficult to read because it was if he was in a state of functional extinction—still alive but remote and unavailable. For me, the hardest questions in his letters should have been the most harmless but took my breath away. When my father asked about our daughters' swim meets or what we ate for Thanksgiving dinner or if I had changed the air filter in our basement furnace, it was a reminder that he would never experience these types of events or activities again.

Our relationship would never be the same again, but how could I continue to communicate with my father without being judgmental or critical? I was so angry at him, but I still loved him. There was no benefit from making an issue of his imprisonment in my letters. He was already there. Instead, I focused on sharing information about our day-to-day life and asked what I could do to somehow make prison more tolerable.

I doubt any parent would want to miss out on twenty years of their child's life from monumental memories, like holidays, graduations, weddings, and birthdays, to miniature memories, like pizza dinners, Scrabble games, and walking the dog. My father's letters profess he was not ready to accept this and move on. His life in prison was a monotonous blur of restrictions and enforcement, numbing and surreal. He needed to let go of the past and adopt a convict culture defined by new unpleasant rituals with very limited contact with friends and family. His letters describe what he missed the most.

October 3, 2008

I enjoyed reading about your teaching conference in Puerto Rico. I miss traveling. I used to go to San Juan once a year back in the 1970s to work with Manual Tobias and his father, Don Pepi. He and his dad were manufacturing representative for Wilson Jones Corporation when I was vice president of marketing. I'm so happy that you are able to travel like your father. When I used to travel around the world, someone would always meet me at the airport with a sign with my name on it and take me to my hotel in Switzerland, Taiwan, Germany, Mexico, the Bahamas, England, and Hawaii. All that traveling gave me confidence so that I cannot be afraid of new environments. It's always interesting to see how others around the world live. But I would never wish anyone to travel and end up here in prison. It is a destination in hell.

February 22, 2009

Congratulations on your new home! Mom and I moved eight times in our twenty-eight-year marriage. One of my favorite phrases is "It's sold!" I don't mean to sound negative, but it's so easy to give up in this place. All the pain, suffering, bitterness, anger, and hatred for our Lord that I live with each day is very hard.

I was not raised to hate, I was not raised without love, and hopefully, I have been able to as a parent love you as my parents loved me. They were not formally educated, and they did not stand on the street corner reading from the Bible, but they did it right. They had the answers. Unfortunately, of the three boys they raised, I was the one who made the horrible mistake. Thank God they were already in eternity when I failed badly. It would have killed them, I know. I thank them in prayer each day for being my mom and dad, and I thank God each day that you are my daughter. If I die in here, it won't be because of anything they failed to do in raising me and anything you did wrong as a daughter.

I don't know when the appeal will be coming, and I certainly don't know the answer if they say "yes" or "no" to the appeal. All I can do is pray. It will be ten years in August that I committed my crime, and here I still sit in prison and maybe for the rest of my life. Please, don't give up on me. I know I have put you through hell, and I will always be sorry for that. I love you and you will always be my daughter, and the outcome of this situation will never change that.

August 4, 2011

My brother wrote me another letter to tell me about his recent hospitalization. He is in his late seventies now, and I do worry about his health. Nobody wants to be alone in life, especially when suffering with illness or surgery. He closed his letter by asking when I would get out of here. I wrote him back and told him it is not possible. The last conversation I had with my social worker ended by him telling me that I could get out as early as 2024, at the ripe old age of eighty-four, if I even last that long.

May 28, 2012

I am so very proud of my two granddaughters. I wish I could be there to be a real grandpa to them. I can tell they are both competitive and support one another in all their extracurricular activities. I used to hero worship my oldest brother when I was their age. I wanted to be a great athlete like him. Why? Because I loved him so much. We were six years apart, so it was hard for me to do everything he did. Your daughters have special attributes all their own. God has blessed them with their own gifts, and they have to realize that and just be themselves, not someone else.

September 30, 2012

The fog that came over me when you called to tell me my brother died remains. It's hard to believe he is really gone, leaving me as the only Colwell left out of our immediate family. I cannot even try to take his place. At this point, it would be best for all if God would take me home to join my family again in heaven. I am a rotten example of what a brother, father, and friend should be in this life.

I have disgraced everyone who once loved me and now has to whisper that I am in prison where so many think I should be for the rest of my life. I have made so many victims of my horrible act that leaves me thinking what good am I to anyone.

I wish I could have been there for his memorial service to hear how much he touched so many people. My brother was such an example of a godly man and one who always put others, especially family, first. He taught me so much growing up as a little brother. His heart was bigger than his mind and filled with God's love. What a blessing he was.

May 19, 2013

Happy twentieth wedding anniversary next month. Wow, I am getting older. I would give away winning the $600-million-dollar lotto ticket to get out of here before I die. I'm three months into my seventh year here plus the three years before I ended up here, or a total of ten out of the last fourteen behind bars. It's getting so old, and I'm getting old along with it. Please pray for me that God gives me a miracle and sets me free of this confinement. I know life is full of ups and downs, but I am ready for an up for a change. I have to be careful lately. I am feeling so isolated and lonely. That combination only makes this journey longer and harder.

As a parent, you'll go through many seasons. Life is a lot like the weather, it's seasonal. It has a way of pushing us into the next season whether we like it or not. And when pushed into the next season, we are often uncertain and even fearful of what it might hold for us. Since my brother's death, I have thought a lot about the later seasons of life when I am haunted by thoughts such as, Will I be left all alone? Why am I now isolated from my family and loved ones? Will my health hold up? Will my mind stay fresh? *As with every season like the one you are going through with your daughters, we have to make a choice. Should we waste a season in fearful thoughts or do as Saint Paul said, "The best use of the time must be made because some days can be evil." Regardless of the season, we can count on God's faithfulness. He said, "I will never leave you nor forsake you." And we must say in response, "The Lord is my helper, I will not fear."*

May 30, 2015

You will never totally understand how much your caring matters. This recent journey in my life could not be tolerated much less survived without your love, prayers, letters, and pictures. I have never before ever been so alone and disconnected from loved ones and family day after day with time dragging slowly and seeming never to change. You have been the only one who has given me hope for the future and kept me from going off the deep end. You will never totally understand how much your caring for me has kept my head above water in this deep pit I have been in. Your rewards are not only here but in heaven. God sees what you are doing, and I believe he also thanks you.

August 9, 2016

I have never been the grandfather to your girls I wanted to be. And now your youngest daughter is leaving for college. I remember moving you on campus your freshman year. I wish I was there with you to share in the excitement of taking your firstborn to college. I have missed out on another lifetime being in this place.

January 11, 2017

All your pictures and letters are so welcomed. They continue to be my lifeline to reality. Money comes and goes, but family lasts for all eternity. I noticed your butterfly stationery. For me, that's a symbol of hope. And hope is Jesus. If he can make a caterpillar into a beautiful butterfly, then I know he can get me out of here to live whatever amount of time I have left in freedom.

February 18, 2017

Congratulations on your Teacher of the Year award. Wow! I can't share my excitement and joy with others here because it could put you at risk. Many are so mad and hurt because of being in here; they like to make others miserable like themselves. They do not like to smile. One day, I hope to see the certificate of honor in person as well as all the others you have earned throughout your teaching career. I have missed so much.

CHAPTER 8

Don't Rock the Boat

*Never tell your problems to anyone. Twenty percent don't
care, and the other 80 percent are glad you have them.*

—Lou Holtz

In this chapter, I include my father's letters that focused on the disconnection and volatility he experienced in prison. My father said he immediately felt like a target was on his back because he was a sex offender. The social hierarchy of prison inmates automatically places sex offenders at the bottom—they are hated, harassed, and abused. Fights and verbal assaults can occur daily, but instead of getting involved, my father quietly sat on the sidelines.

He kept to himself and did not talk about his case even though he was asked repeatedly what he did to go to prison. For protection, he kept as much of his personal information to himself as he could. Rocking the boat is to do something to disturb or aggravate the balance of a situation. Instead of working together on steadying skills to not tip over, inmates' behavior can escalate, leading to grim consequences of boat rocking. Inmates can face further discipline and punishment in many forms, such as withdrawing visitors' privileges, denying purchases from the commissary, penalties in earning wages, segregating in a different area, or confining to the hole (solitary confinement) for rule breaking. My father worked hard to not rock the boat even though he would rather not be in the same boat at all.

Friend or Foe?

Before my father went to prison, he had a large circle of friends that spanned over sixty years. He had friends who shared common interests and values in attending church, training for marathons, and adventures in snowmobiling. My father made friends easily with his outgoing personality and charm. He brought friends together through fellowship in dinner invitations, boat rides, sunset cocktails, and outdoor concerts. He was a loyal, true-blue friend. He also had many acquaintances at work, in the local sandwich shop, and post office. My father honed his practice in socializing. He remembered names and asked genuine open-ended questions. He was likable.

However, when he went to prison, his attitude toward making friendships changed. He transformed into a loner. Like a turtle in his shell, he became introverted in order to protect himself. In prison, he was surrounded with hundreds of inmates, guards, and staff, but this large group of strangers doesn't necessarily create a safe and trustworthy atmosphere for making good friends. He writes a lot about his rotating roommates or cellmates, whom I thought might naturally generate a friendship with him just based on close proximity. It's ironic that he felt alone but was never really alone in prison.

It was difficult for my father to form friendships in prison not only because of his sexual abuse offense but also because of his age. He was at least forty years older than most inmates at Fox Lake Correctional Institution. He also described many of the inmates as immature, rude, inconsiderate, and disrespectful. Their behavior was erratic and not conducive to maintaining friendships because inmates could be calm one day and lash out the next. He talked about dangerous gangs that formed tight circles of friendship, intimidating other inmates who were outside of their group.

Inmates were hard to live with. He could not trust his fellow inmates to have his back like a friend should.

July 31, 2007

They moved me out of what they call intake this week, so I have a new cell and another cellmate. He is twenty-six years old, has been in prison for ten years, and loves to play his favorite loud music all day and all night. That's not too bad. He wants me to sleep in the upper bunk. There is no ladder, so I have to step on a plastic chair and pull myself up to get into bed. Getting out of bed is even a bigger challenge. So today, I wrote to the Health Services people to remind them that I am sixty-seven years old, my collarbone hurts, and I'm having surgery and will not be able to crawl up to a top bunk. I hope this does not offend my cellmate. Let's see what happens.

January 15, 2008

My cellmate has been sleeping all the time when he is not in class, and all weekend he sleeps. I think he is on medication for a bipolar illness. He is very moody and has many negative feelings daily. Sometimes, when I try to cheer him up, he gets very mad and ugly. I back off and pray that God helps him. He has two children and is in his thirties. God has put him in my path for a reason, and I want to help him as much as I can.

February 3, 2008

My cellmate takes eight pills per day. Some to keep him level, others to bring him up, and still others to bring him down. I have to be very careful with his moods. So I guard what I say and always try to support him. I pray and ask God to show me how to help him.

June 6, 2008

My cellmate started his new medication, but it's too soon to notice any changes. He is manic and tries to hurt himself con-stantly. The other night, he rolled up a sheet and told me he was going to hang himself, and I would wake up to the sound of him swinging. I told God the other day to please leave a key to the front gate of heaven under my pillow one night so I can get out of here.

March 6, 2009

I have another new cellmate. My old one was sent to another prison where he can take a six-month earned release program and be home before the end of the year. I pray and hope the best for him. My new cellmate is about thirty years old and has been in prison for ten years. He has two more years until he can go home. So far, he has been okay but still very bitter about being in prison. This place changes people, and many times, it's not for the better. He has no faith in God, so he can only be bitter and angry. I pray that God fills his heart with his love so his time will be less painful.

September 4, 2009

Got another new celli now. He's twenty-two years old, engaged to be married, and starting to settle in. He does not keep our cell clean or organized, so my cleaning will be just that, mine. I guess many people do not share my interest in being clean and organized, so I just bite my lip and find time after school each day to clean the cell. This whole place is a hotbed for colds, flu, and other sickness because people do not keep their cells or the bathrooms clean. I just pray he shows me respect as I try to do to him. I know God wants me to see Jesus in everyone, but I must confess in this hellhole many times this is hard to do. So much hatred, bitterness, and despair. But it is a test for me.

March 31, 2012

My lifelong friends no longer care about me. I am no longer treated with respect, and people I once knew don't waste their time worrying about where I am. I was thinking about a time many years ago when I went to a sales seminar in Kansas City. It was a session on how to manage change. Because I was a young manager at the time, I couldn't remember when change was a problem for me or those working for me. I guess it was one of those areas in my life that I walked over, around, or backed off the difficulty of change.

But after a day-long seminar, I realized change can be devastating to many people, and I was being insensitive. I remember the instructor saying, "Would you be happy if your boss said starting tomorrow you'll have to get up at 2:30 a.m. each morning to go to work?" He went on to say that nobody likes change unless they see the value in making a change. For me, that takes time, but we can control that and make the very best of that change. I tell you that story because of the changes I have been through here in prison. I can't tell a friend this story because there is no one who I want to tell in here.

January 6, 2013

The population here is not one where I can or even want to make friends. Many are filled with hate, and most only want something for themselves and would never think about reaching out to help someone else. The isolation factor is a big part of the hell. The loss of any hope getting out of here before I die is also a big part of the hell.

My TV broke. I am now trying to get it fixed. I talked to other inmates who have the same model TV, and they told me the same thing happened to their TV. The buttons to change the channel don't work, and we are not allowed to have a remote control because of the batteries. The inmates told me to ship the TV to a repair shop, so I did, and it will take about a month to fix. I enjoy watching the PBS channel but can't stop by a friend's place to watch it. I have no friends.

March 1, 2015

Thank you again for sending more money. I was able to buy a special treat—six cinnamon rolls for $8. I went in on it with another inmate who told me he would buy me coffee from the canteen if I gave him two cinnamon rolls. It's a barter system with an acquaintance, not a friend, but this was a deal I could not pass up.

March 7, 2015

I met a new inmate in our unit. He came from a mental hospital/prison in Madison. He had so many questions, and I could easily tell he was afraid. Early on in our conversation, he said they gave him a twenty-five-year sentence. I quickly pointed out that it was a reward that he earned to get out of the mental hospital and into a medium-security prison like this one, living in a general population with no movement restrictions. He said the psychologist told him he cannot go to school or programs. But I felt badly that he was sitting around, so I showed him how to fill out a job application to six different departments here. No one responded to his request for a job, and I realized that he had a security restriction on his record, so he could not work with tools of any kind.

At the mental hospital, he broke the blade out of a razor and cut his eyelids and ripped off all his toenails. But I felt he really could do well in a job here, so I continued to talk with him. I also asked our program director to help this man's job situation. He told him he would try to get the job restriction lifted. And a few weeks later, he is now full of new hope and encouragement. I told him we often need to be thankful and patient as it could take a few weeks or months before this job matter is resolved. God placed him in my path because he needed help. I helped him in the form of listening to his problems and suggested things to solve his problems. It's a pleasure to serve God, and I am thankful he gives me these opportunities.

September 22, 2015

After years of being taunted in here for sexually abusing a child, soon they'll be able to taunt me about my hair falling out because of my cancer treatments. Although I have never told anyone about my crime, most everyone has found out, and so I'm a marked man. I will never get used to the abusive remarks and whispers as I walk by. Chomo! Scumbag! SO! Perv! Skinner! It's hard when people are so cruel. I will not get mad or respond to those who chose to be like the devil.

They threaten to drown me in the shithole (toilet), strangle me, beat me, stab me, kick me. It's especially scary in the shower, which is why I get up at 4:00 a.m. to be the first in and out of the bathroom. Inmates here can really hurt me in the shower. They scream at me if they see my hair is wet and I am coming from the bathroom. They call, "I am going to come and spank you! I will whoop your naked ass! You better run, Chomo. Motherfucker, child fucker!" They ask if I want to be raped, sucked, finger fucked. And the guards just look the other way. It's the way it is. I just keep my head down and walk alone. Please, let the Holy Spirit protect me.

April 9, 2015
Thank you for the Internet information on Social Security. You can imagine all the false talk from inmates who swear that you will receive a $1,350 check the day after you get released and then another $1,000 or more for mental stress received while in prison. So it's nice to see just what is right and to pray for the day I do get out to get my Social Security back on a monthly basis.

Don't Talk about Your Case

My father was very reluctant to talk about the granular details of his crimes with me but did not hesitate in making multiple requests to lawyers to help release him from prison. His letters to me cycled through information regarding court dates, parole board hearings, judges, prosecuting attorneys, and social workers. Each letter would scaffold a myriad of angles in brainstorming possible conditions for his release. He took me on a wild rollercoaster of complicated emotions anchored to the hope of changing his sentence. For over a decade, he held onto the expertise of his criminal defense legal team to succeed in setting him free.

Each time he went in front of the Parole Review Committee (PRC), he truly thought there was an opportunity for him to be released based on his good behavior, old age, and eventually his terminal cancer diagnosis. He told me how he showed the parole

193

board he had been rehabilitated and could once again be a productive member of society. He was convinced that he had been overly punished. He thought the parole board would utilize their discretionary powers in recommending a sentence commutation, a reduction in his thirty-year sentence, eventually resulting in his release.

His delusion in thinking he would be exonerated baffled me. The formula for justice appeared straightforward: he had confessed to sexual abuse crimes and was being held accountable by serving his time in prison. In fact, he was given a second chance at parole early on but squandered it by interacting with kids and amplified it by fleeing to Costa Rica and violating the conditions of his parole. In his letters, my father often twisted court procedures into a form of judicial overkill. His goal was to achieve special concessions for who he was: an elderly first-time convicted offender. He thought the maximum thirty-year sentence for violating parole was severely unfair. "They threw the book at me!" he bemoaned.

I do not want to suggest that I supported his campaign for his release from prison. Although I did not like his confinement because I missed and cared about my father, at the same time, I follow my own moral and ethical compass and believe justice was served in his case. Ultimately, I support the Department of Corrections in containing my father since legally, he was required to serve his full sentence. In his letters, he wrote to me that he was pleading for release because dying in prison was unjust.

August 18, 2007

This may be a very long journey unless I get a good attorney to get me out of here on appeal. Right now, my sentence is for thirty years, which means I would be eligible for a parole hearing in eight years, which is no guarantee that I would get out of before the thirty years. It's a life sentence and against the treaty with Costa Rica, but without a qualified international attorney, I'll never be able to get in front of a judge. So, for now, I pray every day that Jesus will help me to get back to Costa Rica to spend the rest of my natural life, however long that will be. This place is just a warehouse and punishment for me since I have no programs to take. I have no requirements except to sit. So I'm awaiting my interview for the tutoring job which will keep my mind busy and then to take some college-level correspondence courses to again keep me mentally alert. I don't want to turn into a vegetable.

March 18, 2008

I've written this letter five times now, and each time, I cut out more because it hurts to tell you how I was treated in court. It was not a good day. My public defender presented a motion to the court (same judge in Walworth and the same DA) because I was not afforded the same judge who sentenced me eight years ago. We told the court that this judge said at the beginning of my hearing a year ago, "I have not had a chance to read the file as I got the information five minutes ago." So without ever reading my file and strictly listening to the DA and looking out over the courtroom where the victim and fifty relatives and friends were sitting, he said, "I agree with you, Mr. DA, I sentence him to thirty years in prison." I had no witnesses, and the victim and her father spoke, basically saying, "She is okay now, eight years later, but she is afraid for all the little girls out there, so please put Mr. Colwell in prison for life." I could go on, but it is really hard for me to write anything knowing that I will remain here for the rest of my life.

March 23, 2008

I know you wanted to be here in court with me again, but the court date was given only a few days before I knew when it would be. Given what happened in there, I'm glad you did not have to go through more hell with me. I know you want to, but I'm asking you not to. I don't know what else can be done concerning the rest of my life. The public defender is exploring any next steps that can be taken. I've told her I will give up my citizenship, my Social Security, and not return to this country if they send me back to Costa Rica. They want to lock me up and throw away the key. How can I be a threat to anyone here if I don't live here anymore? I'm praying that I may just die in peace, not in this hellhole, but this may be where I will have to find that peace, and if so, I pray I die soon.

Let's hold off on another visit until I have exhausted any other chance of getting back to court. I want to see you, but it's just that this is the first time in sixty-eight years that I can't get this horrible journey to be over.

April 3, 2009

I really thought by now I would have news to share with you about my appeal, but no such luck. I did find out recently that the public defender I have had for the last year will no longer handle my case. If and when the appeal is approved, I will be assigned a new public defender for my next appearance in court. It's very hard when you have worked with one for over a year and then are told you now have a new one and have to start all over again. But I will do what I have to do even when I know these public defenders get paid and work for the state.

I have been given thirty years. So the odds of a state public defender to go against the state that gives him a paycheck is very rare. Once the court knows you have a public defender, the judge can get whatever the district attorney wants, which in my case is thirty years. A private attorney would be hounding the court for a more rapid response, but the state public defender is content with waiting. One thing for sure, I will never get used to this hellhole, and I do not want to die here.

This is the hardest part of my sixty-nine years on this earth. They cannot take away my love for my daughter or you praying for me.

Sorry, my letters have not been positive lately. My emotions are up and down like a yo-yo. The waiting has been wearing on me. I try not to pull you in and know you don't deserve that. This is by far the most painful period in my entire life.

June 13, 2009

Yesterday was the lowest point I have reached over the past ten years. God has shown me how your mom must have felt when she knew she was going to die. That feeling of all hope being withdrawn from your heart and soul. I feel like this is my last lap of the race in this life.

I went to the PRC (Program Review Committee) and the DOC (Department of Corrections). I am required to meet with this committee once a year. The PRC decides whether you should stay here, go to a minimum-secure facility or even to maximum. They told me because my sentence is for thirty years that I am considered a high risk. Therefore, the DOC may decide to move me to a maximum-security facility where you are locked down 24-7 with no school, no jobs, and few if any privileges. And being a sex offender (no matter how serious the offense), the DOC likes to send sex offenders to maximum.

They may decide to leave me here because of my tutoring job, but they said there are no guarantees. So I came out of that meeting with a horrible headache and a sick feeling in the pit of my stomach. I came back to my unit for lunch and mail call. I have not kept any of your letters because I am afraid, so I do destroy them right after I read them a few times. I have less than a box full of my personal belongings. When I die in here, you won't have much to go through and throw out of the box of my whole life. My life is reduced to a box. A little box.

My appeal was turned down. There is virtually no chance now to get out of this hellhole any time in the next twenty years (if I live for twenty years). It's nice that my attorney wants to send a last appeal to the Supreme Court of Wisconsin, but that, too, will be turned down. The Supreme Court will not overrule the appeal court. It doesn't happen.

This is the saddest and most heartbreaking feeling for the second time in my life. The first was the death of Mom. And now, this blow is equal to that, and I am in my seventieth year in this life. Living here in this hellhole is not really living but only existing.

When I die, you will no longer have to hide your shame when someone asks about your dad. And you can tell your girls that I am no longer alive to be their granddad. I was never really their granddad as I didn't get be part of their lives. It's been so unfair to you. This is not the dad you should have had.

September 18, 2009

Thanks for your letter and information about legal help. Unfortunately, Wisconsin Judicare Inc. will not help a person in prison, so I'm sending that back. The other two, American Civil Liberties Union and Legal Action of Wisconsin Inc., I will write to. Expand your search to include free legal services for a criminal in prison from an attorney anywhere in the US that may give me more options. Who knows, someone may say, "This man needs good legal help."

I did finally hear back from my public defender after sending multiple letters for months. She said, "I received your letters, and I'm writing to let you know that we're still in waiting mode. The court will be back in session soon, and at that point, we can expect some news. Until the court makes a decision on the petition, I don't have anything I can offer to you. There are not any motions or briefs I can file. Therefore, I don't anticipate coming to Fox Lake to meet with you because I really cannot put forward any options at this point. I can only hope we have some good news soon. Until then, my position is that we can only wait."

So I just need a good attorney that will get me out of here based on what I did which was to leave the US for two years. Nothing else. What a system. It's all about money.

Can you help me one more time on the Internet? I have the e-mail address for an attorney who worked at the International Court of Human Rights in Costa Rica and is an expert on international law. I want to write her about my case but do not have her mailing address. I feel like I have exhausted all my legal options. Because of my crime, I do not qualify for any early release programs, even for good behavior. So it doesn't matter how I act in here. All sex offenders, regardless of the nature of their crime, are grouped together as the worst scum of the earth and must serve their entire time. With thirty years in front of me, I'll run out of life before I am released. Sometimes, I am surprised I have breath.

October 2, 2009

Enclosed is the last letter I'll ever receive from the State Defender's Office. I had a sick sense in my stomach for the last two years that this public defender was simply going through the motions. After all, she is paid by the state, and the state put me in here for thirty years. I will now die in prison. The sooner, the better. I have nothing to live for, no freedom, no time to die in peace, only time to slowly die in this hellhole.

All the hope I had over the last four years is now totally gone. I can't even hope to wake up tomorrow because I have no reason and no desire to live any longer. I know now how the inmates on death row feel. No hope, no way to change their ultimate reality to lose their life. I think they must also pray all day to die now, not to have to wait for years doing no good for themselves or others, just waiting to die.

Not only am I totally isolated now, but now have absolutely no hope that this will ever change. So please, place your prayers in others who may have hope and are not just waiting to die. They deserve your prayers, and the results will be favorable.

Thank God you did not and will not end up like your dad who at seventy years of age has only death to look forward to. This place is so hard for me. I see others come and go each week. I see others talk about going home in a year or two or five. I see others that this damnation is only a small part of their life. I have never been in such a negative, hateful, and at times unsafe place for a seventy-year-old.

Most of all, thank you for all your love and prayers and encouragement. I am sorry to have been such a disappointment to you. You are so much like your mom, but you have so many virtues that belong only to you. Thank God for all the blessings he has given and will always give to you. My loss of hope and the will to live must be God's will. I must accept it. I pray he takes me soon.

Below is the letter from the State of Wisconsin State Public Defender Susan E. Alesia, Assistant State Public Defender, September 30, 2009

I am very sorry to tell you that the Wisconsin Supreme Court denied the petition for review. I've enclosed the court's order. I've had the chance to discuss your case with some other attorneys. I could not come up with any options for us to pursue. I do not see a federal issue in this case that precludes us from going to federal court, and obviously, we have exhausted our state-court options. Legally, I believe there are no more issues to pursue.

The Department of Corrections is making many changes beginning in October. The DOC and the courts will be releasing people early. The DOC is still working out the details, and most of the options seem to be unavailable to people with sexual offenses, but it is something I will continue to monitor, and if it seems that there is a way that this can favorably impact your sentence, I will let you know.

As we've discussed many times, I don't see any legal issue regarding the extradition from Costa Rica. I know you disagree. The one thing I can and will do for you is have an amended judgment of conviction entered that accurately reflects the sentence credit the judge granted. The record will be returned to the county, and at that point, the judge will be able to enter the order. I will be back in touch with you when I get that done.

December 14, 2010

I wrote to the attorney in California two weeks ago and haven't received a response. She probably thinks, Why respond when he doesn't even have a cell in the state of California? I'm not flying to Wisconsin to help him on a no-fee basis. I guess I'm not surprised. No one else has answered my letters for help either. Probably a conclusion that says here's a sex offender with a thirty-year sentence. Let him be.

The only opportunity to see the parole board is after I have been here for ten years, no matter how perfect my behavior has been. But I am told that the parole board very rarely paroles a sex offender as long as the victim says "no," and we know that will never change. So that door is virtually closed for many years.

I read recently in the law library here that case law shows here people who have left probation and left the US have been given a sentence of no more than twice the time they were gone. So if you were gone for two years, the maximum you would receive is four years.

While researching in the law library, I made it my business to read all I could about revocation, which is why I am here, not guilty of any new crime. In all the revocation cases I read, the attorney was successful in using plea bargain down to 25 percent of what the DA was asking for, so in my case, I should have given a maximum of seven and a half years, not thirty years!

Every street I have gone down over the last three long years has been a dead end. The only conclusion I can draw is that Frank Lettenberger is the only person who could get me out of here. He knows my original case from eleven years ago, knows the DA, and knows the judge. I think he could get me deported out of the US. But that's not going to happen, so let's drop this whole matter. My appeal option has been exhausted.

May 2, 2010

This Friday was a very difficult day for me. Each year in May, I go to a meeting with PRC, the Program Review Committee, and each year, they pat me on the head and say, "Keep up the good work. " *So in preparation for the meeting this month, I asked to have a meeting with our social worker to see what I could do to change my situation. We talked for over an hour in his office in the Administration Building. He removed the very thin thread of hope for me getting out of here. He said according to the rules of the Department of Corrections, my risk level will remain "high" until I have less than fifteen years left on my sentence. Anyone with fifteen years or more time is classified as a high risk. No one is released if they have a high-risk rating.*

He said the next time I will have my consultation is after seven years, which will make me eligible to see the parole board, which will be in 2015, at age seventy-five. When I do see them, I will still be considered high risk, and they never parole anyone the first time you see them. They will give me a forty-eight-month or thirty-six-month recall. So when I am seventy-eight or seventy-nine, I will be able to meet with the parole board again. Even then, he said there is no guarantee that they will consider sending me out because I was still (no matter how perfect my record is here) a high risk and probably will not be considered a candidate to get paroled until at least eighty-two years of age when I reach the fifteen-year mark.

Somehow, I can see myself at eighty-three years old with the health and energy to get out of this hellhole and have to spend fifteen more years on probation in Wisconsin. I kept very cool although I just wanted to cry and say, "Let them send me to death row as waiting fifteen years more is death row!" My heart was hurting, and my chest felt like it would explode. With my best composure, I asked if there was anything in his opinion that I could do to move the time line up so I may have a few years of freedom before I die. He said I would have to hire a good attorney who could convince the judge and the district attorney to bring me back to court and ask for time served and be deported to Costa Rica. So the doors are closed and locked for a very long time.

I have no one else to share this devastating news with except you. Given this news, please do not plan a trip here to see me this summer. Wait until fall when I can slowly process this total loss of hope. Your visit then will be a welcome change for me.

June 9, 2010

This week, I meet with the PRC board. It's made up of a chairperson, a staff member from administration, and an officer that oversees the guards. They are six weeks behind (each inmate gets an interview once per calendar year), so the tone was "Okay, let's get this over with because we are behind." Basically, they said the next step for me is to meet with parole, which will be in 2015. Then parole will give me a thirty-six- or forty-eight-month deferral (recall), so by 2018, at the age of seventy-eight, I will stand my first chance of maybe getting out of here by age eighty if everything falls perfectly in line. Otherwise, it will be a mandatory release in 2037 (age the age of ninety-seven). It was not my best morning.

December 10, 2014

Nothing can happen on my case until the second judge retires, which is scheduled for 2015, although no one knows what month yet. I do not communicate with my lawyer, Frank, on a regular basis because he charges by the hour, and each time he reads my letters, it is an hourly charge. We have worked out an agreement so that I'll be able to pay if and when I am set free. He has been very kind with our agreement, but I don't want to keep running up charges. When I get out, I'll have monthly Social Security checks to pay what I owe. I will not involve you in any way with Frank and going back to court. I have been waiting seven years now to get out of here.

March 14, 2015

I saw my attorney, and we discussed several strategies for our next move. In the meantime, the second judge who was to retire this year has cancer, and my attorney thinks they will keep him on during the balance of this year so he will have insurance to cover the medical costs of cancer treatment. The judge is my age, so who knows, we may end up in front of him again in court. My attorney is trying to figure out the best approach because this will probably be our last time we can appear in court with a motion to dismiss. This place does not get any easier.

April 24, 2015

My attorney sent a stuffed priority mail envelope with more information about parole. He is trying to reach my attorney in Costa Rica to see about taking my parole in Costa Rica. At least they would get me out of here to live in a beautiful country. My attorney is upbeat about parole because it could be done by the Department of Corrections without going to court. Once released, we could go to court with a modification monitor to send me back to Costa Rica. At least I would be able to go to court without handcuffs and chains around my ankles.

January 8, 2016

The fat lady is standing in the wings waiting until this journey is over to sing a song. But nothing is really over when you are under the thumb of a doctor. Please keep the prayers coming. My attorney says he feels I will be released in February by parole. He said the signs are there now, especially since they have produced a prerelease plan for me.

In the meantime, I will be ready for my spleen operation with an estimate of six to eight weeks of recovery. And that means I could potentially walk out of here with the surgery behind and paid for by the state, not me. The sequence of events go like this: operation in January, release in February, and court date in early March to hopefully receive a discharge from my parole, and all the time will be behind me, meaning I'll be totally free to go anywhere in this world as a free man. It makes tears of joy come to my eyes just writing this to you. Your prayers have been, and I know will be, a critical part of this freedom. It's been a long nine years here, so going home will be the all-inclusive answer to our prayers. God is good. Only three steps left: operation, release, and discharge to be free at last.

January 10, 2016

I will need your cell phone number so I can call you when I get out. The puzzle of getting out of here is a lot to think about. Being released in February from this place does not mean I'll be totally free because parole will pick me up and take me to Elkhorn where I'll probably have a bracelet on my ankle because I will still be on parole, not free yet. My attorney tells me parole is working on a plan to house me. Then the next and final step will be court in Walworth to ask for a discharge, which legally means my time is served and I am free to go anywhere in this world. That's the goal. The final piece will hopefully take place during your birthday month of March. So I will be out to buy you a birthday lunch. That to me is my ultimate epitome celebration: a free Dad being with my most loved person in this world on her birthday!

My attorney gave my health records to another attorney who specializes in Social Security Disability Insurance which will pay me a monthly amount for the rest of my life. In addition, I am applying for a Veteran's Disability which would pay in addition to my regular Social Security. When I get these checks, I can live in Costa Rica and maybe even be able to start my ice cream business on the beach. God is good. I am praying not to be a burden on you and your husband. You have already sent me money weekly for nine years in this place. Enough is enough. Mom is really working in God's ear that this whole mess is completely cleared up, and I am a free man, able to live on my own without asking for money.

February 10, 2016

I just received devastating news. I will not be released at this time. The parole board says that I'm not close enough to death to be released to die outside of the walls of this prison. I am sorry to get your hopes up, but it's over. My prayers now are to ask our God to let me die soon so I can finally get out of this prison.

July 17, 2016

I had three letters awaiting me when I returned here to Fox Lake on Friday afternoon. The previous week, I was picked up and driven to Walworth Jail to wait for court on Monday, July 11.

They returned me one full week later to Fox Lake. When they took me to the courtroom, of course, in leg irons and handcuffs, I sat down at the table with my attorney, and he said do not look over my shoulder because the victim's mom was there to testify. My attorney was 90 percent sure she would not show up, but if she did, I knew the compassionate release that I was seeking would be turned down. They called me to the stand, and I was sworn in and sat down. My attorney asked me a series of questions concerning my cancer and my eleven years in prison. It took about fifteen minutes. Then the prosecutor told the judge that the victim's mother wanted to address the court. She read the three-page letter addressed to the court, painting me as a vicious, coldhearted criminal who should not be released ever. She told the court my cancer was nothing compared to the seventeen years of pain her daughter has been put through because of me.

Well, this was over before it even started. Even my attorney said after her telling the court how her daughter still suffers from what I did, what could I do? My attorney said, "Your Honor, my client is here to ask for a compassionate release. He did not murder anyone, he did not rape anyone, he did not commit a crime of homicide. He wrongfully touched the victim." My attorney made a few more comments, and then the judge said, "We cannot accept the motion from the defendant." This is the same judge who both signed off that it was okay for parole to send me out of parole six months ago. But with the mother saying her "perfect" family has been destroyed and she speaks for the entire community that no one wants me to be released from prison.

Afterward, my attorney said he'll call me next week to discuss plan B, whatever that may be. He will not stop until I am released and put on parole outside the walls of this prison. I was prepared for the worst, and that's exactly what happened. All I could think about was when they walked me back to a cell in all my travels throughout this world, I found that people of every nation and culture I met always celebrated the feeling of arriving home because it is a foreshadowing of our final journey home to be with God in heaven for eternity.

July 19, 2016

July has been a tough month with new symptoms and reaction to my cancer, not to mention the court appearance which was horrible. I will continue to fight to get out of here and die in peace.

I've talked with three sergeants and one captain to see what they can put together on my behalf to sign affidavits as to my character over the last eleven years. I have other ideas I'm working on to get out of this place and enjoy a little time before my illness becomes more difficult to handle.

The turnover here continues at a rapid rate, especially this time of year. So many young people are here for drug violations. It's a drug scene with most trying to smuggle in drugs here on the inside from the outside.

January 27, 2017

I am focused in this new year. I'm working with my attorney to set up a time with an administrative judge to get yet another hearing for my compassionate release. This is our next step to overcome the parole officer's decision. I'm not going to wait another twelve months to beg for a release. Also, I do not want to move to Illinois. It is simply not an option. I know that going back to Costa Rica is also not an option anymore. And because I have so many relatives in the Atlanta area, that would be my next best choice. I want to get as far away from Wisconsin as possible while still having family around me. If parole says no to me, I could be here for several more months. Nothing is easy, but one day, soon, it will be easy for me.

Court Week! July 2017

I'm sitting here waiting to go to court, but to my disappointment, the hearing was canceled and will be rescheduled. This let-

ter was supposed to be saying that I have been released, but that will have to wait a bit longer. Good things take longer sometimes.

August 4, 2017

I am waiting for a call from my attorney for a date to go back to court. Let's hope and pray that we hit a home run and be able to get out of here to start my new life. No word yet for a new court date for our hearing, but I'm expecting news any day now. You'll be the first to know when the date has been set.

August 30, 2017

I just spent five days in county jail. The hearing went well. The state is throwing more junk at me to disregard my attempt to be let out of here on parole. This time it had to do with a sealed file which my attorney was able to get the judge to open and pro- vide evidence of why I shouldn't get out of here. So I go back to court on the last week in September to answer what the state is using against me. My attorney and I agree that this secret file is tied directly to the victim's mother, so we will be well-prepared to answer the state who has used this against me, which is prejudice against me and then holding the file as secret. It reminded me that about a year ago you asked the court to share information about my status and they told you the case was sealed. My attorney says this is the greatest break we have had since we started the fight two years ago. It is frustrating, but I will not stop the fight to get out of prison.

September 16, 2017

Thank you for your words of encouragement for my upcom- ing hearing. I still don't have a date yet, but it's coming up at the end of September. My strength and God's mercy will get me through this time.

This is an unusual time in my life, waiting for three to four months between appointments with my doctor and waiting for a final answer from the court.

May 14, 2017

Two days ago at court was the first time I have felt we have a good judge. In attendance was the judge, clerk, recorder, my attorney, the state's attorney, and me. No witnesses, no testimony, no family because this was a discussion on my attorney's list of items that for five years the parole office has said I have not been in prison long enough. The state's attorney was not prepared because she said she needed more time to send a rebuttal in writing to the court. The judge asked her how long that would take, and she told him she was really busy and needed thirty to thirty-five days. My attorney said, "Your Honor, this man is dying. Our time is critical." And the judge said, "You are right, we don't have the luxury of time. Thirty to thirty-five days is not acceptable." The state's attorney then cut it down to twenty-one days. The judge said that was acceptable and set a final hearing for July 12, 2017. I will find out if I finally get out of prison or if I have to stay.

May 16, 2017

I am back at Fox Lake and still thinking about my latest day in court. The good news is I will hear the decision made by the judge in July, and that decision could be in my favor, which will be a release from this prison to parole. At least, that gets me out of this place and outside to then go back to court for a total discharge from my sentence, and I will be totally free of my parole time. My time will be considered "time served." That will remove any further restrictions from the court and the state of Wisconsin. I'll be free to go anywhere. I want to live out whatever life I have left on this earth.

CHAPTER 9

Run a Tight Ship

If a window of opportunity appears, don't pull down the shades.

—Tom Peters

In this chapter, I archived additional excerpts from my father's letters regarding the importance of keeping busy in prison. I sent him several books and crossword puzzles which he liked to pass the time and put money in his account to purchase a mini television for his cell. The monotony of his daily routine also was occupied with going to work and running on the track. The role of engaging in recreation is critical to physical and mental well-being in prison. It is a beneficial outlet to combat loneliness and boredom.

Providing recreation privileges in prison is similar to running a tight ship; it involves close monitoring, account management, and organization for inmates' safety and prison security. There is a process to strictly enforce rules on a boat as there is in a prison in order to run smoothly, efficiently, and effectively. Scheduling inmates to be released from their housing unit to join in recreation programs can be logistically challenging but worth the time and effort. Recreation also teaches prisoners vital skills needed for reentering society. Engaging in cooperative activities with fellow inmates can be a tool that enhances rehabilitation. Most inmates look forward to participating in recreational activities to make positive changes in their attitude and behavior.

Activities for All

Even with minimal resources, prison can provide leisure areas to keep inmates active. Fox Lake had indoor and outdoor recreation areas to walk, play basketball, and organize softball games. My father's favorite form of exercise in and out of prison was training to run marathons. He stuck to a disciplined running routine and would request a daily pass, rain or shine, to go to recreation and run on the track. Within the monotony and stress of living in prison, he found logging miles each lap as a welcome solace. Running was an integral part of his life and one that continued to fuel his need to achieve, to track his distance and times, positively improving his body and spirit. His fellow inmates saw my father working out daily and actually started cheering him on.

May 7, 2010

As you know, I have used running as a stress reliever for years. Although it's different to run here because the exercise track is closed while they electrify the 12-foot high fence, the razor wire on top was not enough to hear security talk, so I don't know when we'll be able to run again. In the meantime, I walk each day on the patio just outside our cell block from 3:00 p.m. until I get back from tutoring around chow time at 5:00 p.m. It's better than nothing!

February 6, 2011

I just came in from walking on the cement patio that they call passive recreation. I took a path the width of the snow shovel so I could walk. I've been out here since 8:00 a.m. when they opened up our cell block to go outside. It's almost 10:30 a.m. now, so in two and a half hours, I probably walked 6 miles. They tell me thirty-one times around is one mile, but I don't count, just fast walk to get cardio benefits and stay warm. Enclosed is my Fleet Feet Project 1,000-mile certificate. It was presented to me this week, and fortunately, they gave me a copy so I could send it to you. It is something I hope you can be proud of.

August 4, 2011

It's been terribly hot here again. I was able to go to 9:00 a.m. recreation as school was closed down, and they had not announced a severe heat advisory so I could run my 3 miles. Shortly after, by 10:00 a.m., they closed down recreation, but I got my run in!

As I was running on my third lap, a young inmate ran next to me and said, "I wanted to catch up with you to tell you two things. First, I'm going home tomorrow as I am done with my time. Secondly, you probably don't remember, but you helped me two summers ago when I first started running this track. You gave me many tips, and I did everything you told me to do. Now I am running 6 to 7 miles each day, and when I get out, I'm going to train for a marathon in the fall of this year. You inspired me to do my best and to use running as a discipline." I felt like stopping and letting the tears flow to think that this young man wanted to thank me and then to know he was being set free the very next morning. I was overwhelmed. I was honored that he would want to tell me what he said. The next morning at 8:00 a.m., the time when people are released, I said a prayer for him that he would complete the marathon and stay free and have a good life.

March 7, 2012

About every three months, the administration takes away another benefit. A recent example we have is recreation each day at 3:30 p.m. That worked out perfectly for many of us who work from 8:00 a.m. until 4:00 p.m. The younger inmates who sit around all day could go to morning recreation. So now on two days a week, I have to run at night. I don't like that because my dinner isn't fully digested. But there's really not that much food I am able to eat anyway. Portions are getting much smaller here. Of course, they blame the budget cuts.

November 4, 2012

I am enclosing my latest certificate for reaching the 3,000-mile running mark. I worked hard for the last two months to reach this goal before my hernia operation as they will tell me no run-

ning for a month, which for me will be probably just as bad as the surgery.

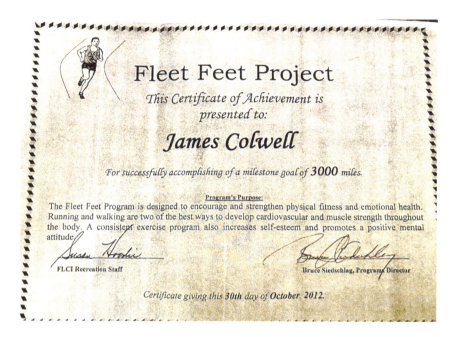

Fleet Feet Project

This Certificate of Achievement is presented to:

James Colwell

For successfully accomplishing of a milestone goal of **3000** miles.

Program's Purpose:

The Fleet Feet Program is designed to encourage and strengthen physical fitness and emotional health. Running and walking are two of the best ways to develop cardiovascular and muscle strength throughout the body. A consistent exercise program also increases self-esteem and promotes a positive mental attitude.

FLCI Recreation Staff

Bruce Siedschlag, Program Director

Certificate giving this *30th day of October, 2012.*

June 4, 2016

When the track opened about a month ago, I knew the first few weeks would be testing my surgery by building up slowly, starting with a mile per day for the first week. The second week I moved it up to two miles. Although my speed has been adjusted, it's okay because I'm out there using my desire to run as a healing agent and to build up my system. I still suffer from a platelet count about one half of what it used to be. This week, I'm up to where I left off last year at 3 miles, a comfortable and realistic goal for this summer. One of the biggest things we must do as we grow older is to accept the fact that we can no longer do what we did five or ten years ago. But I have learned to accept what God has given me and to thank him for my daily runs that are different at seventy-six.

Recently, an inmate about forty-five years old, asked if I could help him to learn how to run. I know God put him in my path because he started with me and today is running 3 miles with me each day. Soon, like a Mama bird teaching her baby birds how to fly, he will be running more than 3 miles on his own. And that's great because he learned the right way for a beginning runner. He's very respectful and tells everyone that I'm his coach. This gives me satisfaction by seeing someone learn and being thankful that I moved him through the learning journey and made the task more enjoyable.

October 17, 2016

This last week, I started wearing layers for my daily run because it's getting close to winter. When I run in the morning, it is about 38 degrees, but with the layers, I warm up after the first half mile. It's still a way to keep moving. Please send sandpaper so I can take off the sharp points from the pins and needles that so far are winning the pain fight.

I will never forget my first marathon when a young man, probably twenty years old, ran with me for a while. He said it was his first marathon, so I asked him how much he had trained. He said he didn't train and he could run the whole race with no problem. He then sped past me, and I lost sight of him. About five miles later, at the twelve-mile marker, I saw him sitting on the curb, looking like he was very sick. I didn't stop because there was nothing I could do. Without training, there's no finish. It's not how fast you run, it's finishing the 26 miles that counts. The discipline of running long distances builds our endurance each day.

Everyday I'm Hustlin'

Working is another positive outlet for inmates. Qualified inmates can work in food service, health care, landscaping, or as educational tutors. The facility my father was in also participated in the Badger State Prison Industries program and allowed approximately forty to fifty select inmates to work in a wood/laminated furniture factory that produced products sold to state agencies. Inmates can make up to $1 per hour depending on their work assignment.

My father had a strong work ethic and was employed in a few different jobs in prison but took the most pride in his work as a tutor in the Fox Lake Education Department. He often told me it kept his brain working, helped to pass the time, and gave him great satisfaction in teaching literacy skills to fellow inmates. Many inmates he tutored in reading and writing did not have a high school diploma or a GED, but they were eligible to enroll in classes. Adult basic education, correspondence courses, reentry/ prerelease programs, and cognitive intervention programs are all offered at this prison. Fox Lake also offers technical training in automotive maintenance, cabinetmaking and millwork, computer drafting, horticulture, custodial services, machining, small engine technologies, welding, HVAC, and masonry.

The caveat in being employed as an inmate is there is a required termination date after two years. In other words, you can't stay in one job for very long before you are asked to apply to a different area within the prison. This particular two-year employee guideline was a restriction that my father felt was arbitrary. He did not like leaving his tutoring job because he was interested in making a difference by sharing the importance of good communication skills. He enjoyed teaching vocabulary, grammar, and reading each week. He also liked that we were both teachers and could share our student success stories with each other.

July 23, 2007

Today, I will turn in my completed application to the academic school here to be considered to work as a tutor in the educational department. The application was six pages long, and I had to write a six-hundred-word letter to the head of the department. My first draft was well over 1,000 words, so I spent a lot of time getting it down to the required amount. I could have written pages on the first question. The topics include:

- *Describe yourself.*
- *What is important to you?*
- *What are your interests?*

- *Who are your closest friends?*
- *Describe your current home.*
- *What else do you want us to know?*
- *What are a few of your favorite books?*
- *How would you spend a perfect Saturday?*
- *What do you want from being a tutor?*

So God willing, if I get the job, I'll not only have the ability to make a contribution but pay will be somewhere in the area of $5 for forty hours of work. Wow! But that's better than zero. I can save it to pay for correspondence courses.

September 11, 2007

No job yet. I've been told that right now there are no openings for tutors. But I'm on a list, and when my name comes up, they will call me. In the meantime, I need to make some money to save for shoes, correspondence courses, razors, and toothpaste. I'm trying to get another job. This one is in the office at the HSU (Health Services Unit) where the doctors, nurses, and health care people work here in the prison. It doesn't pay as much as tutoring, but I would make $4 (10 cents per hour) per week, and then they take out $1 for court costs, so I would clear $3 per week. Not much, but better than zero! I could always get in the kitchen, but now that is not available. Plus, the pay there is the lowest in prison, and I would only make less than $3 per week.

June 4, 2008

I start tutoring next week. I'll be tutoring in vocational math, reading, and a class called Pathways, which helps slow learners get on track for the regular classes. Your visit was so well-timed. I was excited to see you again. I had just taken my final exam. I studied hard to make sure I passed before seeing you. Today, I got my grade, 99.5 percent, and the head of all the tutors gave me an A+. She also gave me a certificate, so now I'm fully qualified to tutor. I'll be working four to five hours per day, which will keep my mind on helping others instead of feeling sorry for myself in this hellhole.

January 15, 2008

I've written to the educational director about a tutoring job again. Let's see what happens. If it's God's will that I help to teach others, then it shall be. There are so many people here who need help. Unfortunately, education and having two loving parents was not part of their childhood. It's not totally their fault, but the result is a hatred and bitterness that goes so very deep in their heads and being. I pray for them, especially the ones I know personally who live in my cell block. I ask God to favor them and heal them and remove that terrible bitterness in their hearts.

August 20, 2008

I have a thirty-hour course certificate to tutor people. I have been trained to help teach the Orton/Gillingham method of reading to people who have disabilities. The teaching method is very complex, but I try to make it easy for a nonreader to learn as an adult how to read. We start with how letters sound then teach syllables. We work a lot with flash cards so students can learn how to sound out letters and simple one syllable words. It is a long process that involves a lot of patience. Some students can learn five or six words and sounds one day, and the next day, they can't remember what they learned. It is frustrating for both the student and the teacher. I am only one of three tutors here at this prison who are certified to help adults to read and spell. Something new and challenging, thank God.

Yesterday, I tutored a man whose parents never sent him to school. Eventually, he was taken from his home and placed with his aunt and uncle who did send him to school when he was twelve years old. He was in first grade at twelve years old and only lasted two weeks in the classroom before he moved again to Wisconsin. And it didn't take long for him to start getting in trouble. He's now in prison for seven years and can barely read or write. We're starting him at the very basic level to learn. I'm trying to help him but often see the opposite of learning here. Many of the young people do not stand a chance in this world because of the lack of education and no mentoring. They return here for the second, third, and fourth time. In and out of prison. How can we work together to stop this cycle?

Besides the tutoring, there's not much in here to stimulate my brain. If I'm going to be in this hellhole, I don't want them to take away my brain.

January 8, 2011

It's back to work this week, thank God. One of the students I've been working with for the past two years elevated to another level this week going toward his GED. He started at the second-grade level and now is reading and writing at the eighth grade level. He tried to quit, but with encouragement he stuck it out. Hopefully he will get out of here with his high school degree.

I also started a new computer literacy class five days a week. We learn to type (I only use one finger) and use the computer, but the Internet is disconnected. I'll never be able to use my new skills in here, but it's still good to learn them. You're never too old to learn, right? Now I'm in school from 8:00 a.m. to 5:00 p.m. five days a week. I get home (well, not exactly, it's more like this 5'×9' box I live in) and eat dinner at 5:00 p.m. then go to the recreation to run 3 miles inside at 6:00 p.m. By the time I get back at 7:15 p.m., I am tired, but, of course, that doesn't necessarily mean I'll sleep at night. It's kind of off and on. But my full day does not leave too much room to feel sorry for myself, and that's certainly positive. I run on Saturdays as well but usually take Sunday off.

June 22, 2011

My work as a tutor is great. I was even considered for the best tutor award. Fox Lake has not nominated a tutor for the past five years. Just being nominated is an honor. We have twenty tutors here, and they are all very good at what they do. I feel it could have easily have been given to any one of the fellow tutors. My nomination will go up against almost thirty tutors throughout the Wisconsin Prison System. I will not make a dent at that level, but that's fine. I enjoy what I do each day to help me from going completely crazy in this place.

It's nice to add this nomination to all the medals, awards, and certificates your family has earned over the years. Maybe, we'll need to build a wall of accomplishments! No grass grows under our feet for lack of activity.

July 22, 2012

I can only have the same job here for two years then must go and find a different job. Two years ago, when my time was up, I wrote the warden to get an extension. Usually with approval, they give you a six-month extension. Well, miraculously, they gave me two additional years as a tutor. So now, that two years is up. And in the meantime, a new warden came to work here a year ago. So I wrote him a few days ago to see if he'll give me an extension. Chances are I will be looking for a new job. Anything except the kitchen! Also, it may be difficult to find a job because the institution has 1,200 inmates and only two hundred jobs available.

> ***Nominee's Name:*** *James Colwell*
> ***Award:*** *Tutor of the Year*
> ***Nominator's Name:*** *Joan M. Knorre, Teacher and Tutor Coordinator*
> ***Organization:*** *Fox Lake Correctional Institution (FLCI)*
> ***Phone and email:*** *920-928-6957 <u>Joan.Knorre@ wisconsin.gov</u>*

> *Can the nominee attend the award cere-mony luncheon on October 19? No*
> *If not, can a representative attend on his or her behalf? Yes*

> *Detailed description of nominee's achievements:*

> *James Colwell is an outstanding tutor, who was certified on 3/3/2008. He demonstrates a commitment to his learners by contributing new*

219

ideas and methods to improve their literacy. He is a patient, quiet man, who teaches struggling, often reluctant low-level readers. Because of his encouraging and nonthreatening approach, he gently nudges them to take risks to improve their reading and writing skills and work to their full potential. Interestingly, the students often develop a positive attitude about school and learning because of James's persistence.

After two years of tutoring, he was promoted to literacy clerk on 8/9/2010. He initiates various techniques to assist student learning. For example, he uses handmade flashcards with spelling and vocabulary words each day to enhance memorization. The students need to say the word and use it in a meaningful sentence. James also suggested weekly sentence writing because his pupils struggle with that. Presently, all the students are required to write three sentences with at least five, seven, and ten words consecutively without a tutor or teacher's assistance. Dictionaries and word lists can be used. When they have completed their sentences, students edit with the teacher and keep these sentences in a portfolio so progress can be tracked.

Besides the Tutor Training course, James also participated in the Orton Gillingham Method in Phonics, which is a thirty-hour Advanced Tutor Training Class held at FLCI. Since James is skilled in phonics, he does an excellent job screening students using a Phonics Assessment and Morrison McCall Spelling Test. These tools give the teacher a better idea of the students' skill level in sound-

ing out words and reading level beyond the TABE test (Test of Adult Basic Education).

In conclusion, James's down-to-earth, positive attitude motivates his students. When new, challenging learners experience his enthusiasm and respectful manner, they soon realize that learning how to read better will improve their quality of life and success in the world of work.

(This letter was written on my father's behalf to nominate him for "Tutor of the Year." Not long after his nomination, he was terminated from his tutoring job because inmates are only allowed to hold jobs for an assigned length of time. He was doing an outstanding job making positive contributions to the inmate population, but he could no longer work in this capacity because of prison rules.)

August 8, 2012

I just found out that my tutoring days are over. I'm in the process of sending out letters to other departments to find another job where I can use my brain, not my physical strength, which at my age is not what it used to be. Please pray I find something soon so I will at least continue a small income to buy hygiene products to make this life a little easier. But if I don't get a new job, I'll have to use state soap and state toothpaste, which are about as good as using nothing.

September 11, 2012

I've only had one interview over the past two weeks, and that didn't work out. Based on my experience, the person interviewing me said I need to find a job using my brain, not my hands. I've written several departments to inquire about a job. It's different to be asking for a job that makes only pennies an hour, but those pennies are very important for life in this place. So far, my job hunting has come up with a big goose egg. If I don't get something soon, I'll probably be drafted by the kitchen, and I don't want that. There's a handful of clerical jobs available:

1. *Tutor/literacy*
2. *Clerk at canteen*
3. *Clerk at Health Services (HSU)*
4. *Clerk at Vocational School Office*
5. *Clerk in the Administration Building*

All are filled, so I'm on a waiting list. Again, I could work in the kitchen, but it's not a good place. Many inmates steal food, and if I work there, I could also be pegged as guilty and sent to the hole. I never want to go to the hole. Unless a clerk position opens up soon, I may have to take that chance. The only other jobs are working in the unit as a janitor or picking up garbage.

October 7, 2012

I started a new job as a clerk at HSU (Health Services Unit) this week. However, it's been trying to put my mind into a new job with the loss of my brother on my heart. The job is heavy in computer knowledge, and I don't feel yet as if I can do it. But I'm going to give it my best possible shot. Maybe, old dogs can learn new things.

October 16, 2012

I quit my job at HSU. My mind could not focus properly, and the amount of typing on electronic typewriters and computer keyboard was overwhelming. After three days, I went to the sergeant and told him I was not the man for the job. He said to give it another week, but I said no. I know I am slowing down a well-oiled system and will not continue to be a problem instead of an asset. So now, I'm back looking for another job and praying that time will help me better focus and not remain in the fog over my brother's death.

October 21, 2012

I took a new job at the canteen picking up orders for inmates all day. I must stand all day, and my back is really talking to me. But I need the job even though it pays only half of what I made as a tutor. I pray for God's strength to help me to be able to keep the job.

January 28, 2013

In many years of travel and visiting distribution centers and warehouses that held thousands of office supplies, I never thought that in my seventies, I would be working in one. But today I do.

The last time I had a hard manual labor job was the summer between my junior and senior year in high school. I needed to save money for college, and my job was driving a lift truck in a hot and dirty aluminum factory, picking up scrap pieces of aluminum off the production line, then driving them into the furnace room (about 170 degrees) and dumping the scrap into a red hot furnace to be melted down and used again to make aluminum pots and pans. That experience gave me the motivation to never again have to work in a factory. To this day, I don't know how my dad spent forty-two years working at the Caterpillar Factory in Peoria. He worked hard to make little money to take care of his family. And your grandmother worked part-time at a department store.

Yes, today I work once again in a meaningless labor job of picking items (soap, soda, snacks) on a line for seven hours a day. And the pay for two weeks' worth of work is enough to put 12 gallons of gas (at $3.50 per gallon) in your car. But it's what God has given me to keep me out of this unit each day and feel a little productive. It buys me shampoo, soap, and toothpaste every few weeks. And a jar of Maxwell House Coffee is now $6.50, so I have to follow a budget to make my money work the best way it can.

May 8, 2013

I finally have something to share. I got a promotion at work. I am no longer scanning (like in the grocery store) at work, I am now the janitor. Yes, it's hard to believe, but the janitor position *is a promotion. And I get a pay raise of 2 cents per hour and or another $1.60 each two weeks when we get paid. I'll use the money wisely. Work is really knocking me out. After using my brain for four years, now I must use my hands in manual labor, not requiring any brain power. But it's a job, and I'm giving it 100 percent each day.*

December 10, 2014
This place can produce some deep negatives. This journey is like what it must be like to be stuck in a time lock where little changes day to day. I still have my private cell, and that is a tremendous blessing. Although I am still waiting to become an official tutor again, I continue to help several inmates with their homework.

Chow Down

My father repeatedly told me that prison food is garbage. Institutionalized, bland slop on plate. He told me it was one step above dog food and not fit for everyday human consumption. In April 2016, while my father was at Fox Lake, there was a report that the tap water was contaminated. The water was described as a yellowish-brown color with sediment in it, making it totally undrinkable. It turns out the water was originally found to be contaminated in 2014, but those reports were either ignored or didn't make it to officials, and multiple water samples going back to 2008 have shown that the water was contaminated. There is bottled water available, but prisoners must buy it, and many can't afford to.

My father was a cook in the Army and had seen his share of food rations, but nothing like the food they serve in prison cafeterias. The dreary atmosphere matched the repetitive menu and requisite times for breakfast, lunch, and dinner. Same food, same schedule. Eat, sleep, repeat. Many inmates, including my father, would rely on purchasing snacks at the commissary, like Doritos, cookies, and candy. It was like buying treats from a convenience store but half the size and less than half of the options. Holiday food in prison was particularly depressing as he really missed home-cooked meals, pumpkin pie with a dollop of whipped cream, and a hot cup of quality coffee.

March 23, 2008

We had beef stew here for Easter, but it tasted more like dog food. Every day, I see anger and hate around me. Thank God you have your family. You are where God wants you to be, so don't waste your productive time worrying about me. Take care of your husband and daughters. For now, that is God's purpose for you, and you must follow his will. Miracles do happen.

November 24, 2010

There is a rumor going around that tomorrow we will get REAL mashed potatoes. We will probably get a fake piece of turkey loaf and canned corn. No word yet on desert, but usually it's a sugar cookie.

January 7, 2015

We just completed our biweekly Saturday hot dog and orange slice (out of a can) lunch. Yesterday, many inmates received a box of Kentucky Fried Chicken. They do that as a fundraiser each year. To me, having a new container of Maxwell House Coffee was more important, so I bought a box of chicken for someone else, and they gave me a new jar of coffee. A win-win situation!

Visiting Hours

Visiting my father in prison was emotionally, physically, and psychologically draining, but for my father, it was a positive outlet of recreation and wellness. We scheduled our visits approximately once a month because of the long-distance drive, child care, and dog walking arrangements. It wasn't easy, but I know how happy it made my father to see me and my husband. It was an eight-hour drive round trip with a three-hour maximum visiting time. Our daughters had no idea we were on our way to visit their grandfather.

Every time we visited the facility, we had to be processed through the prison's visitor's center. It's a small administrative building on the perimeter of the prison grounds. Anyone who wishes to visit an inmate at Fox Lake Correctional Institution must have an approved visitor's application on file. Visitors who do not have a visiting order or who forgot to request a visiting order will not be allowed entry to the prison regardless of circumstance or distance traveled. We witnessed family members being turned away without a visitor application, and it was heartbreaking to watch them leave without seeing their loved ones. Visits for general population inmates occur Monday through Friday from 2:30 p.m. to 8:45 p.m. and on weekends/holidays from 8:00 a.m. to 3:45 p.m. Weekday visits can be up to three hours in duration, and weekend visits last up to two hours.

After our visitor's application was verified, we were asked to sign in with my father's prison identification, number 389188. We memorized his number to expedite the paperwork. We had to produce our driver's licenses and stow all our belongings, including car keys, in a self-serve automated coin locker. We were only allowed to bring in a small plastic bag of coins (one pound maximum, no paper money) to treat my father to snacks from the vending machines. We were required to pass through a body metal detector. During our first visit, I was wearing an underwire bra. I set the metal detector off three times before the guard escorted me to another room, brought in a female guard who patted me down, and asked me to put my bra in a bowl. They ran my bra through the metal detector and shouted "All clear!" before I was allowed to put my bra back on. It was humiliating. I felt like I was being treated like a prisoner, suggesting I did something wrong.

Thankfully, my husband always went with me except for one particular time we had trouble getting clearance to enter the prison. I was wearing a pair of jeans that were bedazzled with extra shiny sparkles on the back pockets. In my defense, I thought these jeans were a stylish denim choice in my wardrobe at that time. Similar to the problems my underwire bra previously had caused, the rhinestones and decorations on the back of my jeans kept setting off the metal detector. I had no idea that my jeans would be considered a security threat, but the guard just shrugged his shoulders and said flatly, "It's your jeans." We were denied the visit. What could I do? I did not have an extra pair of pants, and we had already driven four hours to see my father. He was anticipating our visit, and I didn't want to let him down. Like the families who had been turned away for not having a visitor's application on file, we walked out the door, defeated, and returned to the parking lot without our planned visit.

My husband was determined that I see my father that day. He started unbuckling his jeans in the car and shimmied his hips underneath the steering wheel, undressing. I asked what he was doing, and he said, "If they won't let you in wearing *your* jeans, you'll just have to wear *my* jeans." His jeans fell around my waist like a hula hoop, but I held onto the belt loops, walked back into the visitor's center and successfully made it through security wearing my husband's jeans. I borrowed his jeans for the next three hours while my amazing husband sat patiently waiting in the car in the prison parking lot, wearing only his boxer shorts.

Once processed in the visitor's center, we made our way to the dayroom or visiting hall. We were searched again and assigned a small table with three uncomfortable plastic chairs surrounding it. Seating is dictated by prison staff where visitors and inmates can be best observed. The room smelled like every fragrance an animal might create. The walls were painted a dirty dull green, and the old rusted screens covering the windows let pinholes of light onto the linoleum floors. It sounded like the inside of a cafeteria with a loud cacophony of voices and clanking vending machines. There was no privacy or space for intimate, personal conversation. Correctional officers hovered over the visiting room, watching and listening.

Fox Lake allowed minimal physical contact at the start and end of each visit, such as a handshake or brief hug. I squeezed my father in an embrace as long as I could before we were required to sit down. When we hugged, my father's tears started to spill, but he would swiftly wipe them away on his sleeve. He never wanted fellow inmates or guards to see him cry. Crying was a sign of vulnerability, which often led to gossip and could place a big target on his back. Once seated, inmates were not allowed to leave their chair or move around. He could not go to the bathroom during our visits. If my father needed to use the toilet, the visit was promptly terminated.

During our visits, I could not flood his mind with negatives or hardship because he was already in prison and needed to take his mind away from despair and isolation, so we talked, laughed, and prayed together. In the seventeen-year span of visiting my father, I felt like I had to make every visit a joyous occasion, bringing extra smiles and stories to give to him, like opening presents on Christmas morning. I displayed a heightened sense of happy until the visit was over and I deflated like a balloon on the return ride home. My father told me each visit felt like a scene from the movie *The Wizard of Oz*, where the black-and-white film suddenly turns into vibrant colors. The three-hour visits always seemed like five minutes to him. As soon as it was time to leave, my father said it always went back to depressing black-and-white again.

August 18, 2007

I got the approval back for your visit. Visits are two hours on Saturday and Sunday. I asked one of the captains to get the information. You can't bring books and no food. I understand they have some sort of vending machines in the visiting area. Just being here will be wonderful.

November 11, 2007

The day before Thanksgiving is all set for your visit. But if it is snowing, please do not come. I do not want you in any danger to drive up here. All the visitors' papers are in order, so you'll have no problem getting in. They will probably search you upon entry, so be prepared for that. They get very nervous about people coming in because some visitors try to smuggle in dope and ciga-

rettes. Sorry, you can't bring a photo album, but seeing you will be a blessing in and of itself.

July 25, 2009

Thanks again for being here yesterday for a three-hour visit. What a time we had together. I realized that night that the two of you sacrificed about eight hours yesterday to come and see me. By the time you drop off the girls, drive here, talk with me, and drive home, it's easily eight hours used up. I appreciate the time on your day off to come here and be with me.

October 22, 2011

For almost five years, I have not been able to sleep well, waking up at least every hour or two each night. Last night, after a three-hour visit with you, I only woke up once! Obviously taking me out of this life here for three hours to share, laugh, and be a dad again was the miracle. What a fantastic visit that could only be topped if we could have rescued your husband in his shorts waiting in the car in the parking lot!

Thanks to your husband for driving all the way here and back home after sitting in a prison parking lot for hours. Through all the suffering, you both have stayed by me, and I thank God for you.

November 4, 2012

Thank you so much for your visit. I think I talked way too much and didn't give you and your husband a chance. I appreciate you buying me vending machine snacks with all your quarters. It was nice to hear about what's happening with your family and your plans for Thanksgiving. Your travels will far exceed mine, and that is wonderful. You will have so many memories of places throughout the world to share. God had blessed you and your family with the opportunity to travel.

April 7, 2013

Your visit with pizza, Coke, and ice cream from the vending machine was as close to a birthday celebration that I could ask for. I know it's a sacrifice for you and your husband to drive here and spend a few hours with me. I thank God for the two of you who have stood by me through this very difficult journey. Your visits here are so greatly appreciated. I also received a card from your college roommate. Did you tell her to write to me? She didn't include a return address, so please thank her for her kindness. I really enjoyed hearing from her.

April 11, 2015

I thought I'd sneak by without anyone noticing my seventy-fifth birthday, but again, you are several steps ahead of dear old Dad. Wow! What a birthday visit! The three hours went by in what felt like three minutes. As I glanced around the room upon your arrival, I noticed some people playing board games. We had so much to talk about it would have been impossible to play any games. Thank God we know how to communicate and love one another. Thank you for a great visit.

Walking back from our visit was exciting and sad at the same time. To think about our fun time and then realize it's back to by 7'× 9' cell again was hard to accept. But life goes on, and prayers will one day be answered. I know God has plans for me to be able to enjoy some freedom before he calls me home.

November 8, 2015

I am still basking in the glow of seeing you and your husband during our visit last week. Spending three hours with you talking and laughing takes me away for a while. But then the harsh reality comes rushing back. After our fantastic visit, with tears flowing down my face, I had to go into a closed room with two guards for a total strip search. I had to take everything off, including my underwear. I was standing there in my birthday suit. It was so cold and humiliating. So I offered up my disappointment to Christ as to not spoil the afterthoughts of our great conversation and visit.

April 23, 2016

It's the day after your wonderful visit. and I'm still running many of our conversations through my mind in a slideshow because they were so interesting and upbeat. So much so that my surgery even feels better today, and I believe it has a lot to do with your visit. The time went by way too soon, and saying goodbye is always so difficult. God is showing me that using you two as his messenger that my hope and trust in him will result in the most wonderful part of my life when I am free again. Thank you for making the trip again, so many trips in the past ten years to see your dad and being here to celebrate my birthday.

CHAPTER 10

High and Dry

*Think of life as a terminal illness because if you do, you
will live it with joy and passion as it ought to be lived.*

—Anna Quindlen

Being left high and dry is defined as being stranded, without help
or hope of recovery. It is a phrase with nautical roots which orig-
inates from ships being grounded during low tide. My father was
left high and dry many times during his prison sentence, but he
felt especially overlooked when medical ailments developed as he
grew old.

Prison officials are required to provide inmates with adequate and necessary medical, dental, and psychiatric health care
services. Basic treatment does not include yearly physical exams
or routine six-month dental cleanings. Additional treatment programs like the ones offered at Fox Lake Correctional Institution
included domestic violence counseling and alcohol or substance
abuse treatment. Although inmates have a constitutional right to
health care, the quality of care is often deficient and can be an
exceptionally long wait time. Plus, many prisons expect inmates
to pay at least part of the bill to receive medical treatment.

Medical issues can be exacerbated in prison, particularly for
aging people like my father who grew increasingly dependent on
medication, tests, and frequent exams to sustain his overall health

and wellness. His health deteriorated in prison due partly to an overwhelming amount of stress and a poor diet but largely because of his old age.

The medical care he received in prison was often postponed and sporadic. For example, instead of seeing a doctor immediately for a blistering rash on his leg, it took several weeks to secure an appointment with Health Services (HSU). In the meantime, a staff member told my father to try soaking his leg with wet paper towels to relieve the pain. He was prescribed an antibiotic over a month later before the infection finally started to clear. My father also started suffering from migraine headaches and repeatedly asked for a pass to go to the HSU to be assessed. The HSU is where every inmate goes for initial health care evaluations and screenings. If he was given an opportunity to go to HSU, he was often sent back to his cell with only two Tylenol tablets providing superficial relief as a quick and ordinary remedy.

He also wrote to me about sweating in the middle of the night, vomiting on his bedsheets, or having diarrhea without immediate access to a bathroom facility. In prison, he did not have access to comfortable beds, easy hydration, and or healthy foods that might have enabled him to fight off colds and flu viruses. With delayed or dismissive treatment and a lack of medication refills, many inmates like my father are at risk in missing timely preventive healthcare. As years passed during his time in prison and he was in his midseventies, his medical conditions worsened; he suffered chronic pain and became terminally ill. I felt helpless without being able to provide him with additional medical interventions to promote his physical and mental well-being. How could I provide the best care for my elderly parent in prison?

Trouble with Toothaches

My father had an obsession with clean teeth. He took pride in impeccable oral hygiene and would worry if his teeth were stained with residue from coffee or red wine. He invested in a WaterPik to blast areas he couldn't adequately reach with dental floss. He even gargled with bottles of hydrogen peroxide as mouthwash to reduce bacteria. My father had a regimented cleaning routine. His compulsive toothbrushing stemmed from a fear of germs hidden in his mouth. He would brush his teeth in the morning, after every meal, and in the evening. He even kept a toothbrush in the desk drawer in his office.

In prison, oral health is not a top priority. If teeth are discolored, worn, chipped, broken, or misaligned, a smile makeover is not available. Dental floss is prohibited because it can be used as a weapon to strangle or create rope. Regular checkups are not available to inspect teeth and gums for gingivitis or signs of periodontal disease. My father's routine six-month cleanings with a dental hygienist who removed plaque and polished his teeth were nonexistent in prison. Treatment plans in prison may include tooth extraction and filling cavities, with only basic and emergency services provided. Again, placing a request to see a dentist usually took several months. He wrote about some of the problems he encountered with substandard dental care.

January 15, 2008

When I came here, I had one tooth that was worked on in Costa Rica but not finished, which has left a hole on one side of my mouth. They were preparing it for a bridge. Now I recently lost a piece out of the side of another tooth. I feel pain, so I put in a request to see the dentist. They only have one dentist for 1,500 inmates, so it takes time. I hope it does not turn into an emergency basis.

July 29, 2008

I'm taking antibiotics they gave me after my tooth was extracted to clear up the infection. I am healing well but was disappointed to learn that all they will do here for dental problems is fix a cavity or pull a tooth. No caps, no bridge work, no root canals. So I pray that my teeth stay good until I can one day see a real dentist on a regular basis and don't have to have more teeth pulled. They waited one year to do something about it. I don't want false teeth. I want to preserve what I have. I'm being very protective of my overall health by watching what I eat and keeping up with my exercise. Again, getting out of here will put me back with health care that is reputable. Let's keep praying to get my appeal and be sent home to live out the rest of my life.

October 25, 2012

I have to go to the dentist. Yesterday, while eating, half of one of my teeth broke off. The nerve is exposed and painful. Fortunately, I have $8 left in my bank account, and they will take $7.50 of it that we must pay when we go to the dentist or doctor. Except for your generosity, I have had no checks for working coming in for almost three months. I should get a check for my new job that will be about $15 and not be completely broke.

May 13, 2012

In here, things crawl from day to day, and then something happens all at once. This week, I went to see the dentist. I have had a tooth problem for the last six months under the bridge that was put in almost thirty years ago. The tooth holding the back part of the bridge almost came apart from decay. So they cut the bridge off, the last two thirds of it, to get to the bad tooth and to pull it. When pulling it out, it broke off, so they had to dig the root out of my gum. Now I have a big gap, which they will not fix (the state will not pay for a new bridge). I wonder if it will ever heal. I can't run for the next few days because it may reopen the hole and start bleeding again. But maybe, next week I'll be on the track again. They'll have to try much harder to knock me down.

I Can See Clearly Now

My father's farsightedness started deteriorating in his middle age. He would stretch his arms out into a Frankenstein-like pose, squinting to read a newspaper, novel, or magazine. He had blurry vision without the aid of over-the-counter plastic readers that were scattered like Easter eggs throughout our house on the kitchen counter, sofa, and car dashboard. Several times a day, he would ask, "Where are my glasses?" By the time he got to prison in his midsixties, he relied on an annual updated eyeglass prescription from the local optometrist in order to drive, work on a computer, and scan restaurant menus. His eyes were also easily agitated by dust or dander, and he frequently used eyedrops, which were not readily available in prison. Consequently, he teared up regularly because his eyes were dry and irritated without eyedrops to provide relief. He was embarrassed by his bloodshot and watery eyes because it appeared he was crying, and he did not want to appear weak in front of fellow inmates. He carried a wad of toilet paper to wipe his eyes, which only caused more redness and inflammation.

He had at least two pairs and types of prescription eyeglasses, including progressive lenses and bifocals. He could not see clearly without his prescription glasses. My father became an avid reader in prison and heavily relied on a working pair of prescription glasses. If he didn't have glasses, it caused him headaches, panic, and dizziness. Unfortunately, replacing broken or misplaced prescription glasses in prison is very difficult. It can take several months to receive a new pair of glasses that are often inferior quality. Upgrading prescription glasses is also very difficult.

Again, like the dentist, seeing an optician or professional eye specialist is not available to inmates. My father was also starting to develop cataracts, clouding his vision, which contributed to him tripping and falling more often. Cataract surgery is generally considered elective and nonessential. After he took a tumble on the ice one winter, my father said, "The CO (correctional officer) told me to get up off the ground and if I wasn't blind yet just look out my one good eye." Trying to adequately function with poor vision in prison without proper assistance is another reason inmates are at risk.

October 15, 2007

I need your help. When I was in Dodge (the prison where I started), they examined my eyes and gave me glasses with bifocals. But last week, I accidentally sat down on those reading glasses.

*They broke in half, and no one here can or will repair them.
I went to the records department here and asked for a copy of my
eyeglass prescription. I am hoping you can order them and have
them shipped directly to me. They will not let you bring them to
me or mail them from your home address. They must come directly
from the company that makes them. The state will not provide two
pairs of glasses, one for reading and one for distance. If you can
do this, I will be very grateful. Please get the cheapest pair. This is
no place to wear designer glasses. I am sorry to cause you another
expense, and I will try not to always be asking.*

January 20, 2016

*Can you call about my eyeglasses? I sent in an order over a
month ago and want to make sure they are sent to me on the outside. When you call, can you explain to them that I will be out by
the end of February, and the order was sent in December with a
check for $26.48. I have no way to call the office from here.*

Relief for Reflux?

Acid reflux is another preexisting condition my father had
before he went to prison. His reflux would flare up when we had
spicy food, red meat, or even chocolate cake. These types of foods
would trigger his reflux symptoms. He had difficulty swallow-
ing, his face would turn a shade of red, he would start gagging,
and immediately excuse himself to go to the bathroom. I could
hear him vomiting, and he would return to the table to drink water
or attempt to finish his meal. In prison, his reflux persisted and
was exacerbated by limited choices in the cafeteria and obstructed
access to bathroom facilities due to security measures. He was so
worried about having an acid reflux attack in prison that he often
skipped meals. Over-the-counter remedies he would use before
prison, like heartburn medications or antacids, were cumbersome
to obtain and given only under supervision of an HSU nurse. If
medication was given, it was not regular enough to make a difference in an inmate's health.

March 10, 2010

I have been having stomach problems. At lunch, my stomach backs up and doesn't let me eat another spoonful. Years ago, I went to a clinic in Costa Rica about it. They put me to sleep and put a tube down my throat to take pictures inside of my stomach. The doctor said that the area that opens and closes to empty food out of my stomach was not working right, and when the door does not open, food backs up in my throat and will not let me eat anymore. He said I should have surgery to correct it. But I said "No thank you" and instead used a small white pill before I ate which allowed me to eat without the problem. But now I don't have the little white pills, and I have to leave the chow hall to puke then let my system rest. I guess I'll eat again tomorrow!

August 25, 2010

Health Services called me to review X-rays of my throat. They said because of my age, the nerves in my throat do no act right, and I get a reflex reaction that will not allow me to put another bite of food or drop of water into my throat. That's when I must throw up immediately as the food forces its way up to my mouth and must be released. They told me to eat soft foods, chew well, and drink water with my meals. That's easy to say, but I know it will happen again.

Help! My Hernia!

Shortly after my parents were married in 1962, my father had surgery to repair a hernia in his early twenties. According to my father, it was an invasive surgery, and he almost died on the operating table. Over fifty years later, my father's painful bulging hernia unfortunately returned, causing severe health complications, except this time he was elderly and in prison.

Scheduling a surgical procedure in prison requires a tremendous amount of classified coordination. Incarcerated patients who need to have surgery outside of a correctional facility are not given specific information when they will be transported due to security concerns. Restraints and shackles in a clinical setting seem excessive, especially when a patient is under a general anesthetic. Could my father feasibly plan an escape while a surgical procedure was underway?

The Health Insurance Portability and Accountability Act (HIPAA) of 1996 specifies requirements for maintaining patient confidentiality, but inmate privacy is not always a priority during health care procedures. My father felt exposed in every way from preoperative stress with blood draws, catheter, and IV insertions to postoperative anxiety with nausea, puss, and other bodily fluids exiting his body in the hospital room, all under the watchful eyes of correctional officers. Surgical procedures create a long list of vulnerabilities, including a loss of control. This loss is compounded in prison. Everything is tougher: adequate rest, pain management, and recovery.

September 18, 2012

Bad news. My hernia is back in the exact same place. It's getting very large. It's about the size of a golf ball pushing out after I eat or run. I will have to have another surgery. It is not considered an emergency, so it could be October or November.

October 16, 2012

No hernia operation yet, but I would think any day now. But with the Department of Corrections, it's best not to think in common sense terms and realize everything takes so much time here.

November 4, 2012

This week, I will go in for a blood draw to check out if I am in good shape for the surgery which will be sometime this month, I am told. Last week they gave me a physical, and they'll want to do an EKG this week before surgery to establish a baseline. I think the medical staff are concerned that I am seventy-two years old and want to make sure I'm ready for the knife.

April 10, 2013

I have worn the beads down on my rosary praying to the Blessed Mother of God for good health. This week, they took me out of here to the hospital nearby. It's so nice to be able to see freedom for a brief time to renew that wonderful feeling that there is still another world out there.

However, it's hard to forget this place as they put chains around my ankles so I can't hardly walk, let alone run. And they put a chain around my waist with handcuffs, of course. When I shuffled into the doctor's office with a guard on each side, I could see the fright on the receptionist's face. The doctor is a female surgeon, and she will be doing my surgery. When? Oh, they will not tell me so I cannot plan an escape with someone on the outside. For me, that would have to be a deer, rabbit, or maybe a racoon. Anyway, she said I will require a net to close up the wall tear. She said when the hernia is much smaller, they can simply sew it together, but mine is too large, so they must insert a net to replace the hole. I have to do all of it alone, with nobody waiting for me in the recovery room. Being alone is very hard for me.

May 20, 2013

The guard told me at 9:30 p.m. after final count not to eat or drink after midnight, so I knew my hernia surgery would be happening the next day. Sure enough, I left the facility at 6:15 a.m. the next morning to go to the hospital. They took me into surgery around 10:30 a.m. and had to use plastic cable ties around my ankles in the hospital bed even though two guards were in the operating room. They strapped both of my arms down on boards next to the operating table. One arm was for the blood pressure cuff, the other for the IV. The doctor came in and asked if I knew why I was there. I said, "Yes, to have my hernia repaired, so don't cut off my leg by mistake!" That got a big laugh from everyone in the operating room. After recovery, I was wheeled back to my room with two guards by my side and told by the nurses that the doctor said everything went well. When I got back to my cell, I was in pain. I want to go home. I am so sick of this confinement. It's far worse than surgery.

May 23, 2013

The operation was painful. They made a 5-inch cut just above my belly button to go in and place a net around the hernia. It's hard for me to pull up close to the desk as I am writing because my stomach is swollen. No running for six weeks.

Medicine for MRSA

Infections can be more common in prison because of the communal environment and unsanitary conditions. Lack of hand-washing and attention to cuts or scrapes on the skin can contribute to outbreaks. MRSA (methicillin-resistant *Staphylococcus aureus*) is a staph skin infection and can be very contagious. It spreads through direct contact with another person who has the infection. My father "accidentally" discovered he had MRSA.

August 8, 2012

I woke up a few weeks ago with a knot under my right arm about the size of a plum. It was hard and had a puss pocket in the middle. I squeezed it to drain the poison, and that helped. The next day, it closed up, and the puss formed again. I think it is a spider bite because we see a lot of spiders in this place. I broke it open again to drain but don't have a Band-aid, so it catches on my sheets when I roll over at night. I hope it goes away.

September 20, 2012

I was called up to HSU to get my shingles shot, but the nurse said they sent the wrong shot. While I was there, I asked the nurse to look at what I thought was a spider bite on my leg.

At that point, my leg was swollen and very red. I rolled up my pant leg, and she said, "No, that is not a spider bite. It's MRSA, which is a staph infection." She said she'd start me on antibiotics and told me to check the wound each morning. She said if I have a lot of pain, she'd write me a note to stay in my cell all day and not go to work. These health setbacks are scary.

Cancer Diagnosis

As an only child, the first two most important relationships I had were with my parents. My father wrote to me about his cancer diagnosis when he was seventy-five years old, and a familiar shock wave rattled inside of me. I had already lost my mother to the ravages of cancer at forty-nine years old. The thought of my only living parent suffering with cancer all over again was unbearable. Unlike my mother's cancer battle that was filled with encouragement and peace to help carry her as gently as possible into God's arms, my father's cancer battle would be isolated and anonymous in prison. Who cares about a pedophile who is dying? Many would say he deserves to die in the worst way possible. But he was still my father. He was still human.

A list of questions kept me up at night, off balance, worried, helpless. How could my father take care of himself in a prison cell after chemotherapy? Who would monitor his medication? Were any comforts offered to him to help him stabilize and gain strength? Would he get extra blankets, clean underwear, ice packs, pain medication? When could I begin asking questions about his treatments and procedures? What phone numbers could I call to talk with his medical team? What caregiving options were there for families of inmates with a terminal illness?

My mother was blessed with a substantial support system during her cancer treatments. My uncle and aunt (my mother's brother and his wife) frequently came to our house to cook, clean, and help create a list of key contacts, including doctors, nurses, pharmacists, and emergency personnel. A group of women we called neighborhood angels brought us weekly homemade meals, multiple friends and family took turns driving her to doctor's appointments, walking with her, praying the rosary, dressing her in colorful scarves when she lost her hair, bathing her with lavender scented soaps, playing soothing meditative music, reading magazines, rubbing her feet with peppermint oil, watching television, holding her hand, and delivering flowers, cards, and balloons for encouragement. This circle of support surrounded our family during our lowest points, lifting us up in spirit with prayer and love. My mother left indelible memories for so many.

Despite all the experimental treatments, medications, well wishes, and positive motivation to persevere, cancer still took her. I watched my mother wither away, dropping dramatic amounts of weight from her small frame until she was only eighty pounds, with her shoulder blades rising from her bony back, creating a sprawling map of blue veins underneath her thin skin. Her hair came out in clumps until tiny wisps of black ran across her forehead, and she tried covering her naked head with an itchy nylon wig. She lost control of her bowels, her speech, and her sight. We were there with her every step of the way. My mother was loved, celebrated, and respected. She died at home with comfort and dignity. But what would happen during my father's cancer diagnosis? What type of support would he receive? Would he be left to die alone?

September 20, 2015

Enclosed is my diagnosis telling about my lymphoma cancer. I asked my doctor to give me something to read about the disease and had a copy made. It used to be called Waldenstrom macroglobulinemia, a rare type of cancer that begins in the white blood cells, your bone marrow creates too may cells, crowding out healthy cells. With under ten cases per million per year in the United States, it is a rare but treatable form of cancer.

Between the CT scan and the most recent bone marrow test, the doctor and his staff concluded that this is the type of cancer I have. So now I start chemotherapy for the next month. I have had a few health scares here, but cancer is scarier. Hopefully, the treatment will turn my platelets back to normal because they said they are at a very low count.

My lawyer called, and we are going to move forward with a compassionate release, which requires an age of at least sixty-three years old, which I have already beat by ten years and a serious disease. I would qualify cancer as serious.

I'm not going to stop my life because of cancer. I'm pleased the doctors found out what it is and now can go forward with a plan to slow down the cancer. I don't expect God to do it alone.

September 24, 2015

This past week, I spent eight hours at the hospital. I was given my first series of chemo treatments. The first half hour felt like a burning sensation in my hand, and I had a bad headache. Then out of nowhere, I got some really sharp pains in my lower back. So they had to stop the chemo and give me a steroid shot and a saline solution drip to ease the pain. Then they started the chemo drip again at half of the speed for the next several hours. Finally, in the eighth hour, the treatment was completed. The doctor reminded me that the next treatment was in a week or so and that would be less severe because my system is getting used to the poison. I do not look forward to that. After the next round, my hair will start to come out, and I'll be on my way toward being bald. I remember when Mom lost all her beautiful hair during her chemo treatments.

September 30, 2015

The big "C" is trying to slow me down. The release of certain elderly inmates from this place is very different; even though I meet the guidelines, the release committee does not allow me to be present. The possible release until recently was decided in a court, but now the DOC has taken over that part instead of a judge. My lawyer will submit my story with medical receipts to back up the claim, but even my lawyer can't be there in person. So there is no opportunity to bring in the human part of the request. All they do is look through the cold paperwork and say yes or no. From what I hear, many try, but few are successful in getting a release. So all I can do is pray that there will be mercy in their hearts.

I continue with my chemo treatment. Even though it took months of testing, scans, and blood draws, I can't ask for a second opinion. The prison doesn't allow that. The standard treatment is chemo, surgery, and radiation. There's no guarantee that these will help to slow down the cancer or even force the cancer to grow. I have heard there are alternative therapies, but I can't use the Internet to check them out. Could you do some more research and send it to me?

October 7, 2015

Yesterday, they called me to HSU. They said you had been asking for my medical information, but I would have to sign a release form first for them to give you whatever is in my file or speak with you verbally on the phone. This week, I went for my third chemo treatment. I didn't throw up or have a headache this time. You remember that Mom got sick for three or four days after she had her chemo treatments. But then again, Mom was so far along in her cancer that they had to give her a very strong mixture of chemicals to have any effect on her cancer. My mixture is much less severe. I don't share my health situation with anyone on the inside.

October 11, 2015

Here at the HSU in prison, they can do little for me as I am now a patient of UW Madison. I have not been given a special diet in here, just the same old food. My doctor said if he does not see results in this next round of chemo, he would like to send me to the infirmary at the maximum state prison. But that is where they send people to die. I am not going there! They also offer hospice there, and that I will not need.

May 16, 2015

This past week, I spent most of the day, from 6:00 a.m.–3:00 p.m. riding for two hours one way to the hospital to see a hematologist. I gave blood twice and talked with him to better understand why my platelets have dropped to one third of where they should be. He said he could not give me an answer until we go through the next three months of bloodwork and MRI to scan my vital organs, including spleen and colon to see if the platelets are being used up faster than they should. As my dad used to tell me, the best things in life always take longer, so don't give up hope.

July 30, 2015

The normal platelet count is ninety, and mine has been forty and still dipping. I don't have a lot of energy lately. I'd like to share copies of my medical records with you, but in prison, it is difficult to share anything, much less get a copy.

August 15, 2015

I went to the doctor's office again today, this time in a wheel-chair in shackles on my feet and handcuffed. Before I arrived, I had to get another blood draw at the nurses' station. While I was sitting there with a needle in my arm, two guards hovered over me, but the nurses were singing songs along with the radio. They were smiling and called me by my first name. They were so caring and treated me like a human.

Splenectomy in Shackles

Less than a year after my father's cancer diagnosis, additional underlying problems began to emerge. He told me about severe stomach pain and eventually found out he had an enlarged spleen. The spleen is a small organ located on the left side of your abdomen under the rib cage. This organ is part of your immune system and helps to fight off infections while also filtering damaged cells out of the bloodstream, but this was concerning because the prison environment is unsanitary, and I was concerned he would become even sicker.

My father was facing yet another surgery alone in prison. I could identify with some of the fears he may have had leading up to his splenectomy in 2016. I had my own health scare in June 2020. I was rushed to the emergency room with sudden severe upper abdominal pain and diagnosed with pancreatitis, a painful inflammation in my pancreas. My pancreatitis was caused by gall-stones. Pancreas functions include making fluids and enzymes to break down the food you eat as part of the digestive process. When a stone leaves the gallbladder, it can block the opening from the pancreas to the small intestine and is extremely painful and life-threatening if not treated.

Because of COVID-19 health regulations, I was not allowed any visitors in the hospital. I was alone in a hospital bed for a week before the doctors determined that my pancreas was no longer inflamed and they could perform gallbladder removal surgery. It was lonely and depressing on an isolated floor with almost no one seeing me for hours at a time, to be surrounded by strangers who were also suffering from illness and could not be accompanied by their loved ones for comfort. We were all quarantined with masks on in our isolated rooms, propped up on inflatable mattresses that changed pressure to ward off bed sores.

Walking down the maze of hospital corridors and vast empty hallways was like being in a scene from the horror movie *The Shining* (1980). I thought I would turn the corner and see the Grady twins eerily staring at me in their matching light blue dresses. Even after I came out of the surgical recovery room, no family members were allowed to join me. I faced fear and pain completely on my own in the hospital, but unlike my father, I wasn't shackled to my bed in cold steel restraints, and I got to look forward to my family picking me up, taking care of me, and bringing me home.

July 11, 2015

Finally, some bits and pieces are coming through about my health problem. I'll return to the blood doctor at the hospital, and hopefully, he can tell me about plans for future healing. The tests have shown my spleen is enlarged, which has squeezed the blood platelets, not allowing for more to be produced, which is why the platelets are dangerously low. All the blood tests show that the platelet count continues to go down further from normal. They have analyzed my blood up, down, and in between. So now the key to my spleen healing is to find out where in my body the infection is coming from. The next step is to see a rheumatologist to see if he can find the source of the infection. I have to keep moving to push

*away the temptation to feel sorry for myself. That is not an option!
I've got a lot more to do in this world.*

September 5, 2015

*Thank you for your letter and research about my spleen. I
know you can't contact my prison doctor. Oh, the rules! I have
discomfort off and on, like a sore stomach pain. I have a list of
questions for the doctor already prepared for my next appointment—whenever that will be? They do not tell us in advance for
security reasons, so I will most likely find out at 5 a.m. that I'll be
in a secured vehicle to go to an appointment the same day.*

November 15, 2015

*I saw the doctor again. He does not want to consider radi-
ation on my spleen because like the chemo, it could have more
harmful effects than good on my body. Once I know more about
the condition of my spleen, I'll talk with a surgeon to learn more
about the procedure and risk involved in removing it. All this is
based on the fact that my cancer has no cure at this time, but it can
be treated provided it helps to slow down the disease.*

December 27, 2015

*At my last doctor's appointment, I made the decision to have
my spleen removed instead of waiting for an emergency when I
could start bleeding internally as my platelet count continues to
drop close to zero, which results in bleeding. I would like to have
my surgery in January in order to have a few weeks of recovery
before meeting in February with the Parole Review Board. That
way, if I do win a release, at least I'll be able to walk out of here
on my own power.*

January 20, 2016

*I should be having my surgery by February first. But things
take so long around here. I meet with parole on February 11
to finalize a date for dismissal. I am nervous that it's so close
together, but I do need the surgery before I get out. I want to get*

out of here by February 26 and picked up by the Walworth County Deputy and taken to the probation office.

As I sit here on my plastic chair at my desk writing to you, my back is reminding me of the accident I had two days ago coming back from my job at canteen. I was tired and not paying attention as I crossed the icy street. In a flash, my legs went straight up in the air, and I landed flat on my back. Ouch! Another inmate walking a few yards back ran to my aid and helped me to stand up. I was stunned and a little dizzy. Once I got myself under control, the pain kicked in.

They wanted to take me to HSU, and I said "No" because I do not think anything is broken. I could still walk and wiggle my toes. Needless to say, that night I didn't sleep very well because I could not get comfortable. Thank God I didn't land on my hip because I hear too many stories of old people breaking hips, and they are never the same again. Hopefully, it's just a bad bruise and I'll be back to running after the New Year. My back is getting better, and thankfully, my ribcage is also improving. For a while, I could feel each breath in each rib.

February 7, 2016

I am so excited to leave this place forever. But before I go, I still need my surgery. The surgeon was gone for a month over the holidays, and my doctor misunderstands the urgency of getting this operation done before I get out of here. I won't have insurance for at least a few months on the outside. It's so frustrating to be sick, but even more frustrating to be sick in prison because I have no direct communication with my doctor.

February 17, 2016

This morning, I went to HSU to get a Meningococcal vaccine. My doctor has been ordering a series of vaccines for me lately that will help fend off the disease when my spleen is removed. The spleen serves as a filter to fight off many diseases.

Any obstacles must be put aside because God always finds a way for us to embrace the fruits of our suffering. I will not give up hope, I will keep fighting. Worry will hold back my healing.

February 23, 2016

I have not had my surgery yet. They continue to take blood each week to monitor my cancer. My doctor wants me to fast every Sunday from 6:00 p.m. to 6:30 a.m. before the blood draw on Monday mornings. That's fine with me because I don't eat much in the evening anyway, and it reminds me to keep fighting to control my cancer because I have a lot of things to do when I get out of here.

March 2, 2016

Your letters are so inspiring to my desire to overcome my illness. I learn from each letter and always look forward to the next one. I read recently in a book about Gustave Flaubert, nineteenth century French author of Madame Bovary *(1857), and* Sentimental Education *(1869) that he toiled over word choice. Somewhere in your studies as a Ph.D., you probably read about him. Anyway, Flaubert said, "The art of writing is the art of discovering what you believe." It really is all about choosing words. I know words matter. They matter here in prison. They matter in court documents; they matter in tone and inflection. You have spent most of your life chasing the exact word or right word. It's all about style and expression, right, morning star? So delicate, so true.*

April 9, 2016

My spleen is gone! I was on the operating table for four hours. My lower abdomen is black and blue from the waist down.

April 17, 2016

My seventy-sixth birthday was spent lying down to rest and give my spleen surgery a chance to heal. It's only been a few weeks since the operation, and the surgeon said I will be in recover for at least four to six weeks longer. The work done to remove my spleen moved a lot around, and I am very sore in my midsection. I don't feel well enough for a visit just yet, so please wait.

May 1, 2016

I am spleenless and still kicking. I saw my doctor again this week to see how my platelet count is doing. The surgeon said I could live without my spleen, so I immediately asked, "For how long?" I received another letter from a friend. Being in prison, I often think that the only people who feel I have any worth are you and your husband. So I was surprised to read her opening sentence, "I enjoy and appreciate your nice letters. They are so uplifting, and for you to continue to be strong in your faith is so admirable." Life is full of uncertainties, but God knows what he will give us next. Our job is to position ourselves for a blessing by stepping out in faith.

On Pins and Needles

My father's list of ailments grew. He developed neuropathic syndromes related to his cancer. His newest pain companion was peripheral neuropathy, which caused numbness, tingling, and pain in his legs and feet. He felt like he was constantly being stuck with pins and needles.

June 20, 2016

I have developed a new symptom which is one of the many attached to my cancer. I have peripheral neuropathy, which can be painful. The sensation in my legs and feet is one of needles and pins being stuck into my skin. Ouch! Running each day does not help, but I keep going. I just need to accept the fact that things will get worse as I continue to fight back.

September 15, 2016

The Tylenol I take has little if any pain relief for me. There are times when the pins and needles in my arms, legs, and back wake me up, and I try for an hour or two to get back to sleep. But

251

I am not deterred. I will continue to fight this cancer. The greater pain is not being able to see you on a regular basis and not being able to see Mom at all. I think this is my purgatory right here on earth.

October 2, 2016

I have a good feeling I will see the "pins and needles" doctor sometime this week. It's been almost two months since my doctor made the appointment. Can they wait any longer? The Tylenol has become useless. I just want to get to the bottom of these new symptoms and find out what I can do to get rid of the constant pain. Unfortunately, the hot shower each morning only increases the pain as I think the hot water makes the pins and needles come to the surface of my skin even more. I pray for some relief.

I have completed my comprehensive report that I will present to the parole commissioner at our next meeting. I have included a month-by-month journal of the past fifteen months since my cancer was discovered. He has to know how serious my disease is and why I need a compassionate release. Unfortunately, I can't pin a picture of Mom inside of my suit coat because they don't allow that. But I know she will be with me during the meeting. Let's pray the outcome is favorable.

November 11, 2016

My confidence was shaken this week because I learned from HSU that my next appointment for a test to determine what is causing the pins and needles is not scheduled until February, three months from now. The pain is so bad that when I get out of bed each morning, the pain forces me to sit back down again because I lose muscle control in my legs.

The pins and needles have weakened my legs combined with the meds that are supposed to take the pins and needles away turns out not to be a good mix for my running. At the end of my 3-mile run the other day, the toe of my shoe caught the gravel, and I went face down on the concrete. They rushed me up to HSU to stop the bleeding. With my low platelet count, I bleed very easy, so the doctor said I should go to the ER. He wanted a scan of my brain to make certain I had no bleeding on my brain because I fell on my head.

At the ER, I had to have several X-rays on my arm and shoulder. I was admitted around 11:00 a.m., and by 3:30 p.m., no one had asked if I was hungry. They finally brought me a turkey sandwich. Nothing was broken, so they patched me up and sent me back to prison. The next day, I woke up with both eyes black and blue and an egg-sized bump on my forehead. So the other inmates started calling me names like racoon, batman, the lone ranger because of my black-and-blue face. It's starting to fade, and now they scream, "Yo, gramps, where's your mask?"

February 6, 2017

Please do not worry about my compassionate release. My attorney and I have been working, and it will most likely be a long, tiring, and discouraging journey. Thank you for taking your time to call my attorney so you could better understand why Illinois is not an option for me. Our appeal to the decision will involve why after ten years is the mother of my victim able to stop my release. It's not a question of anyone deserving forgiveness; no one deserves it. That is the point of forgiveness. It is undeserved mercy and grace extended to someone to release them from guilt. Forgiveness removes the need for punishment and retribution. God has forgiven me.

All this is in God's hands at this time. He knows better than I know myself. He knows my heart and my hope in him. He can at his timing release me from this prison. All we can do is not worry, stay positive, and pray.

February 26, 2017

I saw my doctor again, and he asked why I stopped taking the gabapentin, the medication he gave me for the neuropathy pain. I told him the side effects were too powerful for me. I needed something to heal the nerve damage but not this particular drug. In the meantime, my pain is ten times more intense than even after run-

ning my first marathon. So for now, I'll substitute prayer for pain. I believe that will be best for healing.

I finally got my cancer doctor to laugh. I told him laughter is good for you. It heals. He is very bright and also very serious. It's been my goal for the last several appointments to get him to laugh.

April 27, 2017

Please do not plan a visit with me. I will have multiple appointments with doctors and maybe an overnight for testing my "pins and needles." I'm really tired of living with the pain each day, and the drugs are making me so dizzy and loss of muscle control. Crazy side effects.

Don't buy any sewing needles. I have plenty each morning sticking in my legs! No spleen, but I have a lot of needles, and the sensation hurts. It's always something!

May 27, 2017

I went to the neurology doctor today, and she said my pins and needles testing showed that the nerve damage can't be repaired. All they can do now is give me pain pills. I told her I don't want to get hooked on strong pain medication. So we talked about what else could be done. She recommended trying Capsaicin cream and apply it three times per day on my legs. It is made with hot chili peppers, so until your shins get used to it, the burning is tough. But I'd rather have that if it works than take medication every day. So I guess now I'll have hot pins and needles!

June 9, 2017

I refuse to accept the doctor telling me that my nerves can't be healed and I'll need pain medication for the rest of my life. I'm not going to walk around on pain pills, at least not yet. I've been trying to train my mind along with prayer to reduce the pain and even prove the doctor wrong about not begin able to heal the damage. I will not give up! I believe fighting my health problems will be much easier when I am out of this environment. No one knows

I have cancer here. I just thank God I can move. Everything is difficult here. It's hard to heal.

August 17, 2017

I finally got my new medication back from HSU. I think they lost the prescription and had to reorder. Who knows? The name of the drug for my peripheral neuropathy is duloxetine. I have very little information about the drug and would like you to look it up on the Internet so I will know what the side effects are when taking it. My most effective drug is the love of God.

September 22, 2017

I walked to the Administration Building to sign in, but when I arrived, the sergeant told me not to sign in. I told him I was late. He responded, "You're never late." He said all the incoming and outgoing calls were down, and he wasn't sure when they would be up and running again.

No exercise again this week. I have my first cold in the last two years, and it's a doozy. With my platelet count still low, it takes longer than normal to get through any disease. It's in my chest and throat. I'm coughing a lot. The doctor here has me on an antibiotic along with Mucinex to break up the congestion. But if I'm going to court, I'll be there if I have to walk to the Walworth County Jail.

October 3, 2017

I didn't know that this last chemo treatment would be so bad. I have been in the hospital for five days. I could not call you from the hospital. Finally, I did ask the staff to call you and tell you where I am. You can get more information by talking with the nurse on my floor. I hope you are able to call. I thought I would be going back to Fox Lake, but instead, they brought me to the infirmary at Dodge for a few days to monitor the progress in getting the blood count down. I'm sorry I can't call you or read your letters because I am not at Fox Lake right now.

Last Stages of Leukemia

My father was diagnosed with a second cancer, acute myeloid leukemia, in September 2017. One month later, he died in a prison hospice facility in Wisconsin. He was seventy-seven years old. He was never getting out of prison alive.

The hospital-based clinicians I spoke with during that month were compassionate and humane. They provided me with as much detail as possible regarding his condition. It was the first time I experienced a positive collaboration between health care and the prison system.

I called and spoke with a few nurses at Fox Lake Correctional facility. They told me he was diagnosed with AML (acute myeloid leukemia) on September 24. I took notes as the nurse rapidly reviewed his conditions and testing over the phone with me.

His bloodwork was complete, and his white blood count was elevated. On September 27, he was urgently admitted to hematology for an appointment. He was then sent to the infirmary at Dodge, a maximum-security prison. He now needed to wear a mask at all times to prevent possible infections. They would provide him with antiviral medications. He had no prospective time line, but it was fatal.

On September 28, he had another appointment with the doctor for a biopsy. He spent five days in the hospital from September 29 to October 3. His first lymphoma was diagnosed in 2015, but this was another type of cancer, more aggressive and deadly. He would not be eligible for a transfusion and at this point would be made comfortable upon his transfer to a prison hospice facility. The nursing staff told me to start preparing for his death.

This was the last letter my father wrote to me, less than two weeks before he died on October 26, 2017, in a maximum state prison in Wisconsin. A staff nurse called me to tell me my father died. He took his last breath alone on a Thursday morning, chained to a hospital bed. After a decade of being institutionalized, he was finally free.

October 15, 2017

It's been a hectic two weeks for me, but now, I'm back in my room at Fox Lake. The whole time I was in the hospital and one day in the infirmary at Dodge prison. You have been my rock since the day I started here. Always know that Mom and I are so proud of you and your family. I thank God for my beautiful daughter.

I told the hospital to contact you to at least tell you how I was doing. I am back in my cell, getting everything put back in place. I read in your last letter that you would be here on September twenty-ninth. I hope you called first because as you know I went to the hospital on September twenty-sixth and wasn't here.

The last ten days have been a scare for me, and the biggest problem was that I could not write you about what was going on with my cancer. I'll try to explain by use of a time line so you will know my condition and treatment for the past several days.

On September 23, I was called to HSU to see the doctor. My blood draw was processed, and white blood cells skyrocketed to the point that they sent me to the hospital to see my doctor. They would not give me five minutes to go back to my unit to get my reading glasses. When the doctor came to the exam room, he had a somber face.

He explained the new cancer, which was leukemia, an acute growing cancer unlike my first cancer that was a slow grower. He started to tear up and said, "Remember we have talked in the past that you have a few years left on this earth." He said the leukemia at my age is rapid. So I was admitted to the hospital immediately. I had chemo for six days around the clock. This would bring the white blood cell count down because I could not live long at that high count. So after six days (and another bone marrow stab in the back, not fun at all), they released me and sent me to the infirmary at Dodge.

I thought I was going back to Fox Lake. When I arrived, they checked me out, and my first question was, "How do I get out of here?" Dodge is a place they send very ill inmates to die.

There is nothing you can do for me there. They said I could only be released from this doctor who would see me in the morn-

ing. So that's when I said I have no glasses and no stamped envelopes to let my daughter know where I am. So they gave me a stamped envelope and a tiny writing pad, and I struggled for the better part of an hour to at least try to write with my head almost touching the pad.

The next morning, they released me back to Fox Lake. I'm doing okay. I'm not gone yet! I need to stay strong for what I hope will be my last hearing on compassionate release back at court in Walworth on Friday, October thirteenth. But I know that your prayers and God's help will get me to court, and we'll see what happens.

Sorry about my handwriting, but I think all the medication has made it more difficult to print in my old sloppy handwriting. But I will write in a dark room so I never lose our connection. I am so thankful for you.

God bless and remember to love one another. I'm still kicking! I love and miss you.

CHAPTER 11

Mayday, Mayday

The death of any loved parent is an incalculable lasting blow. Because no one ever loves you again like that.

—Brenda Ueland

"Help me!" signals a life-threatening emergency when immediate assistance is needed. One early morning in October 2017, my father made his only emergency phone call to me before he was transferred from a minimum-security prison where he had served over ten years to a maximum-security infirmary, where he would die within two weeks.

The nurse told me prior to his death that my father was no longer permitted in the general population at Fox Lake Correctional Institution because he was at risk for infection, his mobility was limited, and he needed more intensive care during his late stages of cancer. Consequently, he was transferred to Dodge Correctional Institution, the prison hospice facility in Waupun, Wisconsin. Waupun is informally known as "Prison City" because of the four prisons in the area that employ over one thousand security officers. My father resisted going to the infirmary because he knew that was where end-of-life services were available, and Dodge was where inmates went to die.

My cell phone rang at 8:00 a.m., with the caller ID display "Toll-free number." A prison nurse announced this call was com-

259

ing from Fox Lake Correctional Institution, and she held the phone to my father's mouth. He began talking, his breath labored as he whispered, "I left a few things for you. Not much. I don't know when I can talk again. Sorry. Love you." Twenty last words.

I have replayed his words over and over, searching for a deeper meaning. They were not particularly grandiose or profound utterances. In contrast, when Benjamin Franklin died, his seven last words were, "A dying man can do nothing easy." George Orwell's eight last words, "At fifty, everyone has the face he deserves." And Emily Dickenson's nine last words, "I must go in, for the fog is rising." Was I expecting goosebumps listening to my father's last words? Did I want him to perform a more powerful and detailed act of contrition? Was I searching for a deathbed confession? My reply sputtered and stopped when the nurse told me it was time to go. The phone call only lasted a few minutes.

The Department of Corrections (DOC) first started this prison hospice, program ten years earlier in 2007 to assist a growing number of older inmates who needed palliative care. Inmates in the hospice prison program have chronic or terminal illnesses and have opted against extraordinary means to prolong life. The infirmary dedicates six rooms in the sixty-two-bed hospital for 24-7 nursing care. Inmate volunteers receive training in hospice philosophy and are assigned to sit with seriously ill inmates to help provide companionship. Although my father's hospice stay was short, many inmates can linger in the hospice program for up to six months.

When my father went to Dodge, he was in a secured unit within a prison hospital. The medical staff had a wide variety of experience, and a team of nurses was exceptionally attentive in caring for my father. Although protocol requires that nurses do not share personal information with prisoners or ask inmates personal questions, when my father first arrived at Dodge lucid and alert, he provided my contact information to the nurses assigned to his room, and they called me every day, sometimes twice a day, until his time of his death.

During our conversations, the nursing staff appeared non-judgmental and treated my father with compassion. One nurse told me on the third day of my father's hospice stay that he asked for a Sprite, and she offered him a bendable straw so he could reach the drink easily. She told me after eight days in hospice, he was no longer eating solid foods, but he did have some chicken broth and seemed to enjoy the cold sugary soda because he asked for another can of Sprite a few hours later because it did not make him vomit. She told me he had a *Bible* on his nightstand but did not see him read it. She fluffed his pillow. The staff kept the television on for him, but he slept for most of the day and was in and out of consciousness.

Despite being tired and weak during most of the time in prison hospice, my father's ankle was still chained to the bed, and he was under the watchful eyes of multiple security officers at all times. Was his pain part of his punishment? Did he deserve this final humiliation before dying? I didn't want him to be in pain. I didn't want him to be treated unfairly during his last days on Earth. Did some of the prison medical staff feel the same way? Did they also grapple with very complicated emotions like trust and safety while caring for my father?

There are only seventy-five prison hospice programs in the United States but more than one thousand state prisons. The hospice services vary depending on the facility's resources. A professional team at most prison hospices is similar to those outside of prisons, including a physician, nurse, and case manager or social worker. Social workers help connect prisoners and their families with resources and support they need. Could the hospice care my mother experienced really be replicated for my father in prison? Would he truly be cared for, or would he be considered less than? The stakes were high. Dying was his only way out of prison. He still deserved to face death with dignity.

Monarch Mom

My mother died on June 25, 1990, when I was twenty-two years old. According to the medical examiner's report, her cause of death was carcinoma of the lungs with metastasis to the bone and liver. She died at forty-nine. I believe in signs that help us feel like the people we love are still with us even though they are physically absent. Whether it's a song, scent, or line from a movie that resonates at just the right moment, I believe these cosmic signals allow us to make connections with the soul and our surroundings. There are guardian angels looking out for us, and it is comforting for me to visualize the people we love in the heavenly skies above.

It is no surprise now when a monarch butterfly appears at just the right time, my family will look at each other and exclaim in unison, "It's a sign!" The butterfly is a symbol of transformation, hope, and future happiness. I like to think a butterfly's wings are powered by possibility. When my mother died, I started seeing monarch butterflies during rare and beautiful moments in my life. There are many examples over the years, but some of the most memorable include a monarch butterfly landed on the sleeve of my wedding dress while we were outside taking pictures, another monarch flew through the window of an academic building when I was defending my doctoral dissertation, a monarch landed on the car seat as we were buckling our newborn baby to take her home for the first time, and another monarch fluttered around our youngest daughter's painting at a school art exhibit. Even though our daughters never had the chance to meet my mother, they know my "monarch mom" as a sign of protection, love, and faith.

I've often written about my mother in published poems, articles, teaching, and travel blogs. She was my hero because of her influence, her values, her work ethic, her kindness. Her legacy of altruism lives on in our family. On her tombstone, it reads, "A lifetime of giving to others." Additionally, my mother's teaching career was impressive; she gravitated toward teaching in schools in low-income areas where students often had low test scores and high dropout rates. She made it her life's work to try and help students overcome obstacles in their lives that often included violence, drug addiction, and teenage pregnancy. She was a tough love teacher who pushed students to explore their potential and seek opportunities personally and professionally.

The word "education" is derived from the Latin *educare*, literally translated "to bring out of" or "to lead forth." It seemed natural to become enamored with my mother's lessons in endurance. After thirty years of teaching in a variety of settings, her final job title as "educator" was at the Illinois Youth Center (IYC), a level-one maximum-security juvenile detention facility for girls. She taught from 1985 to 1990 with a group of seventy-five girls; their average age was seventeen. My mother worked with academically underprepared students in remediation classes. Many students struggled with literacy required for advancement toward a degree or certificate. The facility provided GED and high school diploma academic services. She inspired students to earn their credentials, no matter what.

My mother refused to stop teaching even when she was ravaged with cancer and tumors peppered her spine, migraine headaches became the norm, and cramps in her fingers stopped her from holding a pen. My mother brought bed pillows with her to the car every morning to help soften the seat as she commuted to work. She persisted in grading every assignment, even if it meant splitting the work between short naps for recovery from multiple aches and pains. Her principal finally had to ask her to no longer come to the classroom because she was falling asleep as a side effect of several medications she was taking. She reluctantly stopped working only nine months before she died. She did not want to leave her students in the middle of the school year. My mother was a warrior.

The funeral visitation for my mother was packed with a sympathy line that stretched around the corner and down the block with former students, teachers, and administrators waiting to express what a positive impact she made in their lives. The students at IYC made a booklet of letters bound with a purple construction paper cover and pink ribbon, and their memoires of her remain in my heart.

When my mother died, I had just graduated from college. I tried to adjust, shifting my focus to pursuing additional degrees in higher education and eventually pursuing a teaching position myself. As her only child, I was inspired by her dedication to teaching, and I returned to school to complete my master's degree in writing and doctorate in education. Over thirty years after my mother taught at IYC, I am currently collaborating with a colleague in criminal justice to teach a learning community course at IYC and follow in my mother's footsteps in the same facility where she last interacted with students. I will continue listening to students' stories in her honor.

My mother left a void in my father's heart he could not refill. In his letters, he often pulled an invisible tether to bring me closer to him, tightening his manipulative grip by using her death as a method of control. He knew how much I adored my mother and wanted to please her. Sometimes, it appeared he used our mother-daughter relationship to make sure our father-daughter relationship continued while he was away in prison.

She's Gone, but Not Forgotten

June 6, 2008

I think about Mom a lot. We shared almost thirty-two years together on this Earth. She was a very brave woman. Mom knew more about her cancer than many of the doctors. She would ask question after question and said it was her body, and she wanted to know what was going on and what the doctors were going to do about it. We love and miss her and will never forget her.

June 13, 2008

It's hard to believe that at the end of this month, Mom was taken from us eighteen years ago. I pray, miss, and love her every day. I will never understand why we had to be separated by death. I know she was in so much pain before God took her home.

Mom loved bright yellow marigolds. If you go visit her grave this month, please take a pot of her favorite flower and set it next to her marker so she knows I did not forget. Remembering all the wonderful times we shared helps me get through the valley of this journey.

May 8, 2010

Another week has gone by. Being here is like winding a clock each day, knowing one day you'll wind it for the last time with nobody ever seeing the clock. Time comes and time goes in an endless circle to nowhere. When I am blessed to join together with Mom again for eternity, I will ask God why he took her home so early. That's the question that's been on my mind every day for over twenty years now.

June 9, 2010

Thanks for your letter and pictures. These are my only connection to life, not simply existence, which is what I have here. During the weeks before Mom's death, we talked a lot about quality of life. Although she was afraid to leave us and wanted to be reassured that we would never forget her, she said that her time near the end was only existence, not life. On this month of her twentieth anniversary of her death, I am reminded of the wonderful life we celebrated together and tell her in my prayers each day that I know now what she meant to simply exist, not live. With hope gone, what is there to live for?

She'll be dancing in heaven and telling the angels about her daughter. Remember, August 4 is Mom's birthday. Don't worry, Mom, we will never forget you or stop praying for you.

Nobody I knew has ever had a love and a wife that I had in your mom.

April 23, 2011

I am sorry to hear about your friends' mom who has breast cancer. It's very hard on her but equally hard on her loving husband. I have memories of your mom's fight to overcome cancer that I never shared. I remember the details such as the time I walked into the bathroom and Mom was crying over the sink with a brush in her hand and clumps of her hair falling into the sink. What a horrible sight after having such beautiful hair since the day I met her at University of Illinois. There she was, twenty-eight years later, losing those beautiful long locks of hair.

Or the time I had to learn how to give her morphine shots in her arm, then stomach, then feet because all areas from previous shots were black and blue. The nights were always the most difficult times when I would sit next to her bed in our master bedroom and talk and pray, trying my best to comfort her and not succeeding. But if there was one thing she understood and heard from me on many of those nights, she knew when I said how much I loved her. I could look into her wide, open eyes, her eyes of pain and despair and see she enjoyed when I told her "I love you." I'm not sure if it helped her physical pain, but I want to believe it took away the pain in her heart. I shared my life with this woman since August 4, 1962, and will never forget her.

January 1, 2013

Thank you for going to Mom's grave with the annual mini-Christmas tree and paper ornament wishes. I loved your daughter's response, "I know she gets the messages in heaven because when we visit her grave again, the messages are faded."

It must be hard for you to walk in town and look across the river to see the back of our house where your vibrant and beautiful Mom was, and back then, I was a "real" father. We are both gone now. I pray that God's tremendous love in your heart will heal.

Last Rites

My father applied many times for a compassionate release, but the courts refused each of his requests. Compassionate release is when inmates may be eligible for immediate early release on grounds of "particularly extraordinary or compelling circumstances which could not reasonably have been foreseen by the court at the time of sentencing." The policy grants judges the authority to order the release of sick and elderly inmates to provide them a chance to spend their final days outside of a prison cell. It was first implemented in the 1970s, but policies vary between states. Some states, like California and Maryland, distinguish between "geriatric release," which is age-dependent and "compassionate release," which offers early release for inmates who are ill.

During the two weeks my father was in the infirmary at Dodge Correctional Institution, I received a flurry of phone calls from his attorney, trying to make a last attempt at approval for compassionate release and request for a state transfer to move in with me during the last few weeks of his life. However, I did not believe I would see my father again outside of prison. Given the length of his sentence, advanced age, and deteriorating health, dying in prison was inevitable. If a release is not possible, some prison hospices allow the family to come sit with their family member in their final days, but special permission and completed visitor forms are required before that is possible.

Before his death, my father had signed a living will with clear wishes regarding his medical care. He did not want feeding tubes to prolong his life and also signed a do-not-resuscitate order (DNR). In addition, he gave me power of attorney, a legal document appointing me as his only agent to carry out his requests.

In making arrangements for my father's last days, I called my cousin, Father J, a Roman Catholic priest, to ask him to see my father to administer last rites. Father J has been a spiritual guide and leader in our family for decades and was very close with my father. In my mind, he was the best family member to officially minister the last rites or final anointing before death.

Prison chaplains are also available to minister to inmates and share God's grace and mercy. Spiritual care is important to many inmates, and prison ministry visits often bring comfort.

Father J was accompanied by his sister who worked with him in tandem at the church office. They made an appointment in advance to meet the prison chaplain who would accompany them once they arrived at Dodge. However, my cousins had never been to this prison hospice in Wisconsin, and the long drive was disorienting. Unfortunately, they got lost along the way, arriving late for their assigned visiting time. The chaplain had already gone home for the day, and they were told strict procedures must be followed in arriving on time for their approved visit.

Thankfully, my cousins' pleas with the corrections officers were considered, and although they were over an hour late, they were still allowed into the prison hospice after a series of security protocols that required gate clearance for all liturgical items. Father J was asked to present photo identification as well as documentation of his clergy status to the corrections officer at the front desk. Appropriate documentation may be a letter of appointment to the congregation, a copy of an ordination certificate, or clergy license.

Father J carried his "priest pack" to prison, which included the *Bible*, oil, crucifix, and holy water. After filling out some additional paperwork in the waiting area, he was stopped because he had a container of holy oil. The officer explained to my cousins the prison is very cautious about contraband being brought into the facility, and they were required to inspect anything that comes in. There are instances where people have tried to bring narcotics hidden in religious books. Father J also attempted to bring in a little round wafer host, holy communion, but was not allowed.

He wasn't aware of the rule "no oils in the facility" and was told he could be denied entry. My cousin did not understand this rule but respected it, and instead of being denied entry into the facility, he poured a puddle of the holy oil onto his hands and placed the empty oil container in a locker along with his wallet and keys. After the holy oil issue was resolved, Father J set off the metal detector alarm three times because his metal hip implant. He said the security officer asked him for a medical form, but he did not have a copy with him. The officer shook his head, but eventually waved him through the gates. But my cousin also got "beeped" in the metal detector for wearing an immaculate conception silver necklace and was told to remove it and place it in the locker.

It was getting late in the day. "I told him we were already late for our visit and kindly asked to let us in," Father J explained. "After all, I had my clerical collar on, but they still rummaged through my bag, scanned my *Bible*, and refused to let me bring in the anointing oil. I just wanted to get in and tend to your father. I told the officers Jesus identifies strongly with the weak, helpless, and outcast. He considers the way we treat *them* to be the way we treat *Him*. He wants us to identify with them as well, putting ourselves in their shoes and caring for them."

When my cousins finally made it through processing in the waiting area, they walked through a series of security checkpoints. They had to hold out their hands to be scanned. The ion scanners used in prison can pick up on small particles of drugs being present. Father J faced another obstacle because he was having difficulty placing his hand flat on the scanning bed. He wasn't pushing his palm down far enough. This took extra time to scan his hand properly, so my cousin (his sister) offered to help, but she was quickly reprimanded and told to step away from Father J.

What was it like to visit a prison death ward? My cousins walked through a maze of corridors before reaching the hospital room. They were directed firmly, "Go to the building on the right." After walking a few hundred feet, another officer yelled, "Stop! You can't go there. You have to go left. You can't go that way." My cousins pivoted, and the officer reached for his walkie-talkie, ordering them to follow the Y-shaped sidewalk and choose the path to the left. They got turned around another four times in multiple caged security areas with curly barbed wire looming above.

Finally, they made it to my father's bedside in an isolated mini cell where the curtains were pulled around his bed like a cocoon. The nurse came in and treated my father as if he were awake, "Hello, Mr. Colwell, I'm here now. I see you have family visiting." She tucked in his bedsheets and replaced the full plastic container of water on the bedside table. She said he was in a comatose state. He had not eaten or drank for the past two days. His hair was shaved short and neatly kept. A sheet covered his thin, gaunt body. There was a plastic rosary on the table since the prison does not allow metal rosaries because inmates may sharpen the crucifix and use it as a weapon.

My cousin lifted the bedsheet to see if my father's feet were swollen and retaining fluid and asked the nurse for a sponge to dab his dry, cracked lips, but sponges were not allowed. She described his face as an ashen color, but his fingers were not yet blue. He twitched when Father J announced, "We are here with you. We know you want to go with God." His eyes fluttered, but he could not talk. Was he in a state of delirium? Was he dehydrated? Overly sedated? Father J asked, "Have you asked God for forgiveness? Just blink your eyes if you can hear me."

They began to pray. An officer was also sitting in the room, a constant security presence. When Father J leaned in toward my father, the officer scolded, "What are you doing? You can't be that close. No touching." My father was in and out of consciousness. There were no tubes or machines. In one of the most holy moments before death, my cousin gently said, "If you are unable to say the prayer with us, it's okay to say it in your mind." He blessed my father and told him all his sins were forgiven. Father J talked about our family members who had passed, reassuring my father, "They will meet you, your wife, your parents, your brother. You will meet them all again in heaven. You can go now. You have permission to go and be with them."

Toward the end of their visit, they told my father, "Danica is coming tomorrow." It was Thursday evening, and I had made arrangements to leave early the next morning and stay the entire weekend at my father's bedside. However, the prison hospice nurse on duty called early the next morning and told me my father had died as he did not make it through the night.

Obituary

When people die, sometimes people awkwardly share platitudes like "Let me know if you need anything" and "Time heals all wounds" or "This, too, shall pass." This is because it is difficult to know what to say when others are grieving. Although these phrases are well-intentioned, the sentiment can be hollow, especially when a loved one has died alone in prison. From my experience, it is more comforting to ask to go for a walk or listen to music or just sit with each other *without* talking. Sometimes, silence can be a healing salve while another is contemplating, "How can I make meaning of this loss?"

Elisabeth Kübler-Ross, a pioneer in near-death studies, references the five stages of grief as denial, anger, bargaining, depression, and acceptance. These stages can sometimes be on a sliding scale or continuum. They don't happen neatly or linearly. Grief is messy, and it is challenging to stay nimble, to move forward, to carry on. C. S. Lewis described grief in his memoir, *A Grief Observed*, the story of losing his wife to cancer, "For in grief nothing 'stays put,'" Lewis wrote. "One keeps on emerging from a phase, but it always recurs. Round and round. Everything repeats."

My father died on a Friday, and on Monday, the prison hospice staff called, asking me what I wanted to do with his body. I did not anticipate things would move this quickly. The prison referred me to a funeral home in the area, and immediately, I was asked a series of questions about making arrangements, starting with publishing an obituary. How could I honor my father posthumously? Was I ready to share news of his death? Would this be the first step in talking about my father who had been in prison for over a decade? There was no guidebook on how to write an obituary for my father who died alone in prison.

After putting my thoughts together, I wrote my father's obituary, and it appeared in local Wisconsin newspapers and our hometown Illinois newspapers. His obituary was also posted online.

> *James "Jim" Colwell, 77, of Fontana, Wisconsin, formerly of Naperville, Illinois, passed away on October 26, 2017, of acute myeloid leukemia.*
>
> *Jim was born April 10, 1940, in Peoria, Illinois. He is survived by his only child, Danica Hubbard, and his two grandchildren. He was*

preceded in death by his father, Allen Douglas Colwell, his mother, Delphine (Paczesny) Colwell, his brothers, Richard "Dick" Colwell and Robert "Bob" Colwell, and his wife of over 25 years, Mary (Bulfin) Colwell.

As a young boy in Peoria, he performed on the radio singing and tap dancing to songs such as "Night Train to Memphis" and "Lulu's Back in Town." Jim graduated from Woodruff High School in Peoria and continued his education at the University of Illinois, Champaign-Urbana where he pursued a degree in architecture. He was a member of the Sigma Pi fraternity and met his future wife, Mary, on campus during their freshman year.

Jim served in the Air National Guard as a cook. He pursued a business career that spanned decades that included a vice president position with Fellowes Brands Manufacturing. While living in Naperville, Jim and his wife, Mary, enjoyed walking their dog every night along the Riverwalk brick pathway which ran along the DuPage River behind their home. He later started a successful cleaning franchise in Fontana, Wisconsin. He was an avid runner and ran several marathons. He enjoyed traveling to Germany, Taiwan, and Hawaii, but one of his favorite places to be was on the boat, watching the sunset, listening to Jimmy Buffett with a cold beer.

Funeral service will be held Friday, December 15, 2017, at 10:00 a.m., St. Thomas the Apostle Catholic Church, 1500 Brookdale Road in Naperville, Illinois.

Memorial Mass

My father's memorial service was dramatically different than my mother's memorial service. When my mother died, we met with the funeral director to coordinate the visitation, mass, burial, and reception. The funeral home staff was gentle and organized, respecting our needs for calm and comfort. The details were overwhelming, and my father responded to questions, completed paperwork, and signed checks. Most of the days leading up to her funeral mass were a blur, except when my father asked me to pick out something special for my mother to wear in the casket. It was a strange request.

In fulfilling this request, I went to my parent's bedroom, opened my mother's closet doors, and inhaled the faint floral fragrance of her signature scent, Estée Lauder's Youth Dew perfume. I wanted to leave her clothes folded and untouched because I expected her to walk back into our lives. It was uncomfortable standing in my mother's closet without her there. I felt like I was disrupting her private space. Eventually, I began looking through her sweaters and pants until I decided on a delicate peach-colored satin garment. Would this become her "death dress?"

In contrast, the days leading up to my father's memorial mass were devoid of these sensory images. Unlike my mother's funeral mass, there was no visitation, church choir, casket, procession, or burial. I wasn't sure how to proceed since many of our friends and family did not know what happened with my father for over a decade before his death as I kept his imprisonment hidden. How could I now announce his passing after not speaking about him for so long? How would people pay their final respects? There was an extra layer of anxiety leading up to his memorial mass as the stress of honoring the "good" man people once knew and exposing the "bad" man people did not know was in fact the *same* man who died in prison. How would my friends and family come to terms with this conflict when I had been struggling with it for over a decade?

We arrived at the church about an hour before the memorial service to arrange mass cards and leave a guest book on a table in the vestibule. I was not expecting a crowd, so I requested that my father's memorial mass be in the small chapel that seats about thirty people. The chapel is separated from the main church with an expanse of etched glass windows depicting guardian angels alongside Archangels Michael, Gabriel, and Raphael. It was the same church where I was married, the same church where we had my mother's funeral mass, my father in-law's funeral mass, and my grandmother's funeral mass. This particular church was an important symbol of what we believe in and where we are called to gather.

I brought a large picture of my father to place on an easel next to the wooden podium. My husband helped me carry in a bouquet of flowers, and I practiced reading through the eulogy. Our daughter rehearsed the song "To Build a Home" by the Cinematic Orchestra.

To Build a Home

> *There is a house built out of stone*
> *Wooden floors, walls, and window wells*
> *Tables and chairs worn by all the dust*
> *This is a place where I don't feel alone*
> *This is a place where I feel at home*
> *'Cause I built a home*
> *For you*
> *For me*
> *Until it disappeared*
> *From me*
> *From you*
> *And now, it's time to leave and turn to dust*

She said she chose the song because of the meaning she found within the lyrics. She told me, "It talks about how family is our foundation, and we build a home for each other in our hearts."

When she sang and played this song during the memorial mass, I held my breath until my heart felt like it was going to burst. I was so proud that she chose to courageously perform this song on a day filled with tears and pain. Her voice and organ playing elevated the somber mood to heavenly heights.

I decided to tell only close family and friends that he died but not necessarily that he died in prison. I still wasn't ready to share this sensitive information, but I could not hide it much longer.

Father J was the officiant at the funeral mass, who had administered my father's last rites a month earlier in the prison hospice. He began by reciting a number of blessings and readings from the *Bible*. It was beautiful. At that point, I felt almost buoyant. I was safe and warm, thinking I may get through the entire memorial mass without hearing the word *prison*.

And then it happened. Father J began his homily. A homily is a commentary that follows scripture readings and makes connections to the lives of parishioners in the church. My cousin was known for his charismatic and animated homilies, drawing his audience closer with thought-provoking, extraordinary stories. But on this particular morning, my cousin decided to unpack every bag of truth about my father with abandon. He embodied John 8:31–32, "Then you will know the truth, and the truth will set you free." From the start, he opened the door, and the words tumbled into the room for all to hear, know, and see. At that point, I should have felt unbound and liberated because the truth was in the air, but instead, I wanted to shrink and disappear.

Father J told *everyone* in the chapel, which included a crowd of family members, my friends, colleagues, my husband's colleagues, neighbors, and daughters' friends. He openly announced where my father had been during the last several years before he died—behind bars.

As Father J continued the homily, his voice sounded to me like radio frequency interference, a loud garbled static in my ears. I could only hear every other word as he told the truth about my father and used specific detailed words: prison, sex offender, hell, heaven, mistake, forgiveness, freedom. I tried to follow his stream of consciousness but no longer had the ability to push the truth away. I was now drowning in truth. I was seated in the front pew and grateful my husband and daughters were anchored beside me because my knees were shaking, and I had a horrible knot in my stomach. Our eldest daughter reached over, took my hand, and squeezed. Did I dare turn around and face all the people who were sitting behind me? Could I run away and not read the eulogy I prepared about my father? Were my words somewhere on the edges of truth?

After my cousin finished his homily, it was my turn to speak. I slowly started reading the eulogy I prepared but then had to address the truth with a capital "T." I wasn't sure how to follow in the wake of my cousin's homily, so I told the story of when we visited my father in prison and I wore bedazzled jeans that set off the metal detector. I wanted to lighten the mood and clear the air. Mercifully, I looked across the room to see my friends and family smiling and nodding in acceptance, encouragement, and love. The truth was out, and there was no turning back.

We had a lunch reception at our house after the memorial mass, and I made an attempt to talk with Father J about the surprisingly candid homily, but I was surrounded with family who had traveled long distances, and I wanted to be present to hear good memories about my father because I was tired of thinking about when he was in prison. That chapter of his life was over. He was free. In one of my father's letters, he talked about what he expected at his memorial mass.

November 4, 2012

I enclosed something for my memorial service after God calls me home. Although I will be there in ashes, I can't help but think many will want to say anything good about me. I hope Father J will be able to lead the memorial mass. He will find kind words to say about me. It will be difficult for you since your father spent the last number of years in prison when most dads are retired and being great granddads to their grandchildren.

When I'm Gone

When I come to end of my journey
And I travel my last weary mile,
Just forget if you can that I ever frowned
And remember only the smile.

Forget unkind words I have spoken;
Remember some good I have done.
Forget that I ever had heartache
And remember I've had loads of fun.

Forget that I've stumbled and blundered
And sometimes fell by the way.
Remember I have fought some hard battles
And won, ere the close of the day.
Then I forget to grieve for my going,
I would not have you sad for a day,
But in summer, just gather some flowers
And remember the place where I lay.

And come in the shade of evening
When the sun paints the sky in the west
Stand for a few moments beside me
And remember only my best. (Mosiah Lyman
Hancock)

Ashes

My father's cremains appeared in a heavy cardboard box on our doorstep a few months after the memorial mass. I transferred his ashes to a biodegradable urn and buried him next to my mother. A few days later, another cardboard box appeared marked "Department of Corrections." In the box were a few pictures I had sent him, his *Bible*, and copies of health and legal documents. How can one fit seventy-seven years of life into a small cardboard box?

My father wrote about being cremated in one of his letters.

August 22, 2009

If dying in prison turns out to be my only option, I want you to have my body cremated. I do not want a visitation because that would cause you more pain. I don't want you to stand next to a casket and tell people that your father was a great man who just happened to die in prison.

When the ashes are returned, ask the funeral home to give you two urns with my ashes in each. Please bury one next to Mom and send the other to my friends in Costa Rica. I have asked them to scatter my ashes in the ocean where I swam while living there. Please have a memorial mass at church.

It's hard to talk about or even think about death, but if I'm left here to die, I am glad I can tell you what is on my heart. You will always be my daughter no matter what happens.

CHAPTER 12

All Hands on Deck

Not all storms come to disrupt your life,
some come to clear your path.

—Anonymous

The core of this book focuses on my father's experience before and
during his time in prison. However, there was no "after prison" as
part of his story because he died while incarcerated. At this point,
I will pick up where he left off, which reminds me of a radio program which premiered in 1976 called "The Rest of the Story" with
Paul Harvey. The classic radio personality with his baritone voice
would begin to tell a tale and dramatically pause before the commercial break, asking his loyal listeners to be patient and wait,
saying, "In a moment...the rest of the story."

Initially, I held back telling the rest of the story which is
really *my* story, the culmination of how my father's incarceration
affected my life. I had a lot of help and encouragement to open
up and share. "All hands on deck" promotes a call to action—
everyone needs to assist in resolving a problem or addressing
a situation. I am incredibly grateful for friends and family who
have supported me in telling this story. Our collective narrative
can either destroy or redeem us. The outcome depends not just on
who's telling it but also on who's listening.

Grieving Is a Gift

Going through the bereavement process is not like microwaving a bowl of instant noodles. It takes time. A lot of time. I relied on a variety of resources in looking at grief from multiple perspectives. Hope Edelman, one of my many favorite authors, has been leading workshops and retreats in the bereavement field for over twenty-five years. She writes extensively about the grieving process. In Edelman's recent book, *The After Grief*, she explains, "How do we allow a major loss in the past to inform us, to guide us, even to inspire us, without letting it consume an identity? We decentralize it. We wait and watch and allow for other life experiences to accumulate over the long arc. We actively search for meaning" (258). I was numb after my father's death, and many days, I went through the motions like a robot, programming myself to get up, taking care of my family, going to work, coming home, going to sleep, and mechanically repeating the routine. I did not leave any room in my day to consider the loss of my father's death, and for a long time, I did not ask for help. From the moment my father got arrested to now, I am still grieving. My father's death was like sitting next to a blazing fire that was too dangerous to face. But now, years later, it feels more like burning embers, and I can sit next to it and invite others to come sit around it with me.

There are many ways to deal with loss. My husband and I became trained facilitators for a nondenominational program called Rainbows for All Children. Rainbows' facilitators are specifically trained to support children of all different age groups in how to cope with loss. Facilitators act as companions to share experiences and help children make sense of loss and as compassionate role models for peer groups. By validating children's emotions and encouraging peer relationships based on respect, facilitators help children to reconcile these adverse circumstances and to look forward to a fulfilling future. I just recently found out that Rainbows for All Children also provides programs for children with incarcerated parents.

Alan Wolfelt, another expert on grief and loss, has written a myriad of literature and developed step-by-step programs on how to make it through the day while walking with grief. He talks about grief overload, or experiencing too many losses at once. His compassionate guide, *The Wilderness of Grief,* is a gold standard for grief and mourning. It's hard to be patient and go through the stages. Grieving isn't a sign of weakness but a healthy way to handle feelings and reactions. It took me a long time to discover it's "normal" not to feel like yourself after a major event, like a parent dying in prison.

Telling Our Daughters the Truth

Another part of the process was finally surrendering the secrets I kept regarding my father's time in prison. My father was dangerous, and I needed to keep him away from our girls by shielding them from harm. I had surrounded them in a protective bubble for eighteen years, from my father's first moment in prison until his last.

I had a habit of placing his letters from prison on the edge of our hallway table each time I carried up a basket of clean laundry. After sorting the laundry, I would go to the attic to tuck his letters away in a metal bin under a pile of blankets. It was a routine I had gotten used over the years until one day our daughter found a letter from my father on the hallway table. I must have gotten distracted and didn't hide the letter in my usual spot in the attic.

It was my mistake, my carelessness that led to the first of many talks about her grandfather. She found the letter on the table, picked it up, and read his letter from prison then came to find me to talk about what she discovered. She was a senior in high school, old enough to know the truth. She was ready, but I was not. She cried. I cried. She was hurt and angry. She wanted more details and pictures to start filling in the blanks and gaps during his lengthy absence. She wanted to conceptualize, deconstruct, and analyze the time line of when he was first incarcerated to the time she retrieved his letter over seventeen years later. She asked a series of questions and sought answers in order to start making conclusions about her grandfather.

I felt awkward and uncomfortable retracing many of my fictional tales over a decade about going for "a drive" when in fact I was traveling to visit my father in prison. "That's where you were? You left me to go see him in prison?" she probed. She was a toddler when he was first incarcerated, and I told her I did not want to bring her into that kind of environment. I wanted to protect her. We sat together for a long time, and after our eyes were too pink and puffy to say any more about it that night she discovered his letter from prison, she asked, "What about my sister? Does she know?" Immediately, she went into protective mode, demonstrating her desire to intentionally offset the negative for the well-being of her younger sister.

I braced myself for telling our younger daughter about my father's incarceration the following day. I couldn't live with one daughter knowing and the other not knowing about my father. I also didn't want my older daughter to carry the same secret I chose to carry for over a decade. I decided to take our younger daughter to my mother's grave and explain it in the quiet and serenity of the cemetery. Maybe, I was unconsciously looking for my mother's heavenly comfort in repeating the story about my father. I kept reminding myself not to rush through the details.

The frequency would come. I would find the words. When the truth came tumbling out about her grandfather, our younger daughter, also in high school at the time, cried and visibly shook when I told her the details of his incarceration.

I told her she wasn't born yet when he was first imprisoned, and she never had an opportunity to meet him. After a long time sitting in the grass near my mother's tombstone holding hands, she hugged me and told me she understood why I kept my "truth volume" on mute until it was time to tell her about her grandfather. She was the editor of her high school newspaper at the time and immediately made the connection in realizing how this story featured in the headlines impacted our family and the victims' families. She took in the information with emotional intelligence and sensitivity, manifesting it into her own writing and empathy for others.

It was difficult for our daughters to see their mom operate less than 100 percent because it is my duty and responsibility as a mother to put on a brave face, to make sure everything is okay. But that "found letter" on the hallway table opened the doors to important life lessons. What could I teach them now that they knew about my father's time in prison? I showed them how their world can get rocked. I showed them how to fall down and get back up. I showed them that even when I thought I was in control, I wasn't. It's okay if I am not 100 percent all the time. I showed them how to speak their truth. It's easier to avoid thinking about why my parent went to prison, but it is important to face it, so I talked to our daughters about pedophilia. I used authentic words. I claimed my strength so we could take steps together to revitalize and repair.

These conversations also invited our daughters to reflect on my role as their mother. Because of my father's crimes, my parenting changed dramatically. I was overprotective. I planned their after-school and curricular activities. I scheduled their playdates at our house so I could monitor their interactions with friends. I wanted to know where they were and who they were with. My family nicknamed me "Panica Danica" because of my worrying and concern. Now our daughters had a better understanding and context of how and why my house rules and safety expectations manifested to become part of our lives.

A year later, my father would be diagnosed with cancer and die in prison, but we are still thinking about him, talking about him, writing about him. The lessons continue. Today, our daughters are pursuing university studies in health care, philosophy, politics, and law. I believe their recent knowledge and awareness about their grandfather changed their perspective and is a contributing factor in how they move in the world, walking in someone else's shoes, treating people with kindness and understanding.

Forgiving My Father

For me, forgiving is a lifelong continuum. It's an exercise in practicing patience. Honestly, it is much easier to give up and walk away. After all, society gives us permission to dismiss and forget people who are incarcerated with a collective rallying call to "lock them up and throw away the key." On some visits to the prison, I wanted to reach across the table, grab my father, and yell, "Why did you do this?" or "How could you do this to our family?"

My anger often simmered inside of me until I would see my father and suddenly feel sorry for him. I watched him shuffle slowly into the visiting area wearing his faded sweatshirt with identification number 389188 stamped in black ink across the front. He was hunched over and appeared broken, a shell of the man he once was. It was disarming as I looked at him and thought, *Prisoners are people too.* My father was a complex man who committed a crime, but there were other sides to him: doting father, churchgoer, community contributor. Capturing a genuine portrait of my father involves accepting contradictions, which made forgiving him challenging.

My ability to forgive my father came in waves. I couldn't forgive him immediately, so it was more like forgiving him on a sliding scale. I didn't have an abundance of emotional capital or psychological assets to offer my father forgiveness all at once. Consequently, I would pour a little tablespoon of forgiveness into his empty cup, then I would have to stop, rest, and regain energy in order to give a little more.

If I thought about it too much, I would shut down and retract, cycling through whether or not to forgive him at all. How could I forgive someone who had a pervert's point of view? I did not want to take his side or sympathize with him. I hated him. I loved him. I was conflicted.

Growing up Catholic, we are taught and trained how to forgive. Forgiveness is expected. But did forgiveness apply to this situation too? I questioned myself. I prayed about it. Was I doing this right? Should I schedule one forgiving moment or ritual or conversation and be done with it? Did I want to let him have all my forgiveness or should I withhold some forgiveness to save for myself?

As I chose to forgive him in small pieces within a letter or during a conversation at one of our visits in prison, I used these three phrases to help guide me:

- I forgive you when you did…
- It is difficult for me to trust you because…
- I would like to try to work together with you on…

Sometimes, I could only forgive in a few sentences, and other times, I could forgive in a few paragraphs or pages. I felt compelled to forgive him because I wanted him to be able to forgive himself. It felt like picking a scab and reopening a bloody wound over and over again. But each time I forgave my father, I needed to come home and have extra quiet time. I nestled under a cocoon of blankets and watched movies, read books, and lit scented candles. I often made online shopping impulse purchases and ended up buying way too many candles, picture frames, and blankets. With each "click here to buy," I envisioned these items could bring me more comfort, more peace, and more joy. I planned multiple weekend getaways and exotic vacations. I was trying my best to escape the reality that my father was in prison. I was trying to fill the void that my father left me with. I was looking for love in all the wrong places. Was I depressed? Possibly. I was never officially diagnosed, but decided to treat my sadness by covering myself with safe and soft images while I cried, screamed, and fought to get up again and face the reality that my father would die in prison.

Forgiving my father depleted me, made my hair fall out, and turned my stomach into knots. I often turned to self-care for comfort and strength. I could have self-destructed by drinking too much alcohol, doing drugs, or hurting myself in other ways to numb the pain. Many people who have loved ones incarcerated can be more susceptible to displacing their stress with a range of raw emotions that can lead to short tempers, road rage, depression, suicidal thoughts, and serious cries for help. I could have subscribed to a defeatist way of thinking that led to confirmation bias: "Like father, like daughter. If he is capable of these crimes and went to prison, I am too. I give up." But I was not my father. I could not give up. I did not feel this way because as a mother of two young daughters, I could not afford to inflict additional harm on myself or my family, so instead, I tried to turn my pain into positivity. I needed to be strong and learn how to take care of myself in order to have the ability to take care of the people I love.

It was difficult to regulate my emotions when I was tortured with the details of forgiving my father: his lies, his crime, his abandonment, his money requests, his manipulation, his neediness. Eventually, I was able to put things into a forgiveness framework, thinking about my father's illness as a disease in his mind compared to my mother's illness, a disease in her body. Ultimately, they were both diagnosed with cancer, but one of the major differences between my parents was my father *became* the cancer, spreading the toxins of his life onto others.

Another reason why my father was difficult to forgive was he did not take responsibility for many of his crimes. My father used this phrase a lot, "No problem." It's a phrase I incorporated into his eulogy because it resonated with me during my childhood and still has long-lasting effects. It was his mantra and a way to diminish or dismiss big or small problems that emerged. Didn't make the varsity team? No problem. Lost a job? No problem. Had an argument with a friend? No problem. Burnt a grilled cheese sandwich? No problem. But I know now that running away from problems can make them bigger and more pronounced. It was not easy to forgive him for the problems he created, but every time I chose to forgive him, I learned more about myself and the importance of sharing forgiveness with others.

I now view the ability to forgive like incorporating a routine health checkup, similar to going to the dentist twice a year for a cleaning. I am grateful that forgiving my father offered me a release in having a more meaningful relationship with him before he died in prison. I waited to write a book until after his death because I wanted to respect his victims, my family, and friends. We are all on our own path in finding forgiveness. I can now offer my experience to help people who have loved ones in prison and are grappling with making choices whether or not to forgive.

Survive and Thrive

I feel like I have survived a waking nightmare that is hard to fathom: discovery of my father's allegations, over a decade of visits to prison, the reckoning, the reconcile. Taking good care of myself, finding a balance, and forgiving were key ingredients in my healing process after my father's death. I also sought refuge through writing. I kept journals and poured out my feelings onto the page before putting them away on a shelf. I went to a therapist for a short time but felt like I ended up teaching the therapist more about having a parent in prison than she could teach me in dealing with the aftermath. I scheduled coffee dates with friends. I hiked in nature. I biked with my family. I sat on the beach and looked at the water. I participated in group fitness classes like yoga and Pilates. I said yes to domestic and international mission trips, volunteered at homeless shelters, and carved out time to read.

I am known for being infectiously happy and have given myself permission to enjoy life, to shed the shame and move on. I could still love my father on the inside and live in the light on the outside. I am striving to spread this light to others who may feel like they are also hiding in the dark shadows because their loved ones are in prison. I am inspired by Barbara Allan, who has been reaching out to families for over fifty years. Allan's husband was incarcerated, and she has been a vivacious, straightforward, altruistic advocate of prison families across the nation. She is the founder of Prison Families Anonymous Inc., a self-help organization for families and friends who have or had loved ones in the criminal justice system.

Another supportive colleague is Julia Lazareck, a leading advocate for promoting positive change in writing her book, *Prison: The Hidden Sentence*. Lazareck's brother died in prison, and she has made it her mission to help families who are struggling within the criminal justice process. She asked me to facilitate two online support groups as part of Prison Families Alliance, including "Coping with Loss" and "Support for Families of Sex Offenders." We gather for an hour or two and talk each month, lifting each other up with stories, inspiration, and motivation to stay positive despite all the negative forces that incarceration can create.

I also feel it is my responsibility as a mother, wife, and daughter to help protect previous victims and potential victims of sexual assault. Reading famous athlete, author, and motivational speaker Diana Nyad's graphic account of abuse by her high school swim coach in *The New York Times* article, "My Life After Sexual Assault," is raw and empowering. She writes, "These often-charming individuals are lauded, presented with trophies for their leadership, from the piggish Weinsteins of Hollywood to the unscrupulous parental figures scattered throughout our suburbs. Statistics bear out the astonishing number of sexual abusers among us. And therein lies the call for our speaking up. We need to construct an accurate archive of these abuses. And we need to prepare coming generations to speak up in the moment rather than be coerced into years of mute helplessness."

Nyad notes that celebrity status does not grant immunity from unlawful contact with minors. Some sensational headlines I recall include recognizable names in the entertainment and sports industry, like Paul Reubens, Kevin Spacey, Jerry Sandusky, Roman Polanski, and most recently Jeffrey Epstein among a long list of offenders in the spotlight. With growing media coverage of sexual exploitation, it is important to heighten awareness and prioritize child protection. But what does that look like? And what if the perpetrator is your father?

This is a piece of my family history I have been reluctant to share, but it has been cathartic to reread my father's letters and extract the most salient excerpts to include in this book. Award-winning American author, George Saunders, in an interview for *Writers Series* at University of Richmond, talks about micro-choosing or making specific choices in our stories, editing thousands of words in order to pinpoint the most relevant meaning.

In writing this memoir, I hope readers come to my story and can make meaning in their own past and present experiences. Perhaps, the audience will respond "I have felt this way too" or "I think about people in prison from a new perspective." My goal is to connect with people who may be going through this process for the first time or multiple times. We can help each other along the way in seeing each other in vulnerable and exaggerated forms. There are many benefits when we participate in dialogue and find ways for our truth to take root.

CHAPTER 13

Safe Harbor

*Society is like this card game here, cousin. We got
dealt our hand before we were even born, and as
we grow, we have to play as best as we can.*

—Louise Erdrich

Having learned of my father's crimes, I wanted to find out more than
I ever knew about him when he was living outside of the walls of
prison. I put in a rigorous effort to communicate with him, to engage
with him, and since letter writing was our main form of communication (he did not have our home or cell phone numbers), I asked him
to complete a complex "assignment." It was a big ask because my
father was not one to willingly share. Instead, he would avoid many
difficult conversations or conflict. In his letter writing, I hoped he
would explore his feelings and share them with me. I wanted him to
write about his meaning of family in the face of ugliness and despair.

Homework for Reluctant Writers

At one point, I was annoyed that our letter writing was turning
into a cycle of regurgitation; my father would simply echo what I
wrote to him. For example, if I wrote that we went out to a new
restaurant, he would simply repeat the list of menu items in his
next letter. It was like looking in a mirror, but I did not want to see

my reflection, I expected to see his. He would also write letters that posed neutral questions like: Did I remember to change the oil? Did the dog's nails get cut when I dropped him off at the groomer?

He was a natural list maker, and I thought his lists were an avoidance mechanism to not fully communicate but focus instead of completing tasks. He liked efficiency and effectiveness. In many of our conversations before he went to prison, my father would often ask me, "What is the bottom line?" I thought this question was part of his marketing and sales background in making the sale or closing the deal. He wasn't interested in flowery details but preferred expediting communication and honing in on the facts. But in prison, he had more time. A lot more time. I wanted him to explore heavier personal topics in hopes of getting to know my father in a more meaningful way.

My goal was to prompt him to revisit his past and engage in some soul searching. I was hoping he could use letter writing as a conduit for introspection and reflection in his own words. His responses would become significant in my life because in his letters, he eventually shared family history and personal anecdotes unique to his childhood, education, work, and marriage. It was like meeting for a cup of coffee and conversation while reading his letters.

This style of writing has no limits or boundaries, no rules to follow. It can be a stream of consciousness, allowing freedom from rigidity. Instead of my father's bullet point lists, I wanted him to respond to my open-ended questions as a therapeutic tool to record experiences. Although letters couldn't replace face-to-face talk therapy, perhaps letter writing could release some emotional inhibitions and welcome expression that may help organize his thoughts more clearly.

So I prompted him to share his memories of growing up and anticipated a peek into his past that helped form his future. I asked my father to write a letter to his future self with these directions:

- Provide a record of your life and who you are now
- Anchor your views, attitudes, philosophies, and outlook
- Unpack how you have changed through the years
- Highlight your most memorable influences and mentors

Similar to the assignments I create for my English composition community-college students, I asked my father to record his memories in multiple parts, prompting an open-ended journal style of writing.

My request to walk down memory lane produced some startling areas of his life that were previously closed off to me. My father poured out *his* version of hopes, fears, dreams, and intentions. I wanted to know what he liked about himself and what made him proud. What bothered him? What scared him? What would he do differently? Would he be honest?

Your Past: Where were you born? Where did you live? Where did you go to school? Where did you vacation? Did you have any accidents? Who were your friends? Who were your teachers? Did you want to go to college? Did you want to get married? What was your dream job? Share your childhood memories.

Your Present: What do you do when you are alone? What do you think about? What do you dream about? What is your favorite food? What are your biggest problems? What are your darkest fears? What do you regret? What do you like about yourself? What would you change about yourself? What bothers you the most? What makes you laugh? What is the best movie you have watched? What is the name of the song or songs that fills your heart? What book is the most memorable to you?

Your Future: What do you predict will happen to you in five years, ten years, twenty years? What are you looking forward to? What are you dreading? How do you view the world today? How do you want people to remember you?

It took extra time, but throughout the summer of 2013, after he had been in a medium-security prison for six years, my father wrote what he called "five installments of my life." He composed five lengthy letters in chronological order. The writing seemed to flow, and I was pleasantly surprised to receive his first installment of seventeen handwritten pages. I was grateful for his recall but felt he left out or sifted through some of the more difficult parts of his life. Although I appreciated his reflections, simultaneously, I felt like he was holding back and only focusing on the good while purposely omitting the bad.

I transcribed each of my father's letters and added pictures from our family photo album to accompany his words. As details of his life unfolded, I chose a variety of images to intersperse among the chronological narrative of my father's life. This reminded me of all the scrapbooks I have created over the years with the primary purpose of preserving memories for future generations. Instead of storing pictures electronically on my computer, in the iCloud, or on a cell phone, I prefer to print out each photograph and house it in a colorful binder labeled by year.

I have scrapbooks for vacations, birthdays, our wedding, honeymoon, baby books, and holidays. Our family has flipped through these nostalgic pages, taking us back to the special times we spent together. The scrapbooks have also come in handy when our daughters were assigned a school project, entered a photo contest, or were asked to gather photographs for a family funeral. Each scrapbook is like an art journal, filled with pictures, anecdotes, dates, stickers, and colorful paper. I love the ritual of browsing the scrapbooking aisles to experiment with new techniques and mediums when putting photos into an album. It is a creative outlet to help mark years, seasons, changes, and milestones.

Here are my father's letters, composed in an autobiographical style in five long letters. His life story is told in the first-person point of view as he incorporates flashbacks and main events with his own personal stream of consciousness. The pages in his letters give context and a colorful background: growing up in a small town, the importance of his religion, dropping out of college, getting married, climbing the corporate ladder, multiple moves across the country, and suffering the death of my mother after twenty-five years of marriage.

He stopped the timeline abruptly at the year 1990 when my mother died. I wish he would have continued, but I will share portions of his letters from a decade in prison to unpack more of his story. As the curator of his letters, my hope is to share his words with dignity, not disdain. I do not want to exploit anyone in the process but instead put aside my anger, sadness, and judgment.

Backyard birthday party, Dad and Danica, 1990

First Installment of My Life

June 2, 2013

I was born on April 10, 1940, at St. Francis Hospital and raised in the town of Peoria, Illinois. At that time, Peoria was the second largest city in Illinois, after Chicago, of course. The population was around 200,000 people. I was raised in a blue-collar neighborhood where most of the houses were on tiny lots to accommodate small houses. Peoria had five or six grade schools, two public high schools, and one Catholic high school.

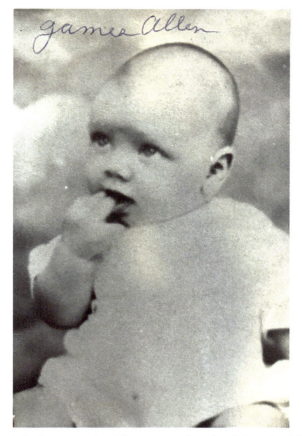

My father's baby portrait with my grandmother's handwriting, 1941

My father was a machinist at Caterpillar, which was by far the largest employer in Peoria. It's been said that Caterpillar kept the Santa Fe Railroad out of Peoria because it may have taken potential employees from Caterpillar. It was basically a one-horse town. Many say that Caterpillar was the controlling factor of Peoria. It all came down to that company as far as how we could live. When Caterpillar closed down each July for two weeks' vacation, the two department stores downtown and many businesses closed because it turned into a ghost town. All the thousands of employees at Caterpillar left town for vacations. We were on the same schedule. Caterpillar was our way of life.

I lived in Peoria with my family for the first eighteen years of my life. For all those years, most trips out of Peoria were to Wisconsin for two weeks in July for Dad's vacation. Once every two or three years, we would travel to St. Louis to visit Dad's sister. All my growing up years were spent in Peoria, which is why I wanted to travel to see the world. All I knew was our little town. I wanted more. Life before my fifth birthday consists of my dad, mom, and two older brothers. I was the youngest of three boys, each six years apart. My mom told me that the stork only came to our house every six years. I used to love going to our relatives' houses. Family was next to God and the most important part of my young life.

At three or four years old, I can remember going to St. Bernard's Catholic Church as a family each Sunday for mass. Because my dad was a Mason, he would drive us and wait in the parking lot for Mom and my brothers to go to mass. I was taught to be silent at mass and sit still and pray. We didn't have any kid's church or activities, instead we sat quietly next to our family for an hour and that was it. But in those early years, I didn't know what prayer was supposed to be.

Before age five, I can remember being disciplined when I did something wrong. I got hit and still remember the sting. If I even looked at my mom sideways, I would get into trouble. I was the youngest, so I got scolded for things my brothers did and blamed on me.

It's funny when you're younger thinking how old some of my relatives looked, hoping that they would be with me for many years. It seems like when we are very young, we look up at the ladder of age and think it will take so long to reach the top, wondering if we will ever grow old. Today, the opposite is true as I look down at my life, wondering how it passed by so quickly. Where did all those years go?

Kindergarten was a big deal for me. What felt like years of waiting to go to school and watching my older brothers, finally, I could walk with my friends each day to attend a half day of school. Our classroom was in the front of the building in the shape of a half circle filled with windows. I always wanted to sit right by the windows so I could look out on the lawn, watching the cars going by. By the age of ten, I could name the make, model, horsepower, and year of every car. I loved cars. I remember not liking naps in kindergarten and thought they were useless and boring. I wasn't tired and felt laying on a small rug for half an hour was a complete waste of time. So I would pull the rug over by the windows, get on my knees, and look out the window. Why would anyone, except perhaps the teacher who wanted a break, force me to take a nap in the middle of the morning? My teacher told my mom that I behaved well, but I never took my nap.

James Colwell and his father, Allen Colwell,
repairing the family car, 1950

Von Stuben Grade School is the same school my brothers attended. Many of my teachers had both of my brothers before I even got there. Many times, they would tell me how smart my brothers were and that I had a lot of work to do to catch up, following in their footsteps.

My mother pushed all three of us to be active in our school, both in class and after-school activities. We didn't have much money, and in those days, after-school activities were free, so Mom wisely took advantage of the opportunity to round us out and experience all we could. Dad, on the other hand, was more laid back and worked hard to keep bread on the table for three hungry boys growing like weeds.

Just before my sixth birthday, Mom thought I had a beautiful voice, so she got me an audition to be on Juvenile Theater each Saturday morning at 9:00 a.m. on WMBD Radio Station. The call letters, WMBD, were taken from an area high up on the cliffs overlooking the Illinois River that President Roosevelt called it the world's most beautiful drive when he visited Peoria. In high school, my friends and I often parked with our girlfriends along the side of the road and looked out at the beautiful view of the river. I knew someday I would buy a big house next to water.

Juvenile Theater was made up of girls and boys between the ages of five to fourteen. The director's name was Wayne West. He was a big man, weighing around three hundred pounds. Wayne would introduce each of us during the hour-long program, and we each had three minutes to sing, play an instrument, or tap dance. It was fun but kind of stressful. We were required to do something new each week. Some of the kids were very talented, and others like me were not as good. However, it was a wonderful experience, and we all had a lot of fun.

As a group, we took bus trips to hospitals and nursing homes to entertain patients. One summer, we traveled by charter bus to Pontiac to the VA Hospital where many World War II men lived. I'll never forget being asked to sing at a man's bedside who had no arms or legs that were lost in battle. I had trouble sleeping that night thinking about him.

After one year of Juvenile Theater, my mom wrote to Morris B. Sachs Amateur Hour in Chicago to get me on the program. I was asked to come to Chicago and make an appearance on the show. It was a contest where the top three winners were awarded prizes. I had never been to Chicago, let alone any big city outside of Peoria. This was really a big deal in the 1940s. The program was a live show on WGN in Chicago broadcasting from the Civic Opera House Stage.

I was so small that I had to stand on a wooden box so I could reach the microphone. The winner was decided through votes from the listening audience. The fourteen-year-old girl who won first prize, $100 and a watch, was from Chicago and a great tap dancer. But my mom got hundreds of her friends and their friends, relatives, classmates' parents from school to muster up enough votes for me to win second prize, which was $75 and an engraved watch. I sang "Down by the Ole Swimming Hole." With that money, I opened up my first savings account at the ripe old age of seven. I was so nervous I thought I would pee my pants before I finished the song. What a tremendous experience that went a long way toward teaching me how to compete and network although I'm not sure I realized it at the time. How could I when I was so scared?

When I got home with my mom, my dad and brothers met us at the train station in Peoria and presented me with a new puppy. Unfortunately, a few days later, my puppy got into some rat poison put out by the owner of Vespa's Food Market about a block from our home. Within a week, my puppy had died. I was devastated that I lost my little companion so quickly after I had gotten him. We buried him in the backyard.

This same year at the age of seven, I received my first Holy Communion. I remember I wore a heavily starched white shirt and dress shorts my mom saved from my brother's first communion.

We didn't have a lot of new things, so all my elementary school years at Von Stuben, I wore hand-me-downs. But my mom had them washed and patched up when necessary. I still got made fun of when my pants were too big or shirts too short. It was humiliating, but what could I do? I learned not to ask for things I knew I wouldn't get.

James Colwell's first Holy Communion, 1947

My family lived in a modest two-bedroom, one-bath home, 30×30. Modest is really a nicer to way to say we were poor. I knew we were struggling financially, but I never realized how much. My parents both knew how to stretch a dollar as far as they could. My dad paid $3,500 to build it with a full basement. Many homes today have a master bedroom as big as our entire home in Peoria. All three boys shared one 8×12 bedroom with a double bed, dresser, closet, and youth bed for me. Fortunately, our bedroom was used only to sleep because with all three of us in the room, we could barely walk around.

By the time I was seven years old, my oldest brother, Dick, left for the Marine Corps, so that freed up some extra space. My parents took the youth bed out, and I started sleeping with Bob in the double bed. I had no problem with the new arrangement, but Bob had grown too tall for the bed. His feet would hang over at the end of the bed. So he started sleeping diagonally, across the bed, which left me the smallest area where my pillow was smushed against the headboard. I learned to sleep with my knees in the middle of my chest to make room for my tall brother.

When Bob and Dick would babysit me, we usually ended up putting on three pairs of socks on each hand so we could have boxing matches. This was Bob's idea. I was so small I could only box up to Bob's knees and sometimes reach Dick's belt line. In turn, they would both box the top of my head. One night, when they were babysitting me, we were boxing in the living room, and Bob grabbed a feather pillow off the bed. We started beating each other with the pillow, and it got caught on the glass ceiling light, bursting it wide open. It shattered, and there were feathers floating everywhere. My brothers bolted to our room when my parents walked through the door while feathers were still coming down around me.

Although my brother, Bob, was six years older than me, he would let me hang out occasionally with him and several of his friends. I thought that was great until one early evening they asked me to go snipe hunting. If you don't know what a snipe is, it's sort of a brown camouflaged bird with a very long pointy bill usually found in wetlands or marshes. They told me a long story about the history of catching this bird—what fabulous imaginations they all had. They showed me how to hold a gunny sack in order to catch a snipe.

As the sun was going down, they took me to a vacant lot next to our house where several years later the Forest Hill Methodist Church was built. The weeds were way over my head. My brother and about ten of his buddies gave me the sack and a bat. They instructed me to follow them deep into what seemed like a scary jungle in order to catch a snipe. Far from our house, they told me to get down on my knees, holding the sack open with one hand and the bat in the other, and left me all alone while they went back to our house.

After about an hour in the dark, scared to death, I could hear nothing except when I thought a snipe might be coming my way. I started getting cold thinking about snakes, rats, and wild dogs or whatever else could possibly kill me. I started crying, but nobody came to rescue me. Finally, after what felt like hours had passed,

I heard my mom calling for me. I yelled at the top of my voice "Here! Over here!" until she found me. I thought she had given up until I heard the weeds bending, and there was my dad with a flashlight. They both found me still holding the sack and the bat. My dad told me it was a terrible trick played on me and he would deal with my brother when we got back home. It was not the first time my dad was my hero.

My two older brothers set the bar high at both the elementary school and Woodruff High School. I saw my role as one to keep up with their successes even though I now know my talents were different. Eventually, it all worked out when I realized I could only do my best and that would have to do. I loved my brothers and wanted them to be proud of me.

Brothers from left: Dick Colwell, James Colwell, Bob Colwell, 1942

I loved being outside riding my hand-me-down bike with my friends, playing cops and robbers. I also loved summers because in July, we would make our annual trip to Spooner, Wisconsin, to fish for two weeks. One summer, I caught a turtle, and Dad let me bring it home. I dug a hole in the backyard about three feet in diameter and used an old sheet of tin metal to line the bottom of a pond for the turtle. I put chicken wire around the area to keep the dogs, rabbits, and other animals out of the turtle's home. Mom bought me a big container of turtle food. About once a week when the turtle was out of the water, I would clean out the water and put in freshwater. Winter came, and the pond froze over, and my turtle didn't make it. We buried him way back on the property and put a homemade wooden cross on his grave.

Each summer, while I was in grade school, my dad took me every Saturday to the motorcycle races at the Peoria Speedway. He was a volunteer medic, so I got to sit in the middle of the field next to the First Aid tent. What a thrill! My knees were bleeding most of the summer as I tried to imitate how the professional motorcycle races would take the turns on the race track, leaning down almost parallel to the track itself so I could try to duplicate the motion. After falling so many times and skinning up my knees, I gave up that stunt. Seems like my mom and dad found ways with little money to give me so many experiences to use throughout my life.

At age eight, when I was old enough to have a better understanding about life, although far from knowing it all, church and my Catholic faith began to grow in my heart. Because I went to a public school, Mom sent me to religious instructions each week at St. Bernard's Catholic School, located across the street from our church. Dad drove me because it was about eight miles from our house. Many times, he would instead drive past the church and to Wisconsin Avenue Tap for a cold beer or two or three.

Dad was a Mason. Mom was a Catholic. But all three boys in my family were raised Catholic, and my dad supported us 100 percent. I remember one particular night in religion class that I came out to Dad's car with tears rolling down my face. Dad knew something wasn't right as he started the car and began our trip home. When I told him what happened, he quickly turned the car around and drove back to the parish house, took me by the hand, and walked up the steps to ring the doorbell. Monsignor Salem answered the door. "What do you need?" he asked.

We went into the parlor, and Dad shared what I had told him. He said to sit tight for a moment as he left the room to find the priest who had told me "Your dad is going to hell." He brought the priest into the parlor and proceeded to tell him he cannot and never will again say anything like that to anyone again. I didn't realize until that moment how well-liked my dad was at St. Bernard's. Dad always went to Christmas and Easter mass with Mom and us three boys. He even belonged to the St. Bernard's Men's Club and one year was nominated to become president of the club. He had to turn down the nomination because he was not a registered member of the church.

At age eight, I was very active in our Cub Scout troop. Many of my friends in the neighborhood were in the troop. We built small race cars for the pine box derby, and my dad helped all of us. He found old wood scraps and gave us nails and hammers. I even had a brake lever notched in, but I never wanted to use it to slow down. I built a derby car on top of an old wagon, and it could really fly when we raced it down the track. It felt like I was going a million miles per hour.

James Colwell's Cub Scouts pine box derby car, 1948

We never could afford a new car, so Dad was always repairing our well-used cars until my sophomore year in high school when he bought his very first new car. I'll never forget that day, the new car smell. That day was almost as exciting as the day he brought home a new black-and-white TV set with a 7-inch screen. We had to sit right in front of it to see a program, but we didn't care. We had a TV!

I got my first job when I was nine years old as a paperboy. In those days, we had to deliver every day—rain, snow, or shine. Once a week, we had to go door-to-door to collect money for the next week's paper. From my earnings, I saved enough to buy wood to build a tree house in the backyard. It had two levels with a built-in ladder to go from the first to the second floor. First class! My paper route money was well-spent and gave me and my friends hours of enjoyment.

To further my music career, Mom signed me up for piano lessons. I took three lessons, but on the third lesson, my teacher said I couldn't play her piano because I had a wart on my finger. How lucky could I be? Saved by a wart! No more piano for me.

Holidays and birthdays were big deals in our house. Mom would invite 30–35 relatives to our home for Christmas dinner, Easter dinner, or a birthday party. She would take the change from Dad's work pants to save for months in order to have enough food and beer for the party. Dad would set up long plywood tables on horses he built to be used outside in the summer and in the basement during the winter. Mom would borrow folding chairs from the neighbors so everyone had a seat at the table. Each dinner was filled with homemade pies, decorations, and love. No one ever said no to my mom's invitations.

At age ten, I began going to my grandma's house in South Bend, Indiana, for three weeks during the summer. Mom put me on the Peoria Rocket train to Chicago where I had to transfer to another train in downtown Chicago to go on to South Bend. Mom gave an extra two dollars to the porter to make sure I got on the right train in Chicago. Three weeks later, I would reverse the process back to Peoria. Much of the time I was at my grandparent's house, I would watch Grandma and her neighbors at what I would call a Pillsbury Bake Off in her kitchen each week. They would make dozens of pies, cakes, and homemade sausage that would hang over the basement rafters to dry out. One summer, my aunt passed away. The visitation for my aunt was held in the house for two days and two nights. Relatives and friends came to see her laid out in a casket in the first-floor parlor to say prayers and the rosary. I didn't sleep too well knowing that my dead aunt was in the casket under the second-floor bedroom where I slept. Spooky!

Every day, my grandpa would send me with an empty case, twenty-four bottles, to pick up a new case of beer. I had to carry it home for three blocks, and it was heavy. Although he could drink twenty-four bottles a day, I never saw him drunk. Sometimes, he would eat a full chicken and a half while drinking eight bottles of beer for dinner. He was a big man, a bus driver in South Bend who by this time was retired.

My grandparents lived in a two-story Victorian home right next to the railroad tracks. Every time a train went by, the whole house would shake. Many bums would walk the tracks and come down the embankment to our front door, begging for food. Grandma always invited them into the kitchen where she would make them two sandwiches and a piece of homemade pie for their backpacks. One day, Grandpa came into the kitchen, and there was Grandma talking to a bum while making him lunch. Grandpa started to immediately scold Grandma in Polish, telling her it's not safe to feed these bums because they may pull out a knife and kill her. As she and the bum walked out the front door with Grandpa steps behind them, the bum stopped and said to Grandma "Thank you for your food. I'm sorry I got you in trouble" in Polish!

And now, I'm going on eleven years old and began to build a train set in our basement against the wall, facing my friend's house. The distance between our two houses was about six feet, almost like a pathway. I painted the tracks black and fastened them down to four sheets of heavy plywood. I built stations and roads, crossing gates, streetlights, houses, trees, and telephone poles. I got a transformer, engine, and cars for Christmas. The whole project took about two years to install. I asked every holiday for things to build my train set. And by the age of thirteen, my train set was complete, but I had no money saved in my bank account.

One night, while running my train set, I looked at the wall facing my friend's house and said to myself, "I bet I could run my train underground to his house." So one day, while walking home from school, I decided this was the day to make a tunnel between our two houses. Nobody was home when we got there, so I took a sledgehammer and began to break a hole in the concrete block wall. About an hour later, my dad came home from work and heard the loud banging in the basement. He came downstairs and saw that I had started to chop a hole in the wall. This was one of the few times my dad used his 2-inch leather work belt on my bottom to teach me that I could not break walls to make a tunnel for my train. Bad idea!

I was very active in Cub Scouts and could hardly wait to become a Boy Scout and earn my Eagle Scout Award. By the grace of God and a lot of work, I was able to reach that goal by my fifteenth birthday. I was happy to accomplish all my goals set in becoming an Eagle Scout. And God blessed me with the desire to go beyond and receive two Palms that few Eagle Scouts go on to earn. This honor is bestowed to those who work in the community and are eventually an asset to the community.

My father's Eagle Scout ceremony, 1955

At this time, I also started flirting with girls in my high school class. One time, I was showboating and dove off a dock to impress a girl but didn't realize the shallow depth of the lake and jammed my neck into the bottom of the lake. My dad ended up carrying me to the car and drove to a chiropractor. After working on me for about an hour, I was able to stand up although I was really sore.

That's all for now. I love and miss you. God bless you.

Love,
Dad

My Comments and Critique

After each of my father's "life installments," I responded to him with compliments, thanking him for shoring up his memories and sharing them with me. I reassured him that I wasn't searching for grammatical mistakes or misspelled words but meaningful stories about his life. I told him this was an important document in our family history, and I encouraged him to keep writing.

This "First Installment of My Life" was easy to follow and a quick read for me. I had spent time in his hometown of Peoria visiting my grandparents during the summer, similar to how he spent time with his grandparents in Indiana during his childhood summers. I wasn't previously aware of this parallel but liked discovering it.

I knew he went to church every Sunday because he often talked about the importance of being a Catholic. I knew he sang on the radio because I have a collection of the records he made. I knew he did not have a lot of money while growing up because he would often reference it in tongue and cheek fashion by saying, "I didn't have a pot to piss in or a window to throw it out of!"

What he did not include, however, was that his father, my grandfather, was an alcoholic. I remember the beer bottles stacked so high in the kitchen garbage bin that it would make a rattling noise when I walked near it. My grandfather would take me to the neighborhood bar after his shifts working on the line as a machinist at Caterpillar. I must have been only five years old, but I still remember the stale smell of beer on his breath and bowls of pretzels he gave me as I spun around on the barstool, waiting for him to finish his drinks. When we got back to the house, he would collapse in his bed until morning. One time, he slept with his boots on! My grandma would always tell me to speak softly because grandpa was tired from working. He may have been tired, but he was also drunk and passed out.

Some personal anecdotes my father wrote I had never heard before, particularly the story about his brother, Bob, and friends teasing him about snipe hunting. It gave me some insight about sibling rivalry, being the baby brother, and how he admired his father who came to his rescue during that harrowing event when he was a child. He tried to emulate his brothers in sports and academics, and I could read between the lines that this was a lifelong competition.

He also highlighted his work ethic and leadership abilities early on with his newspaper route at nine years old and earning the esteemed Eagle Scout Award as a teenager in high school. I thought this first installment of his life may have been a cautious and safe first step in opening up and anticipated more in-depth memories in his future letters.

Second Installment of My Life

July 8, 2013

I think I left off talking about high school and the summers I spent in Wisconsin fishing with my dad. Every year, he laid down the rules for fishing: no radio in the boat, no noise that would scare the fish away. No standing in the boat. My brother, Bob, didn't share our love for fishing, so his job was to pack our lunches. One day out on the water after a couple of hours of silent fishing, Bob broke out the lunch bag and opened potato chips. This was more noise than my dad could take. The next day, my dad rented a rowboat for my brother to keep him off our flat-bottom fishing boat. Bob was not a fisherman, at least not according to my dad's definition.

We caught northern Pike, largemouth bass, and walleye. We'd sit in the boat for hours, lines cast on a cold morning. I could think clearly out there on the water. I remember the lake was like a sheet of glass, and it was the quiet times with my dad that I loved the most. We didn't say much, but it was in silence we said a lot. We'd catch, gut, and fry the fish we caught all in one day. Those two weeks spent on the lake fueled my love of being in nature and near water. You know how much being on a boat meant when you were growing up. This love of water really started with your grandfather. He passed it on to me and my brothers, and I hope I passed it on to you. Being on the water seems to always make things better. I miss it.

My father fishing with his father on Spooner Lake, Wisconsin, 1957

When I came home from the lake that summer, I was energized with all sorts of ideas. Since I failed at building that tunnel for the train to my friend's house, I thought about hooking up my bedroom to his bedroom with a phone wire and walkie-talkie on both ends. To carry out my plan, I bought a big role of phone wire and surveyed how to get across to his house. There was a telephone pole at the end of our driveway and one across the street at the entrance to an alley.

I took my dad's longest extension ladder out of the garage and used it to climb to the first-floor telephone pole. By reaching up as far toward the cross member of the tall pole, I threw a roll of wire up over the cross member and it came down on the ground. Now, I needed to get the wire across the street. My timing was not the best that day. As I was almost at the highest point of the telephone pole, my dad got off the bus and shouted, "What in the hell are you doing?" He ran to the bottom of the pole and shouted, "Those are electric wires. If you touch one or get the wire you are using against one, you will be electrocuted!" I had a bad feeling that Dad was so mad that my bottom was about to feel the bite of his two-inch wide leather work belt again. Sure enough, he hauled me in the house and laid that belt with a healthy swing several times over my butt. I can still remember that pain.

Afterward, he explained the immediate danger I was in being up in the air 30 feet, about to touch electric wires to be thrown down to my death on the street below. Oh boy, me and my crazy ideas. Without knowing that was probably the first clue that one day I would be working with ideas in marketing but not on telephone poles.

The next Christmas, when I was in eighth grade, I received a brand-new Schwinn bike with whitewall tires and shiny chrome fenders and a comfortable, wide seat. Because I was the only one left at home, my brothers were in college, my parents had a little more discretionary money. I had never received anything brand-new, mostly hand-me-down bikes, toys, and clothes. So this was a big event.

I was so proud of that new bike that I kept my old piece of junk and would not use my new bike for tearing through vacant lots while playing cops and robbers with my friends. In fact, for the first year, I would only ride my new bike on Sundays. The rest of the week, I kept it in the garage, covered with one of Mom's old blankets. About once a month, I would wash, dry, and wax the entire bike. When I finished, you could see your face in the chrome fenders. It was like a mirror! Now that I reflect on this, I realize I started taking care of things early on. I'm sure you remember my weekly ritual of washing my car or Mom's car. Also, when we owned a camper trailer on the Fox River, I washed our camper every weekend to keep it looking brand-new.

Our eighth-grade class was a terrific group of about thirty boys and girls. We did a lot of fun things together. The girls would come to our Saturday baseball games on the schoolyard to watch us play other teams in the Peoria area. When any of the girls had a party, they invited all of us. Of course, in the basement, we had a great time playing spin the bottle and making out when someone would turn out all the lights. There was a shift. All of a sudden, my love for baseball and riding my bike were no longer the most important things in my young teenage life.

Girls! Yes, girls began to share that "most fun" thing in my life. Like many young teens, I fell in and out of puppy love several times before the school year was completed. Sometimes, we were all just crazy kids sharing our lives with each other, other times we experienced the broken heart feelings when the "love of our life" decided she loved someone else or just got bored dating the same girl. I especially remember Sandy, who was my main crush at the time. We went to art class together and used to wash out all the paintbrushes. We turned the water on and closed the door and started kissing each other until the door flew open and our teacher screamed, "Get back to class!" I'm not sure, but I think those paintbrushes had to be thrown out because they never did get washed.

That summer after graduation, I had to leave the Juvenile Theater because at fourteen, you had to make room for the younger kids to be on the radio each week. I was sad because I had been with pretty much the same group of friends for years, and I would no longer be able to see them each week on the show.

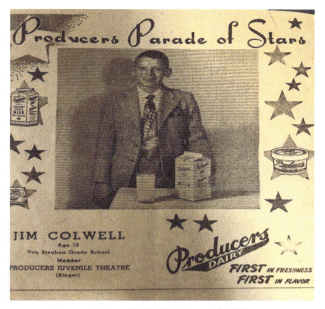

James Colwell, 1952, Juvenile Theater

In high school, my friends and I liked to go to the Beverly Theater each Saturday afternoon. My dad would take us, drop us off, and pick us up hours later. I loved the movies because I learned about how other people lived. In those days, almost all shows were available to children. Not many were rated "R," so we watched anything we wanted. After the show, the theater had a raffle and gave out prizes. I filled out a slip on the way in and dropped it into a box.

The theater staff drew three winners each week, but you had to be present to win. One weekend, I had the mumps, so my friends went to the movies without me, and they put my name on the slip. Sure enough, they pulled my name out for the first prize—a new three speed bike. My Schwinn bike was only one speed. So, they came to our house to tell my mom I won but could not get the prize because I wasn't present at the theater. I learned then that luck was not on my side. I proved that many times later in life during business trips to Las Vegas where I always lost.

Several of my teachers already knew my brothers, so here we go again. I had to prove myself. I started my first year signing up for football, basketball, and baseball. My best sports were baseball and basketball. I got letters in both sports in my sophomore, junior, and senior years.

Besides sports and girlfriends, I was able to maintain honor-roll grades and became a member of the National Honor Society in my junior year. This award for outstanding grades was usually reserved for seniors. I was also in Key Club, and it gave me valuable leadership skills that I used later on in life.

Until my senior year when I got a car, I would start very early for school each morning. The walk with a couple of friends took about an hour, depending upon the weather. The walk was a little more than three miles each way. During baseball season, we played and practiced at Glen Oak Park, which was about halfway between school and my house. I would walk home after the game. There was no bus service, but my friends and I didn't complain, except when it was below zero with snow. On those winter days, we would hitch hike, and many times a driver would feel sorry for us and help us get a ride at least part of the way.

During the summer, I took a job mowing lawns in addition to my paper route. By the end of the summer, I had saved enough to buy a brand-new lawn mower. Now, I was king of the yard mowers. I used that mower the next summer and started getting jobs in fancy neighborhoods out by my aunt's house. I started making $20 each week. That was big money in those days. The following summer, between my junior and senior years, I painted one of my customer's houses and started working in his aluminum factory. This helped me start to pay for college expenses.

By the time I left for college, I had enough money to buy my first car, a 1950 Plymouth two door that cost me $300. There was not a scratch on it, and the interior was perfect. My dad checked it out—he was a skillful mechanic. I drove my new car home under my dad's watchful eyes in his car right behind me and parked it in the driveway. I was so proud. But then Dad told me to give him the keys. I could not drive the car until I had insurance. My heart dropped to my toes. I bought my first car and now could not drive it. He called his insurance company and put the car in his name as a second car, which made the insurance much cheaper. He told me what I owed, so between mowing more yards and the little money I had left in savings, I finally put together enough money to pay my dad for the insurance.

My father's senior high school picture, 1958

I was going steady with a girl named Barb and couldn't wait to show her my new car. I was really excited about washing and waxing it, and when I pulled up, she shouted, "It's our first new car!" Well, that was the wrong thing to say because it was my new car that I earned, not "ours." We ended up breaking up before the start of our senior year.

My best friend and I decided that senior year, we would date at least every girl that belonged to "the spread." The spread was a group of about fifteen popular girls who did everything together. Each was more beautiful than the next, including the president of our class, yearbook editor, and captain of the cheerleading team. It took all school year, but we took each girl on one date. This was a year to be remembered and my best year in high school.

In high school, I was taught love and respect for others. I was normal. I was blessed with friends who helped shape my personality and love for life. Almost all my experiences were happy, but there were a few sad times as well. One of my good friends who sat in front of me in Algebra left early one Friday afternoon to take a bus from Peoria to Springfield. He was going to pick up the used car of his dreams. He liked cars even more than me, if that was possible.

His last words to me on that day were, "I'll see you on Monday to show you my new car." On his drive home, he missed a blind curve in the road and ran off the road, hitting a tree that killed him instantly. That hit me hard. He was not supposed to die at seventeen. The other very sad time was when I was a senior. We were sledding and tobogganing down a long, steep hill in Detweiller Park. No one was drinking. But one of the sophomores riding the toboggan with five other kids on it was going very fast down the hill and lost control. The toboggan veered off the hill and headed for the trees. The kids in front yelled to roll off, but this kid couldn't roll in time and ran into a tree. He was killed instantly. What a horrific sight. The school closed the day of the funeral. Life is never perfect, even though I really wanted it to be.

At eighteen, I was ready to go to college. I was ready to be on my own to make or break my way. None of my friends went to the college I went to, so I would have to start over when it came to making friends. Going to University of Illinois, a school of thirty thousand, was a far cry from being in a high school of one thousand students. And as I found out, bigger is not better. I chose a state school because it was the best price for tuition. My parents paid $100 per semester to help me. I had to pay for my housing and food.

I didn't want to live in a dorm, so I looked for a small inexpensive apartment on campus. It was a modest one-room apartment with a shared bath down the hall. My first semester of classes was scattered all over the campus, so I had to walk what seemed like ten miles between classes.

I decided to major in architecture, again, to be like my brother, Bob, who had graduated from University of Illinois and was already a successful commercial architect who helped design the chain of Howard Johnson restaurants. I studied until midnight seven days a week and got up for my 8:00 a.m. classes each morning. I did nothing socially except for a movie, my treat, about once a month. I had to watch my food budget because I had no way to prepare a meal in my room. To save money and time, I did not eat breakfast and had a candy bar at lunch in order to save for a decent dinner.

I looked for a job after class in the evening, so I applied for one at a fraternity house as a waiter. I had to serve breakfast, lunch, and dinner, and my pay was a free meal three times a day. For an eighteen-year-old living in a shoebox with no private bath and being broke, this job was like a gift from heaven. During the first semester between my job and studying, I earned a 3.7 GPA—a good start for a ungifted student. I enjoyed every subject except for calculus. I was never good at math. Eventually, math became my downfall.

The second semester was packed with many hours in the classroom while keeping up with my studying. I returned home for the summer and returned to lawn mowing. When I went back to school in August as a sophomore, I decided to be in a fraternity but only if they could guarantee me a job in their kitchen so I could focus on studying and having somewhat of a social life. I asked Sigma Pi, the same fraternity my brother, Bob, was in six years earlier, and they let me work in the kitchen to not only receive free meals but not have to pay any room rent. Such a deal!

By the middle of my first semester sophomore year, the fraternity elected me social chairman. This position took a lot of my time because I had to set up social exchanges where a sorority would come to our fraternity for dinner. At the time, there were twenty-eight sororities and fifty-two fraternities, so the competition to get a popular sorority to share a social event like a homecoming parade was really keen.

One of the sororities was the one your mom was in. The night we had them over to our house for a dessert exchange, it was raining, and your mother pulled up in a car full of girls. I walked down to meet them with an umbrella. I had never seen your mom before, and she stood close to me underneath the umbrella. I had the strongest emotional feeling I had ever experienced in my nineteen years.

University of Illinois sweethearts, 1959

She was absolutely beautiful. At that moment, I said to myself that I wanted to date her. So during dessert, I was able to find out mom's name, Mary Therese Bulfin. I didn't get a chance to talk with her because she was like a firefly buzzing around the room, but she found out who I was, and I got the courage to introduce myself to her when desserts were finished that night.

I knew from the moment I saw her that Mary was going to be my wife. Love at first sight. It wasn't high school puppy love this time. It was a deeper feeling and one I knew would last forever. God brought me an angel, and I wanted to be the best man I could for her and our future together. I couldn't wait to start.

I have to close for now because tears are running down my face. I have to wash my face and run because I'll miss chow otherwise. Years with your mother were the best of my life.

I love you,
Dad

My Comments and Critique

In this "Second Installment of My Life," I started to see more prominent patterns in my father's childhood stories. He talks about his love of cars and how hard he works to purchase his first car, a 1950 Plymouth for under $300. He also features his foundational leadership positions in the National Honor Society and Key Club, preparing for a lengthy future in striving for titles while climbing the corporate ladder. My father had a strong work ethic and truly believed that if he worked hard enough, he would achieve all the goals he wrote on his list. I remember my father working late nights and going upstairs to the bedroom office in our house every Sunday after dinner to prepare for the upcoming work week. He was ambitious and dedicated to success, just like he was in his high school years.

In high school, my father was also at the peak of puberty and mentions his attraction to girls in his class. He also suffered tragedy his senior year when one of his high school friends died in an unexpected sledding accident, and he revealed, "Life is never perfect even though I really wanted it to be." This line resonated with me because my father worked so hard to promote an image of perfection. In his letters, he was still not receptive to sharing his shortcomings, fears, or frustrations. Instead, he wrote about an idyllic childhood and phenomenal high school experience, often glossing over experiences with a shiny coat of varnish. What was he omitting and why?

In the final paragraphs of this letter, he introduced my mother into his life story. I took notice and reread these parts because he refers to her with terms of endearment, calling her his angel and professing his love at first sight.

Third Installment of My Life

July 15, 2013

After I met your mom, I couldn't stop thinking about her. I talked to the girls in her sorority, and she was very popular. She had several dates lined up with guys for months. After all, she was on the university homecoming court and captain of the underwater dance team, synchronized swimmers. People told me she was like a fish underwater and could hold her breath longer than anyone on the team. She was awarded "The Dolphin Queen," the only one on campus, for her excellent underwater ballet dancing. She was also in the court for Miss Illini during her first at University of Illinois. Having spent almost thirty-three years with Mom, I realized early on, as beautiful as she was on the outside, she was even more beautiful on the inside.

There are those who give and not take, but each time I thought about Mary, she set the bar high in giving to others constantly. Since the day I met her in 1958 and until the day I am called home, I will always love and honor Mary who showed me what God meant when he said, "Love one another." I will never reach the bar she set so high, but I will keep trying.

The tradition in the 1950s was to ask a girl for a "Coke date" between classes to get to know her before asking her on a real date. Now that I am writing about my first conversation with your mom, many emotions are flowing through my mind like an instant replay of that time in my life. At age nineteen, our romance began and lasted for thirty-one years. When I married your mom on August 4, 1962, my life changed forever. I was twenty-two years old and the proudest man to be with your mother.

After a few months of dating on campus, I pinned Mom in front of her sorority house with all thirty-five girls who lived there and fifty fraternity brothers from my house looking on. We serenaded the girls with our Sigma Pi Girl song, and they sang back with a beautiful love song.

Mary and Jim, nineteen years old, Sigma Pi
fraternity pinning ceremony, 1959

We weren't on campus for long. Mom and I both left University of Illinois at the end of our sophomore year. I had to drop out for at least one semester to change majors and put my academic probation behind me. My grades had suffered because of my time given to Sigma Pi as the social chairman and my decision to drop out of the School of Architecture.

Mom went back to Chicago to live with her parents while teaching in a Catholic grade school. She went to night school to earn her degree in education. I ended up moving to Cleveland to work with my brother, Dick, selling encyclopedias door-to-door.

I learned how to think on my feet and develop a management style that served me well into my marketing and management career. The initial fear of speaking in front of a group or convincing parents to buy $500 worth of books for their children's education was easy for me. Eventually, I managed six people at the age of twenty and three thousand people by the age of thirty-five because I learned so much during that first sales job. But despite my success, I never wanted people who worked for me to think I got a "free ride" because I was the brother of the owner of the company.

I moved on to Kansas City with my brother and rented a bug-infested apartment with a bed that pulled down out of the wall. It was cheap and basic. Every other weekend, I would leave Kansas City and drive for eleven hours to see Mom in Chicago. It was worth the trip to spend time with Mom.

Then I started working for Kraft Foods in Kansas City. I sold Miracle Whip, Kraft Macaroni and Cheese, and Pillsbury refrigerated, powdered biscuits. I was working hard to climb the corporate ladder.

Becoming a corporate executive, 1970

To save for a better place to live, Mom took a part-time job at a drugstore at night. Mom was never afraid to work. We both worked hard to make ends meet. Mom's parents came to visit us one weekend from Chicago. We prepared all the food for three days that they would be staying with us. We even splurged on a gallon of ice cream for the occasion. We were proud to show them our first place, our home.

Your grandfather asked to talk with me by his car. I went downstairs to meet him, and he opened his trunk to show me about twenty bags of groceries they had bought for us. I was angry. I closed the trunk and said, "Please go back to the apartment, and I'll take your car to the gas station to fill it up because gas was only 25 cents per gallon." I convinced him and took his keys. No, I did not get gas. Instead, I drove to the nearest church and donated all those groceries to the food pantry.

When I returned to our apartment, your grandfather found out I didn't fill up his tank with gas. I told him, "No, I didn't. And our refrigerator is full of food we bought for your visit. We do not need your charity or groceries." This was the first time I lied to your grandfather and told him how I could take care of his daughter. But from that day forward, I know he didn't trust me. And I wanted to live up to his trust. Even though we were only twenty-two and had no money or "no window to throw it out of," we had each other.

Another year passed, and I took a better position with General Foods in Kansas City with more responsibility and a larger territory so I could make more commission. Mom went to night school at Rockhurst College, and we started shopping for a nicer place to live. I hope these letters are making sense. I'm not sure. I don't want to leave anything out. Tired and going to close for now. I love you. God bless you.

Love,
Dad

My Comments and Critique

This "Third Installment of My Life" unfolds with my father professing his young love for my mother. She created a base of stability for him, but I sensed he was the one being erratic. He was failing his college classes because he spent too much time planning and attending parties as social chairman of his fraternity. He liked the fantasy escape route of having fun. Consequently, he dropped out of college but always regretted that decision. My mother soon followed him, and her decision caused a rift in the family because she gave up her dreams to follow his. They rushed into an engagement after only a few months of knowing each other and quickly got married.

My father began working with his brother, Dick, selling encyclopedias door-to-door, but my father had a chip on his shoulder. He didn't want others to perceive he was "given" this job by his brother. He wanted to prove himself, and he manifested this need in both his personal and professional life. I believe this is one of the reasons he enjoyed training for marathons. In running past people, he could feel a sense of dominance and control.

Fourth Installment of My Life

July 31, 2013

Your mom and I were so pleased to move into our first apartment. Mom was teaching, but she quit her second job. Instead, she went to night school to add hours toward her undergraduate degree. We met several young couples in our apartment complex. It seemed like someone was having a party in their unit every weekend. We were all in the same boat financially, newly married and starting our careers. We finally had some discretionary money if you call two beers and a pizza shared with friends left over money each month.

Mom and I worked hard to build a nest egg for a home one day. My job took me out of town much of the time, so we really looked forward to being together on weekends. We didn't have enough money saved up to buy a home because in those days, banks wanted 20 percent down. Rather than continue to pay rent, we wanted to build some equity in something we owned. We talked with your grandfather about borrowing one half of the total dollars needed for a down payment on a townhome.

Grandpa had the money, but he guarded it in order to give to his family when he died. He offered to give us half of what we asked for. Mom and I were both upset even though we told Grandpa we would pay him back each month. He said we would appreciate it more if he only gave us half of what we asked. After a couple of days of crying and discussions, we told Grandpa, "Thanks but no thanks." I went to the bank, and they agreed to give us a second and separate mortgage to cover what we needed for a down payment. I often told your mom I would work a second job pumping gas if that's what it would take to buy this new townhome. By this time in our marriage, she knew I would always take care of her. We bought that first house with a lot of love and belief in each other. Sometimes, we didn't agree one hundred percent, but when we did, nothing could stop us. Your mom was so special to me.

Jim and Mary, Kansas City, 1964

On Sunday mornings, we would always go to mass to receive communion and thank God for the many blessings he gave our marriage. Although the townhome was nice, our next dream was to have a home with a patio for barbecues and entertaining. I was on a mission for a house we could afford. I told Mom it probably would not be new, but I would make it look like new.

I had changed jobs again and was now working for General Foods in Kansas City. I was promoted to manager of retail products in the state of Missouri. My main account was Maxwell House Coffee. We sold related commercial products to hospitals, schools, and restaurants throughout the Kansas City metro area. After a lot of searching, I finally found a house we could buy, a ranch style with slump brick, meaning the concrete between the joints of the brick squeezed out and became the appearance of a slump, an unusual and interesting way to lay brick. The owner was motivated to sell, and I felt we could get a good deal. After seeing the house on my own, I brought Mom with the realtor. The outside was really sharp, and I knew she would like it. The problem was the inside. The living room was painted a dark purple, the kitchen orange, and the bedrooms were green. The fireplace was filthy and had used tampons at the bottom which were partially burned.

I had to really convince Mom to look past the dirt and paint colors and we would offer $20,000 less than the asking price. I promised her it would look brand-new by the time we moved in. So we made our offer and got the house! I painted every room and installed new carpet. The day we moved in, Mom was thrilled. She trusted me that I would give her a nice home.

When you get older, you can look back on events in your life that were good and some bad. The first and greatest life-changing event was our marriage. This was the good and the best yet.

Unfortunately, after five years of wedded bliss, we received a call from Grandpa Colwell telling us that my brother, Dick, was killed in an automobile accident. He was on his way home from JCPenney headquarters where he worked and fell asleep at the wheel, crashing into an overpass bridge on the expressway, less than 10 miles from his home. He was only thirty-six years old. He left his wife and four boys behind. It was such a sad time. Hundreds of friends and relatives came to pay their respects and take part in the tribute to Dick's life. He was so loved and had been my hero since I learned how to walk.

Colwell brothers on my parent's wedding day, 1962

Your mom agreed that we should sell our first house, change jobs, and move back to Chicago so we could be closer to family, especially after I lost my brother. Working through a headhunter, I obtained a position with Eagle Pencil Company as a district manager in Chicago. Mom got a job teaching. But right before we moved, my appendix ruptured. I was initially told by the doctors that I had the flu. When I came out of emergency surgery, Mom said I was a pale-gray color. The doctors said the next twenty-four hours would be critical. They made a hole in my right side to drain the poison, which meant that the dressing had to be changed every two hours. God must have had more for me to do because I healed and worked with a bag on my side for another eight months before it was removed.

We moved to Alsip shortly after that time, and Mom became pregnant with our "morning star." You were born around noon. In those days, fathers were not allowed to be in the delivery room. They came into the waiting area to announce that we have a beautiful, healthy baby girl. I was so happy I burst into tears. And that's all for now, my dear daughter. My morning star. I love you. God bless you.

Love,
Dad

My Comments and Critique

In his "Fourth Installment of My Life," my father talks about married life. He catalogs the first of many moves we made as a family as he was always itching for a bigger and better place to live. We moved constantly. My mother was a saint to pick up and move across town and across the country to follow my father's promotions in the corporate world. She was put in the position to find a new teaching job each time we landed at a new address.

My father also briefly talks about his brother, Dick, who died suddenly in a car accident. I was hoping he would go deeper into how Dick's death affected him and his family. I wanted him to expand and stretch the narrative about loss and how it impacted his choices in life. He spoke briefly about Dick to me, saying he liked to live fast and drive faster but didn't fully elaborate. Again, I thought he was whitewashing the topic of death in his letter and avoiding it altogether.

He quickly pivots to my birth and then ends the letter abruptly but on a happy note. Could he have expanded and explored how having a baby changed the dynamic of the family? What was it like to raise a child in 1968? I searched for development of these ideas from my father, but came up short.

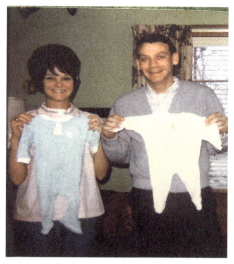

Mary and Jim, parents to be, 1967

Fifth Installment of My Life

August 4, 2013

I hope these letters about my life do not come across as too prideful or bragging about myself. I am only unique in that I try to be who I am and live with what God gives me each day. I am far from perfect.

Now at the age of twenty-six, Mom and I had a beautiful daughter, our one and only morning star, Danica. Our family was complete. Most of your first three years on earth were safe. A few banged-up knees, cuts, scrapes, and bruises, but for the most part, no life-threatening situations.

When you were just a baby, we took you on your first boat ride on the Cal-Sag Canal, short for Calumet-Saganashkee Channel, connecting with the Little Calumet River and onto Lake Michigan. We named our boat Happy and Carefree because that is exactly how we felt riding in it. I was able to purchase a new boat because of my record-setting sales at Eagle Pencil Company in Chicago.

Our first family boat, Summer 1969

My name was starting to be recognized throughout the office products industry. A headhunter called me to set up a lunch to discuss a new opportunity at Wilson Jones Company, a manufacturer of ring binders and office products. They were searching for a product manager for their marketing department. They had a beautiful building east of O'Hare Airport on Touhy Avenue. It was $10,000 more than I was making, and I quickly agreed to the interview with their vice president of marketing. In the 1960s, that was a lot of money. My career just got another jump, and I set a goal to make twice my age in income by the time I was thirty years old.

Once again, Mom and I celebrated the new job and started looking for a bigger home. This would be the third home in our marriage. My career at Wilson Jones was going well. The president came into my office one day to tell me they were grooming me to become the vice president of marketing. The meeting gave me incentive to create a totally new program for the office-product industry. I designed a stand-up presentation supported by a multimedia slideshow to solve paperwork and data-processing problems with the use of our product available from a cosponsored dealer. The concept was unique and soon to be the talk of the industry with other manufacturers trying to imitate my idea. For the next few years, I crisscrossed the United States and Alaska with two assistants, giving this presentation in every major city in the country. We developed a consumer sales team who took our products directly to the end user, creating new business in large markets for the dealer and wholesaler.

I was promoted to vice president of marketing! The presentations were so successful that we were invited to Canada, Europe, and South America for me to teach them during a seminar in Chicago. I learned so much from that experience that helped me years later when I traveled for another company to Taiwan, China, Germany, and Austria to do business. Mom loved my work and was my greatest cheerleader, but she never got used to me being gone all week. But I could have never moved up the corporate ladder of success without Mom.

I was very active in NOPA, the National Office Products Association headquarters in Washington, DC. At thirty-two, I was asked to join the YEF, Young Executives Forum, a nationwide group of executives from manufacturers, dealers, and wholesalers. I was the youngest member at that time to be asked to share in quarterly meetings in major cities throughout the USA. Within a year, I was honored to be asked to be on the board of directors for YEF. A year later, I was elected president of YEF.

The next promotion was when I was asked to become the executive vice president of Marvel Lighting. Their offices were in Philadelphia and New Jersey, so we would have to move to the New York area. This opportunity was awesome. Marvel had a plant with over one thousand employees, another plant in Toronto and five hundred direct to consumer salespeople.

Our move to New Jersey was traumatic. Your mom didn't want to leave her family in Chicago, but she once again supported me in my career path. The following year, I was named cochairman of the National Office Products Annual Convention at McCormick Place in Chicago. With more than four thousand dealers and wholesalers from all fifty states and international guests, I introduced President Ford at the opening-day breakfast. I was humbled and honored.

Mom and Dad meeting President Gerald Ford at the National Office Products Annual Convention, Chicago

Although I loved your mom's parents, moving back to Chicago was not as critical for me as it was for her. Mom's idea of living after marriage was to be living next door to her parents. And eventually, we did. I took a job with Fellowes Manufacturing Company as a vice president. It was a challenge and a rewarding change.

My corporate experience was helpful, but I learned so much about how decision-making was very different in a family-held company compared to a large public organization. Many of the politics of a massive corporate structure were now a part of my new responsibilities. After traveling domestically for all those years, I now started traveling internationally. I spent many trips to Germany and Taiwan, setting up another manufacturer to make a line of storage products for the home called "Next Ideas." I was able to get this new product line into Walmart and was honored to meet Sam Walton, the owner of Walmart. He was an inspiration to me.

Learning from books is nice but not as beneficial as learning from people. I didn't graduate from college, but I learned from meeting people nationally and internationally. Travel was my education. I really did get out of Peoria after dreaming about it all those years ago. And as corporate jobs come and go, I made another move to Sanford Corporation in Chicago. They wanted me to help them market new products beyond the famous Sanford Sharpie pens.

Today, as I sit in a place that is horrific, writing about my life, the next part is a life-changing event, and my throat starts to close, my heart hurts, and tears fall down my face. I will never forget the day Mom was taken away from us at age forty-nine. Some say, "Gosh, she had cancer and you had two years to prepare for her passing." I could have had a hundred years to prepare, and nothing would have stopped the ripping and tearing apart my heart when she died. The moment she died in my arms, I became lost. My partner, my cheerleader, my strength, my everything that was good in this life was lost, never to be replaced.

The last picture my parents took together before my
mother died of cancer a few weeks later, June 1990

I can never work back to center. I am just existing now and am thankful for your blessings. I pray that what came from my heart in writing about my life has given you a better understanding of many parts of my life that you did not know because they took place long before you were born. I'm glad I got to write this while I'm still here. I hope I delivered what you asked for. I certainly don't possess the gift for writing that you have but can only give you what God has given to me. I love you. God bless you.

Love,
Dad

My Comments and Critique

In the last long letter from my father, "Fifth Installment of My Life," it read like a lengthy résumé. He focused mostly on his corporate executive positions and leadership within the office-supply industry. He was obviously very proud of this part of his life as this is the most detailed account of all five installments in his letters. It seemed like he was always carrying his résumé in his back pocket, ready to talk about his various achievements and sales experience.

The time line he created in his "life installment letters" stopped abruptly at 1990 when he would have been fifty years old and my mother died of cancer the same year. I wondered why he omitted the next few decades where our family became fractured. Did he adopt someone else's memories because they seemed more reliable than his own? Was it some sort of blackout or loss of time that had affected his memory? What caused him to stop writing about himself?

My father did briefly address what my mother's death meant to him and dovetailed that loss with being in prison, writing, "I can never work back to center." This was a poignant statement that brought me to tears. I wished he explored this idea about the loss of his moral compass and ultimately losing his way. I wanted to know, was his compass already broken long before my mother died? Did my mother know about his alleged crimes of sexual abuse?

Tough Questions Remain Unanswered

I was hoping my father's letters archiving his childhood, teenage, and early adult years would offer a revelation as to why he became a sex offender. I was waiting for him to come out and say something like "I was abused" or "My interest in pornography led me down a dark path" or "I was bullied and felt like I needed to fight back." I thought his writing may unpack old problems from new angles. Was he a victim who later in life took part in victimizing? Was he capable of recognizing the life-altering decisions he made? Was he censoring himself? Did he find writing to me liberating or limiting?

His letters painted an idyllic childhood full of love as he matured and married my mother, his college sweetheart. His letters raised additional questions about what really happened in his life.

Was this the truth or his version of the truth? In reading, I sought a neatly packaged formula, a data point to track what led to his crimes against children. I thought retracing his life through letters may help him move him forward in understanding why and where his urges originated.

Danica and Dad, 1985

CHAPTER 14

Lifelines

As soon as healing takes place, go out and heal somebody else.

—Maya Angelou

After my father died, I began telling people about the trauma of his prison sentence and soon discovered there was a significant population who also needed assistance in understanding and connecting with one another. How could I offer comfort when I didn't know how to first comfort myself? Part of me felt invisible, existing quietly in the shadows while my father was behind bars. However, I learned shame and silence do not have to coexist when a parent goes to prison.

When a loved one is in prison, families can often feel helpless or hopeless, and lifelines can help. A lifeline is a cable or line used to prevent people or equipment from falling overboard on a boat. Through reading and asking questions, I learned how to grasp lifelines for myself and also throw them to others who needed help. There have been several agencies and organizations developed over the years available to help formerly incarcerated people or victims of crime, violence, and abuse. But in 1999, when my father was arrested, convicted, and sentenced, I could not find a support group or organization for families with loved ones in prison. Specifically, the father-daughter adult relationship in prison was rarely closely examined. Few asked the question,

"What impact does an incarcerated father have on a daughter in her thirties, forties, or fifties?" There is a lot of room for improvement in rethinking and strengthening assistance for families domestically and internationally who are left behind when a family member or friend is incarcerated.

Walking a new path alone can be frightening, but I learned to seek out specific community groups and resources to give me positive energy and spiritual nourishment. Author Rhonda Britten in her book *Fearless Living* proclaims, "You can't be fearless alone." Instead of choosing to be exhausted and depleted individually, lean in to a support network to energize and recharge collectively.

Road Map to Resources

There are at least 1.5 million adult children of incarcerated parents in the United States, yet the relationship between an adult child and incarcerated parent has not widely been questioned, explored, analyzed, or recorded. Where could I find a support group or a national database for adult children with parents in prison so we do not remain a hidden group? What tips and recommendations were available in wading through a vast amount of information? Where were the guidebooks to fit this niche?

I searched for existing literature about adult daughters with fathers in prison, but there are very few materials available to help discuss and come to terms with having a parent in jail as an adult. The main focus appears to be on parent-child relationships prior to age seventeen. I found a number of children's books with colorful illustrations and titles, such as *But Why Is Daddy in Prison?*, *When Dad Was Away*, *Andy: Another New Dad-less Year*, and *An Inmate's Daughter* with sample chapters, "Keep it Simple," "What do people in prison eat?" or "Is it my fault?" The content of these books was sensitive and straightforward, focusing on guidance in dealing with stigmatization and teasing children may experience on the playground or at school. The books also touched on single-parent families, abuse, and social issues stemming from a parent's absence due to incarceration. Most of the books were authored by department of corrections divisions, community service organizations, or religiously affiliated groups.

Even the childhood television series *Sesame Street* developed an initiative in 2014 called "Little Children, Big Challenges" to help adults and children ages 2–5 build lifelong skills for resilience. One of the shows focused on incarceration, introducing Alex, the first character to have a parent in prison. The dialogue is heartfelt as Alex, the puppet, hangs his head low in shame and says to his friends, "This talk about where my dad is got me really upset."

His puppet friend asks Alex, "Because your daddy's away?" Another puppet friend asks Alex, "And you miss him?" And Alex responds, "Yeah, but because of where he is too. My dad is…my dad is in jail." This episode created an opportunity to discuss sensitive information with others. Bringing the conversation out into the open is acceptable and can be helpful at any age.

There is also a genre of what I call self-help "lite" books that may provide an optimistic approach to the darkness of having a parent in prison. I gravitated toward titles like *Survive a Prison Sentence for Dummies: Do you Have What it Takes to Survive?*, *Chicken Soup for the Prisoner's Soul: 101 Stories to Open the Heart and Spirit of Hope, Healing, and Forgiveness*, and *How Prison Really Works: An Idiot's Guide to Surviving a Prison Sentence.* These publications offered some salve for the open wound while dispensing a new vocabulary list of prison slang that could apply to my father: old timer (anyone over twenty-five), grandpa (anyone between twenty-five and thirty-five), and fossil (anyone past thirty-five). My father added to the lexicon when he told me that one of the favorite nicknames he had in prison was "Old Style," like the beer he used to drink. This may lighten the mood momentarily, but being incarcerated is, of course, no laughing matter.

Books

I searched for books specifically in the memoir-nonfiction genre, hoping to find universal stories with a focus on families. I suggest this reading list as a good start, but more needs to be written and published to uncover the realities adult children encounter when a loved one goes to prison.

- *A Tortuous Path: Atonement and Reinvention in a Broken System* by Christopher Pelloski (2019)
- *Conversations with a Pedophile* by Amy Zabin (2003)
- *Doing Our Time on the Outside* by Barbara Allan (2018)
- *Hummingbird in Underworld: A Memoir* by Deborah Tobola (2019)
- *Learning to Sing in a Strange Land: When a Loved One Goes to Prison* by Wesley Stevens (2009)
- *Letters to an Incarcerated Brother: Encouragement, Hope, and Healing for Inmates and Their Loved Ones* by Hill Harper (2014)
- *Long Way Home* by Laura Caldwell (2010)
- *Mother California: A Story of Redemption Behind Bars* by Kenneth Hartman (2009)
- *Prison Baby: A Memoir* by Deborah Jiang-Stein (2014)
- *The Sentence: A Family Prison Memoir* by Gene Kraig (2006)
- *The Unvarnished Truth About the Prison Family Journey* by Carolyn Esparza (2013)

Social Media, Blogs, and Podcasts

A lot has changed in the digital world since 1999 when my father was first incarcerated. Today, I can rely on support from social media tools, like joining the private Facebook page "Prison Family Support Group" launched by the platform www.PrisonInsight.com. The website offers an archive of information via a blog that answers questions, like "Can you get newspapers in prison?" or "What is prison hooch and how do inmates make it?" Another Facebook group, "Prisoners are People Too," includes many informative video vignettes, advocacy, and support for families. Their motto is "To deny their humanity is to deny your own" www.prp2.org. There is also an online community called PrisonTalk that offers family support with a variety of informational tabs, including blogs, resources, a gallery, and forums at http://prisontalk.com/forums.

In addition, YouTube has a robust archive of videos geared toward primary- and secondary-school children, with titles such as "What's it like having a parent in prison?" and "Parents in Prison: Collateral Consequences" and "Connecting Kids with Incarcerated Parents." But again, the focus is on children and teenagers, not adult children. There are current YouTube videos, "What to Bring When Visiting Prison" and "What to Know When Visiting Prison," as well as video conferencing support groups offered monthly through the nonprofit organization, Prison Families Alliance at https://prisonfamiliesalliance.org/, with groups I facilitate called "Support for Losing a Loved One in the Prison System" and "Support for Families of Sex Offenders."

On Twitter, the hashtag #parentinprison is a space to exchange ideas for children and families impacted by parental imprisonment to share articles and workshops in exploring difficult emotions to help make sense of feelings. Yet there are few hashtags offered that categorize Tweets about how adult children create an identity outside of their parents' prison status.

Instagram is another social media platform to find information, like Prison Fellowship, a Christian based nonprofit organization founded in 1976 that offers support to families torn apart by incarceration. Prison Fellowship believes that a restorative approach to prisoners, former prisoners, and all those affected by crime and incarceration can make communities safer and healthier.

Cellular phones are considered contraband in most prisons. I'm not sure how inmates are able to record and distribute TikTok videos, but at the same time, they are promoting the message for criminal justice reform by posting on this particular video-sharing service. There's even a prison TikTok account with hundreds of thousands of followers, watching inmates record fifteen-second to one-minute videos of the conditions at their facilities as well as choreographing dance routines and performing lip syncs.

Free-streaming podcasts can also open a whole universe of appealing and lively conversations, engaging a community of listeners. Some of my favorite podcasts include "Ear Hustle" https://www.earhustlesq.com, "The Secret Life of Prisons" https://secretlifeofprisons.libsyn.com, and "Uncuffed" https://www.npr.org/podcasts/772030875/uncuffed. "Inside Prison Walls" and "Prison Life" are also available to download on Apple or Android devices. The podcast interviews feature candid stories that shine a light on effects of incarceration. Each podcast episode reminds me there are many people in this invisible "club" and it's okay to honestly express our experiences with one another, although sometimes, I want to rescind my demoralizing lifetime membership of being a daughter of a father behind bars. Another robust catalog of podcasts with interviews of family members and social justice advocates is featured at https://prisonthehiddensentence.com with author Julia Lazareck, currently in season 2 of recording podcasts with compelling content.

Is There an App for That?

Prisons are notoriously low-tech, but nearly half of all state prisons now have some form of electronic messaging. JPay offers a fast and secure method of sending money, communications services, and entertainment options, as well as a variety of parole, probation, and post-release services. Downloading free apps like JPay via the Apple Store or Google Play is convenient but costly (www.jpay.com). Unlike Forever stamps sold at the US Post Office, which are always the same price as regular First-Class Mail stamps, fees for sending e-mail, video conference, or money wiring can fluctuate. Prisons charge a fee or a token JPay calls a "stamp" to send each outgoing message. However, each "stamp" only covers a page of writing. If a photo is attached to the e-mail message, an additional stamp is required. A video message could cost up to three stamps.

Pelipost is another free app available to upload pictures. The website www.pelipost.com promises "Staying connected has never been easier. Smile, snap, and send your favorite memories in seconds directly from your smartphone. Photos are mailed directly to the love one's institution." The services charge from four to ten dollars for up to twenty photos. Each photo is printed on 4×6 glossy paper, but again, restrictions may apply depending on each prison's mail rules and regulations.

Communication Is Key

There are a variety of resources offering general information, but more can be done to share the stories of families who are trying to maintain relationships with those incarcerated. Although these stories can be difficult to tell, their value cannot be underestimated. Embracing opportunities to share narratives in how families play a vital role in the prison system is important. Ultimately, collaboration between prison systems and families can make this unique experience more humane for all involved.

AFTERWORD

When I told one of my friends that I was writing a book about my father's conviction as a sex offender, she said, "Well, it's only one version of the truth anyway." Maybe, she is right. We have our own interpretive lenses in how we see the world. A singular narrative can contain flaws and not fully represent the web of experience that makes up the past, but it is still my story. I did not adopt someone else's memories because they seemed more reliable than my own.

In the 2018 season of Malcom Gladwell's podcast, *Revisionist History*, he says that every time we take a story down from the shelf, we're more likely to change it because our memories become distorted. We may add or subtract details to a preexisting memory and begin to mesh ideas that do not necessarily belong together. Collecting traumatic memories of my father prompted me to revisit and remember my past. When I transcribed my father's five hundred letters, I captured a snapshot of what it was like to have a parent in prison by using his words woven together with my words to create an authentic tapestry. I realized this was not only my story to tell but a narrative to develop that can be read and retrieved by many trying to navigate the criminal justice system.

After years of silencing myself, I learned how to come out of my comfort zone and talk about what happened in our family. I finally stopped sabotaging myself and found my voice in facilitating multiple groups with the organization Friends and Family of Incarcerated Persons (FFIP) https://theffip.org/, which began as Prison Families Anonymous, Inc. in 1974. Recently, in 2021, the name of this impactful nonprofit organization changed to Prison Families Alliance at https://prisonfamiliesalliance.org, and I was invited to become the new Board Secretary, participating in quarterly meetings, recording meeting minutes, and volunteering time. It has been an amazing group of people to interact with, sharing information and stories about our loved ones within the prison system both domestically and internationally. I have also been selected to present, "Dying with Dignity: How Prisons Can Connect Families with Support" in October 2021 at the International Prisoner's Families Conference. More information is available at https://prisonersfamilyconference.org/. Barbara Allan, author of *Doing Our Time on the Outside: One Prison Family of 2.5 Million*, started this nonprofit organization over fifty years ago when one of her loved ones went to prison. She led the way for families of inmates to gather in a safe place to vent, share ideas, and foster hope.

Today, "Families with Incarcerated Loved Ones with Disabilities (Mental/Physical)" and weekly general support meetings bring hundreds of people together via video conferencing weekly in an open-anonymous format. Most everyone involved in these meetings knew someone arrested, tried, and sentenced to jail or prison.

I am also collaborating with criminal justice colleagues at College of DuPage and the Illinois Department of Juvenile Justice to offer a new learning community course to juvenile offenders called Rehabilitation Prairie Project: An IDJJ Youth Center to College Pipeline through Eco Composition, Sustainability, and Service. This course will pave a pathway for youth to become college ready and achieve access for participation in the College of DuPage and IYC-Warrenville College Credit Program. Students will work outside with a COD Prairie manager to engage in ecological restoration and write about their experiences harvesting seed, cutting invasive plants, and learning about the ecosystem.

I continue to seek answers to questions for myself and anyone who is also going through this process. As a survivor of sexual assault, I know firsthand the emotional maneuvers a sex offender can make in order to perpetuate self-doubt in victims while working every angle to diminish the severity of his crimes. This book is not meant to normalize what happens but to understand ways to adapt, cope, and survive. I didn't choose what my father did, but I can choose how to respond to it in a constructive way by reaching out to others and sharing my story.

My father's letters inspired me to reach out to families of incarcerated people to let them know they are not alone. It is important to let go of shame. Brené Brown, a professor at the University of Texas at Austin, has spent her career researching courage, vulnerability, and shame. Brown describes shame as "The intensely painful feeling or experience of believing we are flawed and, therefore, unworthy of love and belonging. '*I am bad. I am a mess.*' The focus is on self, not behavior, with the result that we feel alone. Shame is never known to lead us toward positive change."

I have finally said goodbye to shame. Living through this tragedy for decades transformed me and made me sensitive and strong in creating a multilayered memoir. I hope I was able to turn my private pain into a safe space for universal growth and understanding. I was tossed around in rough waters for far too long and can now fully appreciate the rainbows that appear after the storm.

ACKNOWLEDGMENTS

I used many nautical terms as metaphors for chapter titles in my book. I have one last term to include: boat draft. A boat draft refers to the minimum draft of water that is needed for a boat to safely operate without dragging along the bottom. Essentially, it means making sure the boat stays afloat and doesn't run aground. In my case, an entire crew of people paid attention to my boat draft. They enabled me to stay buoyant during the often painful and difficult telling of my story.

Staci Haen-Darden, professor of Justice Studies, committee chair extraordinaire, and fellow faculty member at College of DuPage. Staci, your expertise and positivity are a tremendous gift. David Fierst, attorney at law, author, rigorous researcher, and fellow Re-Member Pine Ridge Reservation volunteer, who carefully edited several drafts, encouraging me every step of the way. Bev Guidish, a brilliant friend who leapt into action the moment I told her I was drafting a manuscript. Throughout our marathon phone conversations and editing line by line, she recommended a variety of solid resource materials. She is a word warrior. Kessea Wieser, an amazing friend with a keen ability to conceptualize each chapter with meaningful, humorous, and in-depth responses. And Diana Hubbard, my sister-in-law who held my hand while I poured out the words and tears. She gently asked me to explore the depths of my story, and I am so grateful.

And thank you to my publisher who walked me through the complex process of publishing a book. Your patience and compassion helped me realize my goal of finally writing my story and sharing it with the world.

I also want to thank all the supportive people at Prison Families Alliance. We have shared our collective pain and positivity in many monthly meetings, and I hope this book honors the journey we are on together, with patience, tolerance, and understanding.

Finally, I have so much love and gratitude for my husband who read every word and walked on this path by my side. Big hugs for our daughters who bring constant joy into my life. I am honored and blessed to be their mother. You all inspired me to find my voice and come out of the darkness into the light. Onward!

GLOSSARY

Arraignment. charges are read and an initial plea is entered (also referred to as initial appearance)

Bench trial. trial by judge where the judge makes the final decision in the case after hearing evidence

Compassionate release. process in which inmates may be eligible for immediate early release based on grounds of "particularly extraordinary or compelling circumstances which could not reasonably have been foreseen by the court at the time of sentencing." Examples include advanced age or health-related issues.

Corrections officer (CO). responsible for enforcing rules and regulations in a prison or jail

Defendant. a person accused of committing a crime

Felony. a crime, typically involving violence, regarded as more serious than a misdemeanor and usually punishable by imprisonment for more than one year or by death

First-degree sexual assault (Wisconsin State Law)
- sexual intercourse or sexual contact without consent which inflicts great bodily harm or pregnancy
- sexual intercourse or sexual contact without consent accomplished by using or threatening to use a dangerous weapon
- sexual intercourse or sexual contact without consent while aided by one of more persons by use of threat of force or violence
- sexual intercourse or sexual contact, with or without consent, with a person under the age of thirteen

Indictment. in felony cases these hearings are held before a grand jury (indictment) or judge (preliminary hearing) to determine if there is "probable cause" that a crime was committed by the defendant

Jail. a place of confinement for persons held in lawful custody who may be awaiting trial. Jail is usually the first place a person is taken after they are arrested. Many jails are used for short-term incarceration of persons convicted of minor crimes.

Judicial release. a mechanism by which the sentencing court may release an inmate from prison prior to the completion of his or her sentence

Jury trial. the prosecutor and criminal defense attorney present evidence of guilt or innocence

Justice. he quality of being just, righteousness, equitableness, or moral rightness

Maximum-security prison. a prison that does as much as possible to keep prisoners from escaping. The prison watches them very closely.

Minimum-security prison. a prison with the lowest levels of restrictions on prisoners' movements and activities

Misdemeanor. a minor wrongdoing

Motion to suppress. it is a request made by a criminal defense attorney on behalf of the defendant in advance of a criminal trial, asking the court to exclude certain evidence from the trial

Parole. a conditional release of a prisoner serving an indeterminate or unexpired sentence

Pedophile. a psychosexual disorder, generally affecting adults, characterized by sexual interest in prepubescent children or attempts to engage in sexual acts with prepubescent children

Plea. a formal statement by or on behalf of a defendant or prisoner, stating guilt or innocence in response to a charge

Plea bargaining. the prosecutor and criminal defense attorney meet to discuss possible pleas and exchange information

Presentence investigation. in felony cases, an interview is conducted by the probation department, and a report will be prepared for the judge

Prison. an institution of confinement for persons who are in custody by a judicial authority following conviction for a crime

Probation. the action of suspending the sentence of a convicted offender and giving the offender freedom during good behavior under the supervision of a probation officer

Sentencing hearing. if charged with a misdemeanor, this may happen immediately after a plea bargain or trial. For felony cases, there is a separate hearing. The judge will review the circumstances of the case and impose a penalty, which may start immediately after the hearing.

Sex offender. a person who has been convicted of a crime involving sex; referring to any person convicted of rape, rape of a child, child molestation, sexual misconduct with a minor, sexual violation of human remains, incest, communication with a minor for immoral purposes

Supervised release. in the federal system, supervised release (also called special or mandatory parole) is a period of freedom for recently released prisoners

BIBLIOGRAPHY

Allan, Barbara. *Doing our Time on the Outside: One Prison Family of 2.5 Million.* The Publishing Pro, 2018.

American Bar Association, Standard 23-8.6 "Written Communications." *ABA Standards for Criminal Justice: Treatment of Prisoners, 3rd edition.* Washington, DC: American Bar Association, 2011, 266.

American Correctional Association. *Manual of Correctional Standards.* Washington, DC: American Correctional Association, 1966, 545.

American Correctional Association, Resolution 2010-1. "Supporting Family-Friendly Communication Policies." Passed February 1, 2010. Published in American Correctional Association, *Public Correctional Policies 2012*, 13. https://www.aca.org/government/policyresolution/PDFs/Public_Correctional_Policies.pdf. Accessed 4 November 2012.

American Jail Association. "Adult/Juvenile Offender Access to Telephones" Resolution. Adopted May 3, 2008. http://www.aca.org/government/policyresolution/view.asp?ID=2&print-view=1 Accessed 4 November 2012.

American Psychiatric Association. *Diagnostic and Statistical Manual of Mental Disorders DSM-IV,* fourth ed. American Psychiatric Association, 1994.

Angelou, Maya. *I Know Why the Caged Bird Sings.* Ballantine Books, 2009.

Barton, Gina. "Walworth County Sex Offender Who Disappeared 2 years ago Turns up in Costa Rica." *Milwaukee Journal Sentinel*, 23 December 2005.

Britten, Rhonda. *Fearless Living.* Tarcher Perigee, 2002.

Brown, Brené. *Braving the Wilderness: The Quest for True Belonging and the Courage to Stand Alone*. Random House, 2019.

Brown, Jackson H. *P.S. I Love You*. Rutledge Hill Press, 1990.

Buffett, Jimmy. "Changes in Latitudes, Changes in Attitudes." *Changes in Latitudes, Changes in Attitudes*. January, 1977.

Burke, Edmund. "On Moving His Resolutions for Conciliation with the Colonies." *The Speech of Edmund Burke, Esq; on Moving His Resolutions for Conciliation with the Colonies, March 22, 1775*. Burke, Edmund, 1729–1797. London. Printed for J. Dodsley, 1775.

Caldwell, Laura. *Long Way Home: A Young Man Lost in the System and the Two Women Who Found Him*. Free Press, 2010.

Canfield, Jack. *Chicken Soup for the Prisoner's Soul: 101 Stories to Open the Heart and Spirit of Hope, Healing and Forgiveness*. Backlist, 2012.

"Captured Fugitive Endeared Himself to Co-Workers." *Inside Costa Rica—National News*, 23 December 2005.

"Child Abuse Prevention and Treatment Act. CAPTA Reauthorization Act of 2010 (P.L. 111–320)." *Child Welfare Information Gateway*, 2011. https://www.childwelfare.gov/systemwide/laws_policies/federal/index.cfm?event=federal-Legislation.viewLegis&id=142. Accessed 1 June 2014.

Clark, Chris and Gillian Mezey. "Elderly sex offenders against children: A descriptive study of child sex abusers over the age of 65." *The Journal of Forensic Psychiatry*, 8:2, 357–369, 1997. DOI: 10.1080/09585189708412017.

Compassionate Release/Reduction in Sentence: Procedures for Implementation of 18 U.S.C. 3582(c)(1)(A) and 4205(g)" *(PDF). United States Federal Bureau of Prisons. Archived from* the original *(PDF) on 3 September 2013*. Accessed 9 March 2021.

DeYoung, Kevin. *Crazy Busy: A (Mercifully) Short Book about a (Really) Big Problem*. Crossway, 2013.

DiBennardo, Rebecca. "Ideal Victims and Monstrous Offenders: How the News Media Represent Sexual Predators." *Socius:*

Sociological Research for a Dynamic World. Vol. 4, 2018. ttps://doi.org/10.1177/2378023118802512.

Edelman, Hope. *The After Grief: Finding Your Way Along the Long Arc of Loss*. Ballentine Books, 2020.

Erdrich, Louise. *Love Medicine*. Harper Perennial Modern Classics, 2013.

Esparza, Carolyn. *The Unvarnished Truth About the Prison Family Journey*. Create Space Independent Publishing Platform, 2013.

Faller, Kathleen Coulborn. "Forty Years of Forensic Interviewing of Children Suspected of Sexual Abuse, 1974–2014: Historical Benchmarks." *Social Sciences Journal*, 2015, vol. 4, 34–65.

Florence-Houk, Amanda. *Andy: Another New Dad-less Year*. Publish America, 2004.

Friends and Family of Incarcerated Persons (FFIP). https://theffip.org/. Accessed 3 February 2021.

Gladwell, Malcom. *Revisionist History*. "A Polite Word for Liar." 2018, http://revisionisthistory.com/episodes/23-a-polite-word-for-liar-memory-part-1.

Hancock, Mosiah Lyman. "When I'm Gone." *Autobiography of Mosiah Hancock 1834–1855*. Compiled by Amy E. Baird, Victoria H. Jackson and Laura L. Wassell. Brigham Young University. http://www.boap.org/LDS/Early-Saints/MHancock.html. Accessed 15 March 2021.

Harper, Hill. *Letters to an Incarcerated Brother: Encouragement, Hope, and Healing for Inmates and Their Loved Ones*. Avery, 2014.

Hart, Matt. "The Geriatric Sex Offender: Senile or Pedophile?" *Law and Psychology Review*, vol. 32, 2008, 153. Accessed 28 January 2021.

Hartman, Kenneth. *Mother California: A Story of Redemption Behind Bars*. Atlas, 2009.

"How Does it Feel to Spend Christmas Day in Prison?" *The Secret Life of Prisons*, 24 December, 2020, https://secretlifeofprisons.libsyn.com.

Human Rights Watch. "No Easy Answers: Sex Offender Laws in the US." 17 September 2007. https://www.hrw.org/report/2007/09/11/no-easy-answers/sex-offender-laws-us#. Accessed 20 February 2021.

Inside Costa Rica "Trio a Force at Finding Fugitives." 3 January 2006. https://insidecostarica.com/dailynews/2006/january/03/nac05.htm.

Interstate Commission for Adult Offender Supervision Advisory Opinions. "Rule 3.101-3—Transfer of supervision of sex offenders." Adopted September 26, 2007, amended October 9, 2019, effective April 1, 2020. https://www.interstatecompact.org/icaos-rules/chapter/ch3/rule-3-101-3. Accessed 16 February 2021.

Jiang-Stein, Deborah. *Prison Baby: A Memoir*. Beacon Press, 2014.

Jordon, Aaron, Editor. *Survive a Prison Sentence for Dummies: Do you have what it takes to survive?* John Wiley & Sons Inc., 2014.

Kerik, Bernard. "Prison is like 'dying with your eyes open.'" *Law and Regulations Commentary. CNBC.* 29 April 2015. https://www.cnbc.com/2015/04/29/bernard-kerik-prison-is-like-dying-with-your-eyes-open-commentary.html.

Kirk, Jay. "Welcome to Pariahville." *GQ Magazine.* 28 April 2015.

Kraig, Gene. *The Sentence: A Family Prison Memoir.* Greenpoint Press, 2006.

Kubler-Ross, Elisabeth. *On Death and Dying: What the Dying Have to Teach Doctors, Nurses Clergy & Their Own Families.* Scribner, 2014.

Lamott, Anne. "12 Truths I Learned from Life and Writing." www.ted.com. February 12, 2019.

Lawson L. "Isolation, gratification, justification: offenders' explanations of child molesting." Issues in Mental Health Nursing.

24 (6–7): 695–705, 2003. doi:10.1080/01612840305328. PMID 12907384. S2CID 13188168.

Lazareck, Julia. *Prison: The Hidden Sentence. What To Do When Your Loved One Is Arrested and Incarcerated*, 2020. *https:// prisonthehiddensentence.com.*

Levenson, Jill and Richard Tewksbury. "Collateral Damage: Family Members of Registered Sex Offenders." *American Journal of Criminal Justice*, vol. 34, 2009, 54–68.

Marshall, WL. "The relationship between self-esteem and deviant sexual arousal in nonfamilial child molesters." Behavior Modification. vol. 1, 1997, pp.186–96. doi:10.1177/01454455970211005. PMID 8995044. S2CID 22205062.

Mince-Didier, Ave. "Consequences of a Child Molestation Conviction." *Criminal Defense Lawyer, Crimes Against Children*, NOLO. https://www.criminal-defenselawyer.com/resources/criminal-defense/sex-crimes/consequences-child-molestation.htm. Accessed 31 January 2021.

Mott, Kendra. "Colwell Could Face 40 years for Each of Three Counts Against Him." *Green Bay Gazette Newspaper*, 10 September 1999.

Muller, Robert. "What if Your Father Were a Pedophile?" *Psychology Today*, 20 August 2018.

National Conference of State Legislatures, Denver, Colorado. "Significant State Legislation 1996–2004 on Sex Offender Sentencing January 2006." https://legacy.npr.org/programs/morning/features/2006/oct/prop83/ncsl_sentencing.pdf. Accessed 3 March 2021.

National Center for Missing and Exploited Children. "Case Resources." www.missingkids.org.

News Release, "Walworth County Sex Offender Who Disappeared 2 Years Ago Turns Up in Costa Rica." *Milwaukee Journal Sentinel*, December 22, 2005.

Nyad, Diana. "Diana Nyad: My Life After Sexual Assault." *The New York Times*, 9 November 2017.

Pelloski, Christopher. *A Tortuous Path: Atonement and Reinvention in a Broken System.* CreateSpace Independent Publishing Platform, 2019.

Peters, Thomas and Robert Waterman. *In Search of Excellence: Lessons from America's Best-Run Companies.* Harper Business, 2006.

Prison Family Support Group. www.PrisonInsight.com. Accessed 5 January 2020.

Prison Talk: Prison Information and Family Support Community. http://prisontalk.com/forums. Accessed 13 July 2020.

Prejean, Helen. *Dead Man Walking.* Random House, 1993.

Quindlen, Anna. *A Short Guide to a Happy Life.* Random House, 2000.

"Rebuilding Family Relationships." Uncuffed. 4 November 2019, https://www.npr.org/podcasts/772030875/uncuffed.

Ribon, Pamela. *Why Girls Are Weird.* Downtown Press, 2003.

Ruiz, Erika. *But Why Is Daddy in Prison?* Strong Family Bond, 2019.

Saintcrow, Lilith. *The Devil's Right Hand.* Orbit: New Mexico, 2007.

Sakala, Leah. "Postcard-Only Policies in Jail." *Prison Policy Initiative,* https://www.prisonpolicy.org/postcards/report.html#_ftn48. 7 February 2013.

Saunders, George. *Writers Series.* University of Richmond interview. 15 April 2011.

Schiffer B., Paul T., Gizewski E., Forsting M., Leygraf N., Schedlowski M., and Kruger TH. "Functional brain correlates of heterosexual pedophilia." *NeuroImage. 41 (1): 80–91,* May 2008. *doi:10.1016/j.neuroimage.2008.02.008. PMID 18358744. S2CID 3350912.*

Staff Writer. "Sexual Predator Worked Real Estate in Flamingo." *A.M. Costa Rica,* 22 December 2005.

"Statistics–Offenders." *Crime Victims Center.* https://www.parentsformeganslaw.org/statistics-offenders/. Accessed 10 June 2019.

Stevens, Wesley. *Learning to Sing in a Strange Land: When a Loved One Goes to Prison*. Resource Publication, 2009.

"Sugarbutt's a Snail." Ear Hustle. https://www.earhustlesq.com. 3 March 2021.

Taylor, Elizabeth. "Elderly Sex Offenders: What Should Be Done?" *The Elder Law Journal*, volume 18, 12/23/2010. Note.

Tofte, Sarah and Jamie Fellner, ed. et al. "No Easy Answers: Sex Offender Laws in the US." Human Rights Watch News Release. September 11, 2007. https://www.hrw.org/report/2007/09/11/no-easy-answers/sex-offender-laws-us.

Turunen, Tarja. "500 Letters." *Colours in the Dark*. 30 August 2013.

Tobola, Deborah. *Hummingbird in Underworld: A Memoir*. She Writes Press, 2019.

Ueland, Brenda. *Me: Signal Lives*. Ayer Company Publishers, 1980.

Villanueva, David. *How Prison Really Works: An Idiot's Guide to Surviving a Prison Sentence*. David G. Villanueva, 2016.

Walker, Jan. *An Inmate's Daughter*. Raven Publishing, 2006.

Waukesha County Sheriff's Department County Jail Facility. "Waukesha County Sherriff Department County Jail Facility Inmate Rules, Regulations and Information Packet." June 2020, pp. 1–13.

Weir, Liz and Karin Littlewood. *When Dad Was Away*. Frances Lincoln Children's Books, 2013.

"West Coast Realtor Arrested on U.S. Charges." *The Tico Times,* 23 December 2005.

Wisconsin Department of Corrections Sex Offender Registry. https://appdocwi.gov/public/faq#A20. Accessed 7 May 2018.

Whitman, Walt, John Nash, and Walt Whitman. *From Whitman's Song of Myself*. London: Poetry Bookshop, 1924. Print.

Whitney, Brian. "Facing Disturbing Truths About Pedophilia Could Help Us Keep Kids Safer." *Pacific Standard*. 14 June 2017. https://psmag.com/social-justice/facing-disturbing-truths-about-pedophilia-could-help-us-keep-kids-safer.

Wilde, Oscar. *The Picture of Dorian Gray*. Dover Publications, Reprint edition, 1993.

World Health Organization. "Pedophilia. International Statistical Classification of Diseases and Related Health Problems 10th Revision (ICD-10) Version for 2010," Section F65.4, 2010.

Wisconsin Circuit Court Access Program. https://wcaa.wicourts. gov. Accessed 10 February 2020.

Wolfelt, Alan. *The Wilderness of Grief: Finding Your Way*. Companion Press, 2007.

Zabin, Amy. *Conversations with a Pedophile*. Barricade Books, 2013.

ABOUT THE AUTHOR

Danica Hubbard, Ph.D., has taught for over twenty-five years as an English professor at College of DuPage, a public community college near Chicago, Illinois. Her field of studies include rhetoric and composition, creative writing, professional writing, and developmental reading. She has traveled the world for professional and personal growth and has written extensive travel blogs highlighting her adventures. An advocate of global education, her passport has been stamped in Croatia, Hungary, Czech Republic, Germany, England, Italy, France, Switzerland, Scotland, Austria, Ireland, Spain, Canada, Costa Rica, South Africa, New Zealand, Mexico, Jamaica, Puerto Rico, Grand Cayman, Slovenia, Bosnia, and Herzegovina. She helps facilitate monthly support groups with Prison Families Alliance and has developed learning community curriculum with the Justice Studies Program faculty at College of DuPage. Dr. Hubbard loves to hike, bike, and listen to indie folk music. Her family is the most important anchor in her life. *Sex Offender: My Father's Secrets, My Secret Shame* is her first book.

CPSIA information can be obtained
at www.ICGtesting.com
Printed in the USA
LVHW071410010422
715074LV00021B/819

9 781638 604044